DOING DISCOURSE ANALYSIS

DOING
DISCOURSE
ANALYSIS

Methods for Studying Action in Talk and Text

Linda A. Wood
Rolf O. Kroger

Sage Publications, Inc.
International Educational and Professional Publisher
Thousand Oaks ■ London ■ New Delhi

For information:

Sage Publications, Inc.
2455 Teller Road
Thousand Oaks, California 91320
E-mail: order@sagepub.com

Sage Publications Ltd.
6 Bonhill Street
London EC2A 4PU
United Kingdom

Sage Publications India Pvt. Ltd.
M-32 Market
Greater Kailash I
New Delhi 110 048 India

Printed in the United States of America

Library of Congress Cataloging-in-Publication Data

Wood, Linda A.
    Doing discourse analysis: Methods for studying action in talk
and text / by Linda A. Wood, Rolf O. Kroger.
        p.   cm.
Includes bibliographical references and index.
    ISBN 0-8039-7350-0 (acid-free paper) — ISBN 0-8039-7351-9
(pbk.: acid-free paper)
    1. Discourse analysis.   I. Kroger, Rolf O.   II. Title.
    P302 .W66   2000
    401´.41—dc21   00-008063

02   03   04   05   06   7   6   5   4   3

Acquiring Editor:	Margaret H. Seawell
Editorial Assistant:	Sandra Krumholz
Production Editor:	Astrid Virding
Editorial Assistant:	Victoria Cheng
Typesetter:	Tina Hill
Indexer:	Terri Greenberg
Cover Designer:	Candice Harman

Contents

Acknowledgments   vii

Introduction   ix

PART I: THEORETICAL BACKGROUND

1. Language, Discourse, and Discourse Analysis   3

2. Varieties of Discourse Analysis   18

3. Examples of Discourse Analysis   34

PART II: METHOD

4. Discourse and Data   55

5. Data Collection   69

6. Preparation for Analysis   82

PART III: ANALYSIS

7. Analysis I: Strategies of Interpretation   91

8. Analysis II: Patterns and Context   117

9. Identities in Talk: Research Examples   143

PART IV: EVALUATION AND REPORTING

10. Warranting in Discourse Analysis   163

11. Writing the Report   179

12. Postscript   187

Appendix A: Transcript Notation   193

Appendix B: Selected Varieties of Discourse Analysis   195

Glossary: Terms for Discourse Analysis   213

References   217

Index   231

About the Authors   240

Acknowledgments

No book is written in a social vacuum. Like all authors, we are indebted to overlapping circles of support—intellectual, social, financial. We wish to thank our students who, over the years, have taken an interest in alternative critical approaches to social psychology. We owe a special thanks to Clare MacMartin, whose sagacious comments on the book and on our work in general have been immensely helpful.

We are indebted to the editorial and technical staff at Sage Publications whose work has greatly eased our own responsibilities in bringing the manuscript to completion. Thanks are also due to the Social Science and Humanities Research Council of Canada for its continuing financial support.

Introduction

What most people do most of the time is talk a lot. To do anything—to build a boat, to launch a rocket, to start a war, to begin a love affair, to initiate a divorce—requires talk and, often, texts. And then more talk. Talk is what moves the world, both in the private and public spheres. "Darling, I love you" moves events along, sometimes with fateful consequences, such as divorce and custody battles. Almost all we do is accomplished by talk. To punch another person out is to regress to uncivilized conduct. War has been described as the continuation of diplomacy by other means; it, too, is a retreat from civilized conduct. It is sometimes said that talk is cheap but talk is always better than pushing and shoving. Talking protects us from the often horrendous consequences of aggressive physical action. Physical moves can also be good, as in romantic encounters, but they too are often brought about and accompanied by talk.

Nevertheless, we still know relatively little about talk. Historically, the social sciences have concentrated on correlations between abstract social conditions and isolated aspects of the behavior of groups or individuals (e.g., suicide, aggression, prejudice). Until very recently, little attention has been given to what people actually say or do in particular everyday circumstances. What they do is to talk, often incessantly—about the world, about work and play, about others (parents, spouses, friends, bosses, colleagues, etc.) and their relations with them. And, in talking, they do things. That was Austin's (1962) revolutionary insight into an aspect of language that had not been fully recognized, the pragmatic function of language, what language does to make social life as we know it possible. Before Austin, social scientists had concentrated on the descriptive or literal function of language, how it transmits information. That function has its own importance, but it is not the whole story.

The story involves a fundamental shift in the social sciences that started some time ago (principally, with Wittgenstein's philosophy of psychology and language in the 1950s), although this shift had a major impact on the practice of the social sciences only in the 1980s. This change promises an advance in our understanding of the human condition, comparable to other turning points in intellectual and cultural development. The shift we are talking about has been called "the turn to language" in recognition of what is most uniquely human, the power of language and the possibilities it affords in the understanding of social life. It amounts to a celebration of what is uniquely human as opposed to the biological grounding of human nature: the contrast between the fully realized cultural being (Harré, 1979) and the "social animal" (Aronson, 1992).

The turn to language, or to *discourse,* as it has come to be known (Kroger & Wood, 1998), has had the salutary effect of breaking down the artificial barriers between the various social science fields concerned with the analysis of everyday social life. Investigators and students have come from communication research, social psychology, linguistics, sociology, anthropology, philosophy, English literature, political science, and other disciplines. They have come to meet at joint international conferences, and they publish in both specialized and interdisciplinary journals to forge a new area of inquiry.

The turn to discourse has been accompanied by the development of new methods, and these methods are primarily what this book is about. The methods are designed for the close analysis of talk and, of course, writing. The methods are sometimes called *discourse analysis,* but discourse analysis as we view it is not only about method; it is also a perspective on the nature of language and its relationship to the central issues of the social sciences. More specifically, we see discourse analysis as a related collection of approaches to discourse, approaches that entail not only practices of data collection and analysis, but also a set of metatheoretical and theoretical assumptions and a body of research claims and studies (Potter, 1997). Data collection and analysis are a vital part of discourse analysis, but they do not, in themselves, constitute the whole of discourse analysis.

The reader may well ask: Do we need yet another set of methods? The social sciences already have a wide variety of methods. Most are mundane because of their very pervasiveness (e.g., interviews, questionnaires, surveys, multivariate analysis), and some are highly esoteric in being confined to a small circle of specialized practitioners (e.g., the Rorschach inkblot). The short answer to our question is a resounding "yes"; a longer answer necessarily takes us a bit farther afield, to a consideration of discourse analysis as a conceptual enterprise. The turn to language has also involved changes in the conceptual framework underlying contemporary inquiry into human behavior. We pause here to look briefly at these changes and their implications for the modes and methods of inquiry.

SCIENCE: NATURE AND CULTURE

We are persuaded by Hampshire's (1978) argument that psychology and, by extension, adjacent disciplines face two essentially different tasks requiring different forms of explanation and different forms of method. Hampshire's proposal has the virtues of being thoroughly grounded in the contemporary philosophy of mind and of being in tune with postpositivist developments. It deserves an extensive quotation:

> Human beings, while studying themselves and their own kind, must pursue at least two irreplaceable types of inquiry because of their own nature as embodied and self-conscious thinkers. One is an inquiry aiming at a purely theoretical understanding of their own physical functioning, in which human beings are seen as objects that conform to universal laws of nature; the other is an inquiry aiming at an understanding of their own thinking, and the thinking of others, in various normal social settings and in different languages. (p. 67)

The first project formulates the objects of inquiry as *res naturam,* natural things located in the realm of nature. In the natural realm, human beings may be taken to be no different from the objects studied by the physical and natural sciences (the particles of physics, the elements of chemistry, the cells of biology). Specifically, the study of human beings as physical beings involves the calibration of our biologically based capacities as a species (how we see, hear, taste, smell, etc.). In short, this line of inquiry concerns our relationship to the physical world. It is classically located in the study of sensation and perception, psychophysics, brain and behavior, and similar endeavors. Conceptually, studies in res naturam are amenable to the kinds of causal explanations that have worked so well in the older sciences. The researchers who pursue this line of inquiry need not be troubled, in their day-to-day practice, by philosophical doubt. They are on safe ground, unless they begin to believe that their mode of inquiry and their mission embrace all science, including the social sciences, and that they can reduce human beings to mere physical beings, governed by their genetic endowment and by chemical and electrical processes in the brain, important as these are. Such reductionist accounts have once more been rendered suspect and indefensible by recent theoretical developments (Bickhard, 1992).

The second project concerns *res artem,* events constructed in the realm not of nature but of culture and, as such, wholly enmeshed in the complexities of language. The study of human beings as social beings is concerned with our relations to the symbolic world, not to the natural world. Such study involves examining how we acquire and use language; how we solve problems; how we manage to live with others; and how individual differences, both normal and abnormal, are created and perceived. This line of inquiry is historically connected with the humanities; with certain subfields in psychology, such as social, developmental, abnormal, and psycholinguistics; and with other social sciences, such as anthropology, communication, and sociology. Conceptually, human activities as res artem are not amenable to explanation in terms of causes, in the natural science sense, but in terms of the ways in which they are produced and recognized as intelligible and sensible (Pomerantz & Fehr, 1997).

These projects entail a shift in the ontological basis of the social sciences.[1] In res naturam, the nature of the entities under study is that of material things located in space-time producing a world locked together by causal relations. In res artem, the nature of the entities is that not of material things but of conversational acts located at people points or in interactive encounters (Harré, Clarke, & De Carlo, 1985). People points are the nodes of interaction created by people as social beings who must act in concert with their fellow social beings; in so doing, they create a world that is locked together not by causal relations but by conventions, shared rules, story lines, and narratives. The rich fabric of social life is woven not by physical beings whose actions are caused by mental entities harbored under their skulls, but rather by social beings who, by virtue of their capacity for language, are engaged in an endless "conversation" and so create and maintain their relations with each other (Harré & Gillett, 1994). It is in this realm that discourse analysis finds its home.

Consider how we look at the death of a person. There are two ways to do so. As a matter of res naturam, we have a dead body. Pathologists and forensic experts can establish the "cause" of the death by the procedures of the natural sciences, and the cause of death will be stated in terms of disease, gunshot wounds, and the like. This is not problematic, except sometimes in a purely technical sense, as when the accuracy of some biological test is questioned. But we also look at the dead body as an item in the social world, in res artem. For example, we need to decide whether the firing of a gun that results in a deadly wound should be considered an accident, suicide, manslaughter, or homicide; we make this decision through the procedures of the social sciences and of jurisprudence in an institutional, social context involving police, lawyers, judges, and juries. There may be disagreements, but these disagreements are of a different sort than those involved in determining the cause of biological death. Their resolution requires discourse par excellence. It is through talk, through discussing biological assays, chemical tests, and the like that we come to an agreement. Death as a social matter is purely a matter of discourse, in terms both of the construction of the death and of how we accomplish that construction.

SCIENCE: ONE METHOD OR MANY?

A book about new methods cannot skirt more general questions about methods in science. In this area, we have accumulated both certain illusions about science (Boulding, 1980) and a panoply of myths or misconceptions about the nature and the methods of science (Bickhard, 1992). We have gained a good deal of understanding about these misconceptions through the work of the sociologists of scientific knowledge who look at what successful scientists actually do to see how science is done (Knorr-Cetina, 1996; Latour, 1987). But the illusion endures that there is a single scientific method, "a touchstone that can distinguish what is scientific from what is not" (Boulding, 1980, p. 833). Shorn of its shibboleths, scientific work is a form of problem solving that in its essentials is no different from the problem solving used by ordinary folk, even though it is highly refined and technical in its particular applications. Even the most exalted of scientific methods, the experiment, reduces to a common procedure. Etymologically, to experiment means to test, to try something to see how it works. It is as simple as that. The only difference between the problem-solving methods of the plumber, of the politician, and of the scientist is that scientists do their problem solving under the special social conditions imposed by the scientific community, which include, foremost, its stringent rules for veracity. In the cathedral of science, to lie, to fudge, or to plagiarize is to commit a mortal sin, punishable by excommunication. It is the ultimate sin, because scientists must be able to rely on the record created by others if they are not to be forced into recreating the wheel in each generation. Boulding (1980) puts the matter of scientific method succinctly:

> Within the scientific community there is a great variety of methods, and one of the problems which science still has to face is the development of appropriate methods corresponding to different epistemological fields. . . . There has to be constant critique and evaluation of the methods themselves. Perhaps one of the greatest handicaps to the growth of knowledge in the scientific community has been the uncritical transfer of methods which have been successful in one epistemological field into another where they are not really appropriate. Furthermore, many scientific methods are not peculiar to science. The alchemists had experiments, the astrologers had careful observation, the geomancers and diviners had measurement, the theologians had logic. These methods are not peculiar to science and none of them define it. (p. 833)

If anything in general can be said about methods in science, it is that they involve imagination and fantasy (to form expectations or theories) coupled with testing. Testing entails logic, observation, and the records of others. As Boulding (1980) puts it, "Without fantasy, science would have nothing to test; without testing, fantasy would be unchallenged" (p. 832). Science is neither Baconian—the endless perusal of facts unleavened by leaps of the imagination—nor can it be science fiction—the unbridled deployment of fantasy unchecked by empirical constraints and rigorous testing.

Perhaps one of the most misguided transfers of method from one field to another is the introduction of the laboratory experiment into social psychology for the simulation of aspects of culture. An outstanding example is Milgram's

(1974) attempt to study in the laboratory the kind of obedience to authority made infamous by the Eichmanns of the Nazi regime. Apart from more general ethical and methodological issues, the failure of the traditional experiment to simulate aspects of culture in the laboratory with any degree of verisimilitude lies in its inability to take into account the pragmatic functions of language, what is being "done" through the talk of the experimenter and the subject. Traditional experimenters take language literally, unaware of its performative, discursive functions. But if the talk within experiments is not fully understood for what it is and for what it does in the pragmatic, discursive sense, the results become contaminated and opaque, and the interpretation of the results becomes ambiguous. The culture-simulation experiment may be good for studying the actions of undergraduates in the peculiar setting of the psychological laboratory, that is, their coping with the rules and conventions of that setting, but not for much else (see Harré et al., 1985; Harré & Secord, 1972, Chapters 1 and 2 for critique).

For all of these reasons, it may be time to examine the possibilities inherent in discourse-analytic methods that fit the epistemological requirements of social inquiry in the postpositivist world.

PURPOSE AND ORGANIZATION

There is no question that there is growing interest in discourse analysis. However, this interest is also accompanied by a good deal of confusion. What exactly is discourse analysis? What are the methods of discourse analysis? One of our goals in writing this book is to acknowledge the extensive variety of discourse-analytic perspectives current in the field. But our main purpose is to consider those approaches that we find most useful from our perspective as social psychologists working within a social-constructionist, discursive framework. And although our focus will be on discourse-analytic methods, we also want to stress, along with other authors (e.g., Edwards & Potter, 1992), that discourse analysis is not simply another methodological tool but a perspective that needs to be understood within a wider epistemological context. Nevertheless, concerns about theoretical issues must go hand in hand with concerns about methodological precision.

Our general purpose then is to identify a limited set of discourse-analytic perspectives and to explicate the methodological procedures we see as most central to the concerns and projects of newcomers to discourse analysis. We will consider examples of discourse-analytic research, but, as befits a text on methodology, our emphasis will be on methodological detail, not on results and findings. We do not intend to provide a critique of empirical studies with respect to their interpretations or to the approach they have taken, although we do try to point out the advantages and disadvantages of specific strategies. We hope that the book will serve foremost to present a range of possibilities. We believe that it is as yet premature to close off judgment or to be overly prescriptive, in terms of both the spirit of discourse analysis and the stage of its development. We also believe that the overall tone of an introductory book should be positive. Nevertheless, discourse analysis encourages reflectivity and reflexivity, so we shall shun neither relevant critiques nor constructive disagreements. The notion of reflexivity is a complex one and is intimately tied to the nature of discourse. Put simply, talk is not only about actions, it is part of those actions—because actions involve talk, and talk about talk is talk about itself. Handel (1982) provides a helpful concrete example: "The first few pages [of his book on ethnomethodology] serve as an introduction to ethnomethodology and are also about introductions. That introduction, then, describes itself. It is reflexive" (p. 35; see also Potter, 1996).

The book is organized as follows. Chapter 1 addresses fundamental assumptions about the nature of discourse and identifies the major features of the discursive perspective. Chapter 2 briefly identifies selected varieties of discourse analysis and then focuses on some general methodological issues. In Chapter 3, we present some examples of discourse analysis that we hope will give readers a taste of what is involved before they wade into the formalities. Chapters 4, 5, and 6 address questions about the nature of discourse data and cover basic procedures of data collection and of preparation for analysis. Chapters 7 and 8 concern analysis and are the methodological core of the book; we examine a variety of specific analytical techniques and overall analytical strategies. Chapter 9 presents examples of research on identity that exemplify different sorts of analysis of different sorts of data. In Chapters 10 and 11, we discuss issues related to the evaluation of discourse-analytic research (reliability and validity) and offer suggestions for the writing of research reports. The last chapter offers suggestions for the development of discourse-analytic skills and considers selected methodological and theoretical issues in the practice of discourse analysis. Appendix A presents the system of transcript notation used in the book. Appendix B discusses those versions of discourse analysis on which we draw most centrally. Finally, we provide a Glossary of various terms (and sample readings) used in relation to discourse analysis, some of which describe work similar to work we have discussed under other headings and some of which refer to forms of discourse analysis to which we give little or no attention.

NOTE

1. We can comment only briefly on the suitability of the term *science* for res artem projects. The German term *Wissenschaft,* or disciplined knowing, avoids the value-laden connotations that have accumulated around the English term *science.* In the German language, everyone who engages in the disciplined pursuit of knowledge is a *Wissenschaftler* or "scientist," whether she pursues literature, anthropology, or physics.

Boulding (1980) distinguishes between secure and insecure sciences partly in terms of the completeness of their knowledge bases. Thus, geology and paleontology are insecure sciences, because the record of the past is fragmentary and may be altered at any time by new discoveries. In contrast, the study of literature constitutes a relatively secure science because of the relative completeness of the record. Boulding's criteria would obliterate in part the vexatious distinctions between the humanities, the social sciences, and the physical sciences. A more neutral term would forestall a good deal of needless rhetoric and misspent emotion. This would seem to be particularly true for psychology, where invidious comparisons between the "hard" and the "soft" parts of the discipline contribute more to rancor and status wrangling than to useful cooperation and understanding.

PART I

THEORETICAL BACKGROUND

Language, Discourse, and Discourse Analysis

Discourse analysis is a perspective on social life that contains both methodological and conceptual elements. Discourse analysis involves ways of thinking about discourse (theoretical and metatheoretical elements) and ways of treating discourse as data (methodological elements). Discourse analysis is thus not simply an alternative to conventional methodologies; it is an alternative to the perspectives in which those methodologies are embedded. Discourse analysis entails more than a shift in methodology from a general, abstracted, quantitative to a particularized, detailed, qualitative approach. It involves a number of assumptions that are important in their own right and also as a foundation for doing discourse-analytic research. Our purpose in this chapter is to cover these basic principles. We note that there are actually multiple versions of the discourse-analytic perspective. For our present purposes, we present one particular version, which is our take on the version originally developed by Potter and Wetherell (1987). The Potter and Wetherell version is one of the better known approaches; furthermore, it is accessible, and its central principles are common to a number of versions.

Multiple perspectives on discourse mean that there are multiple definitions of discourse and of what counts as discourse (e.g., spoken language, written language, language use above the level of the sentence, etc.). What we want to stress here is an approach to definition that views discourse not just as an object, but as a way of treating language. In general, we find congenial the definition offered by Potter (1997):

> [Discourse analysis] has an analytic commitment to studying discourse as *texts and talk in social practices*. That is, the focus is not on language as an abstract entity such as a lexicon and set of grammatical rules (in linguistics), a system of differences (in structuralism), a set of rules for transforming statements (in

Foucauldian genealogies). Instead, it is the medium for interaction; analysis of discourse becomes, then, analysis of what people do. (p. 146)

In other words, language is taken to be not simply a tool for description and a medium of communication (the conventional view), but as social practice, as a way of doing things. It is a central and constitutive feature of social life. The major assumption of discourse analysis is that the phenomena of interest in social and psychological research are constituted in and through discourse. "Discourse theorists maintain that talk is constitutive of the realities within which we live, rather than expressive of an earlier, discourse-independent reality" (Sampson, 1993, p. 1221). Talk creates the social world in a continuous, ongoing way; it does not simply reflect what is assumed to be already there.

The discursive perspective does not deny physical reality. As Wetherell and Potter (1992) note, a mountain is no less real for being constituted discursively as either a volcanic eruption or as a result of tectonic shifts. You still die if your plane crashes into it. They add, "However, material reality is no less discursive for being able to get into the way of planes. How those deaths are understood . . . and what caused them is constituted through our systems of discourse" (p. 65). As Sampson (1993) puts it:

The very objects [and events] of our world are constituted as such in and through discourse. There is no meaning to reality behind discourses that discourse represents; in the representation lies the constitution of what we come to accept as the real. (p. 1222)

These ideas require elaboration. To grasp the nature of discourse in the sense that we use the term means confronting a number of assumptions, assumptions that are usually taken for granted by both social scientists and laypersons. This view of discourse entails (at least) three major shifts from conventional orientations: (a) from a distinction between talk (discourse) and action to an emphasis on talk *as* action, (b) from a view of talk (discourse) as a route to internal or external events or entities to an emphasis on talk as the event of interest, and (c) from a view of variability as an anomalous feature of action to an appreciation of variability both within and between people (Potter & Wetherell, 1987).

BASIC ASSUMPTIONS ABOUT DISCOURSE

Language Is Action

A major source of the view that language is action is Austin's (1962) theory of speech acts. Austin pointed out a feature of language that is known implicitly by all language users: Utterances not only have a certain "meaning" (i.e., they refer to states, persons, events, etc.), they also have force, that is, they are not only about things, they also do things. In other words, talk (and language use more generally) *is* action. Specifically, utterances can be considered in terms of three features: (a) their locutionary or referential meaning (what they are about), (b) their illocutionary force (what the speaker does with them), and (c) their perlocutionary force (their effects on the hearer). For example, if we say to someone, "You stole the money," we are not only describing an event—and the statement could thus be judged as true or false—we are also accusing the hearer (who may be hurt by the accusation, become angry, etc.). The emphasis in discourse analysis is on what talk is doing and achieving.

Further, we need to recognize that talk has multiple functions. For example, the speaker of the above statement might also be said to be insulting the hearer, constructing the identity of the hearer as a liar, and so on. Finally, what a person might be doing with talk depends on the other persons involved, the circumstances, and so on. These factors are captured in Austin's notion of *felicity conditions,* that is, the conditions that must obtain for an utterance to have force as a certain speech act (accusing, etc.). For example, an imperative statement can only be an order if uttered by someone with authority over the hearer. In sum, the discourse analyst will look at discourse for what is being done, not primarily for what it is about.

To appreciate the wider importance of language, language must be seen as action, but this is not always easy to do. In part, this is because both social science and everyday discourse make an unfortunate distinction between talk and action. Both systems privilege action and tend to downgrade talk. There are numerous examples of this tendency, for example, the dismissive reference to utterances as "just talk" or expressions such as "We've talked enough—it's time for action" and more recently, "He can talk the talk, but can he walk the walk?" Nonetheless, people do recognize that talk has a performative quality, that we can do things with words. Let us look more closely at a frequently used expression to emphasize the importance of the distinctions drawn in Austin's speech-act theory. The statement "actions speak louder than words" appears to make a distinction between talk and action, giving primary importance to actions. But the verb that carries the notion of importance and the idea of action is "speak"; the expression appears simultaneously to deny and recognize the importance and action nature of language. The seeming paradox can be resolved by distinguishing between two senses of *talk: talk* as words, and *talk* as what people are doing with words. Similarly, the utterance "talk doesn't count" would reflexively render itself pointless unless we interpret *talk* as referring to words rather than to what can be done with them.

What are speakers doing with their utterances? We can say first of all that they are recognizing the performative quality of discourse. But if we consider such utterances in context, we can identify other functions. For example, a newspaper article reported that China would observe the 50th anniversary of the Universal Declaration of Human Rights while continuing to crack down on dissidents (Cernetig, 1998). The headline read, "China's words on human rights louder than its actions." The claim that China supports human rights in words but not in actions not only serves as an accusation that China is behaving badly; it marks that behavior as particularly egregious. China cannot reasonably offer an account that it is unaware of the Declaration and what it involves. By combining reports of China's observation of the anniversary with reports of the crackdown, the journalist presents China's actions as a mockery, not simply a neglect, of human rights. Or consider the headline of a report on Canadian chartered banks: "Banking and Poor People: Talk is Cheap" (see Philp, 1998). The article also includes a quotation from the report: "When it comes to serving the needs of poor people, their record is lots of talk and not much action" (quoted in Philp). In this case, the emphasis on talk versus action serves as an accusation that the banks have failed to keep their commitment to open their doors to low-income people. In this case, we have *talk* in the form of a promise; clearly, such talk is not inherently empty, or we would pay it little attention. This talk serves to commit the speaker to a future action. In this case, the action is not forthcoming. But what is the nature of that action? The phrase "open their doors" does not appear to refer to talk, but it is also not used literally. That is, no one is suggesting that poor people are not allowed to come into the bank. Rather, they are not permitted to engage in the sorts of conversation and exchange of texts (checks, signature cards, account agreements, etc.) that would give them access to the banks' services.

We can extend our analyses if we consider phrases such as "Actions speak louder than words" and "Talk is cheap" as idiomatic expressions. Drew and Holt (1988) have shown that idiomatic formulations are difficult to challenge, both because of their generality, that is, their independence of the specific details of the particular situation or person to which they are applied, and because they invoke and constitute the taken-for-granted knowledge shared by all competent members of the culture. Because they are difficult to resist, they are rhetorically effective.

These samples of discourse analysis are by no means complete; we demonstrate later how to provide a much more thorough analysis and how to warrant that analysis. Our main goal here has been to illustrate that discourse analysts are not uninterested in content but that their aim is to go beyond content to see how it is used flexibly to achieve particular functions and effects. The role of content requires some elaboration, because people sometimes take the action emphasis of discourse analysis to mean a lack of concern for content. On the contrary, discourse analysis can be said to take content more seriously than do conventional approaches in which the focus is on the psychological processes ostensibly underlying content (Potter & Wetherell, 1995a, p. 82). The misunderstanding also reflects a narrow view of content, whereas the conceptualization of content in discourse analysis is very broad. Thus, discourse analysts do consider the referential and propositional content of discourse, although not in terms of its truth value. The analysis of how language is used also involves the identification of content at a number of different levels: lexical, pragmatic, discourse, and social. For example, the utterance "You're not going out again tonight, are you?" might be a reprimand, an initiation (of a conversational exchange), and a threat to the face of the other. All of these involve the performative force or function of the talk and might all be said to be the content of the discourse. In some instances, a word might be semantically empty in that it has no representative or referential meaning. But it can function as a speech act. For example, in the instance above, if "Well?" were to follow the failure of the other person to respond to the "question," it might serve as a challenge. Thus, there is no reason to restrict the term *content* to the referential aspect of utterances.

Another comment we hear quite frequently is that discourse analysis is not concerned with content, only with "style." *Style* is sometimes referred to as the how versus the what (content) of language use. But the two cannot be separated. Style is how we (both users of language and discourse analysts) get from one type of content to another; doing something in a certain way makes it into another sort of thing. For example, the linguistic or intonational form of an utterance as a question versus a statement has implications for the content of the utterance as a request rather than as a command. This does not mean that pragmatic content is always discernible from semantic content and style; for example, a *hint* is by definition not obvious from the semantic or propositional content of an utterance, regardless of how it is uttered. The recipient and the analyst must also consider the context in which it is uttered. There is a further complication. Style is sometimes thought of only in relation to the nonverbal aspects of discourse. But verbal features, including content, may also contribute to style. For example, the use of formal language (e.g., Latinate, nominal forms) produces a very different style from the use of informal language (as is apparent to anyone who has listened to the remarks to the media by a police officer at a crime scene). In sum, just as form or style is part of content, content is part of style. As soon as we move beyond the level of content as usually understood, we cannot separate content and style. "One cannot properly analyse content without simultaneously analysing form, because contents are always necessarily realised in forms, and different contents entail different forms and vice versa. In brief, form is a part of content" (Fairclough, 1992a, p. 194).

Function

The concept of *function* is central to discourse analysis. It requires some elaboration, in part because, like *discourse* and *text,* the term is used in a number of ways. For example, *function* may be construed in terms of relationships between units (e.g., a linguistic form and the other elements of the system in which it is used). The term *function* as we use it refers to action, or to what it is that people are doing in and with their talk and text (or more casually, what the talk or text is doing). *Action* may refer to anything that can be done using words, from connecting words and phrases to speech acts, including the communication of ideas, attitudes, meaning, and so on. Particular units may have characteristic or expected functions, although the interpretation must always be confirmed in the particular instance. For example, we expect that *and* will usually be used to connect two words or clauses, and it usually does. In some cases, there may be agreement about function, for example, that the function of a phrase such as "I'm not prejudiced, but" is to disclaim. The discourse in question may have no characteristic function in that its action varies from context to context. For example, "That's not a good idea" may be used to evaluate in one context, but to warn in another. Function as action may entail the idea of a specific consequence, as in "persuading," which requires not only activity on the part of a speaker, but a particular effect on the hearer.

We can distinguish types of function in several ways. For example, functions may be linguistic (e.g., to connect two phrases), pragmatic (to convey nonsemantic meaning, e.g., the use of *well* to mark the insufficiency of a previous utterance), or social (e.g., to save face). Functions may be specific or global (e.g., requesting vs. self-presentation; see Potter & Wetherell, 1987, p. 33). Functions may also be described in terms of the type of domain to which they are relevant, for example, legal or religious functions. As we noted above, there is also a connection between content and function in that the former is often described in terms of the latter, particularly when function involves meaning. For example, a request may be viewed as both the content of an utterance and its pragmatic function.

We add a brief comment on structure. Most discourse-analytic approaches can be described as structural in that they do not treat specific elements of discourse in isolation from other elements, but rather attend to their combinations and arrangement. Structure may be sequential or hierarchical, within or across utterances (e.g., in examinations of turn taking). The emphasis, however, is not simply on the arrangement of elements, but on structure as an active process, that is, on structure in the sense of construction.

Discourse as Focus or Topic, Not as Route or Resource

The emphasis on discourse as action and as constitutive of phenomena entails a shift from the usual focus of interest in the phenomena to which the discourse refers to a focus on the discourse itself. Ethnomethodologists (e.g., Garfinkel, 1967) view this as a shift from using features of talk to explain behavior (talk as resource) to a focus on the features of talk as the behavior to be explained (talk as topic). For many, this is a difficult move to make. It means that the emphasis shifts away from a concern with talk as a description of or route to what people "really" think. This is not because it is impossible to gain access to the internal in any direct way, nor is it simply a behaviorist escape hatch (Potter & Wetherell, 1987). But it is an essential move if we accept the proposition that mind (vs. brain) is constituted discursively (rather than existing as an entity prior to and independent of language) and that the separation of thought and talk (and the privileging of one or the other as more "real") is therefore problematic (Harré & Gillett, 1994). Similarly, the argument from discursive metatheory, that events in the world are constructed discursively, means a shift in concern from what "really" happened to how those events are discursively constructed in the social world. The discursive orientation constitutes a counterpoint to the current emphasis on cognition and perception (on things "in there," under the skull, in the mind) rather than on events in the world, including talk as action (see Edwards, 1997, for an extensive discussion of the problems with the prevailing cognitive approach).

The idea of looking at talk or discourse as a topic for research in its own right can be problematic for a different reason than that discussed previously. It is sometimes taken to mean a focus on language as language, that is, in terms of such features as phonology, syntax, or semantics. Some discourse analysts do attend to such features for specific purposes. But generally speaking, the topic for discourse analysts is more properly framed not as language or talk, but in terms of the phenomena that are constructed discursively (e.g., racism, abuse), that is, in terms of what people are doing with words. So, discourse analysts generally do not focus on words as such, as linguistic objects. Nor do they focus on the referential function of words. (We take up the issue of topic in more detail in Chapter 2.)

As a brief illustration of these views about talk, consider the response in the following exchange (from a telephone conversation between Wood and a 75-year-old family friend): "Would you like to come for tea on Sunday?" "I'm sure I can make it." Our interest is not in the literal truth of the friend's statement, in whether the woman is really sure. Both analyst and inviter will be more concerned with what the woman is doing with the words, that is, accepting the invitation. But utterances almost invariably have multiple functions. For example, the phrase "I'm sure" is not required as part of the acceptance of an invitation, so we need to ask what it is doing there. It suggests (and simultaneously discounts) the possibility that the woman might not be able to accept, perhaps because she has a conflicting social engagement or because she has health problems. Both possibilities can serve in different ways to construct the identity of the woman as an active social participant. The second possibility also serves another function, the provision of a potential excuse should she fail to turn up. There are a number of other possible functions that we shall not discuss here (see Wood & Kroger, 1995); rather, we wish to emphasize the way in which talk works as action. The example raises two further points. First, talk is produced for a particular occasion, as are the identities it constructs; this means that we cannot adequately analyze single utterances in isolation from the context in which they are produced. We discuss this point in detail in later chapters along with issues related to the selection of interpretations. Second, in contrast to conventional views of traits and identities, discourse analysts do not assume that identities transcend occasions, or, that personality traits, as conventionally defined, determine actions in a variety of different situations.

Variability

The third major assumption of the discursive perspective involves a recognition of variability as a feature of discourse. Talk constructs different versions of the world and is oriented to different functions; variability is therefore to be expected not only between persons, but within persons. Variability is a problem for the standard social science approaches, because in their search for general laws and consistency, any sign of variability is a nuisance, an error. Vast amounts of statistical computing time are therefore expended in the identification and suppression of variability. But consistency can be had only if we ignore the critical (and interesting) details of everyday life (see Potter & Wetherell, 1987, for discussions of both the extensiveness of variability and traditional attempts to eliminate it). In contrast to conventional approaches, discourse analysis thrives on variability; variability is something to be understood, including the way in which participants use variability to construct their talk for different purposes, for different audiences, and for different occasions. Thus, in the same way that discourse analysts see talk as their subject matter rather than as a resource to give them access to the putative inner person, they see variability as an essential feature of their subject matter rather than as a problem. The goal is to understand variability and to employ it for analytical purposes, not to eliminate it.

The idea of variability is important with respect to the second assumption we have made about discourse, that the discourse itself should be the focus of interest. We have argued that because discourse is constitutive of the phenomena of interest, not merely a reflection of phenomena, it cannot serve as a route to the inner workings of mind or as a tool to reconstruct events. That is, in discourse we are dealing with a version, and it is this version that is important, not the inferences that we (cannot) make from it. And we are not simply dealing with a single version, but with multiple versions. It is not possible to employ some standard against which we can compare versions so as to select the correct one, because that standard will itself be another version (see Potter & Wetherell, 1987, who also point out that the dichotomy between events in the world and linguistic representations of those events is itself a construction and a problematic one). This does not mean that there might not be criteria other than correctness or fidelity to the world for selecting a preferred version. At this point, readers might want to say that they may be able to accept the argument with respect to mind (i.e., that discourse is constitutive of mind, not a reference to mind), but that surely there are instances within the social sciences in which one wants to say something about events in the world. We quite agree and will consider in a later section some of the issues involved in making such statements.

There is one further point about variability that relates specifically to the idea that language is action. As long as discourse is viewed as referential, as merely descriptive of some internal structure or event in the world, it tends to have the status of a "thing," that is, of a material object that is constant across time and space. It is relatively easy then to discount notions of variability and versions and to view discourse merely as a basis for inferences about the cognitions and so forth to which it refers. In contrast, to see language as action is to see it as an event, to accept its variability, and to question it as a basis for inferences. It could be argued that to see language as action is to see it as behavior. Such a view might make the discursive position seem more acceptable or more familiar. Conventional researchers have no trouble recognizing the variability of behavior (although such variability is by and large the bane of their existence). But the discursive position is not that language is behavior. Such an interpretation reflects some fundamental confusions about language and discourse, action and behavior. We address these confusions next.

Language and Behavior

We focus here on social psychology because we know it best and because we think that it provides some of the best examples of confusion. The problem with seeing talk or language use as behavior is that this conflates two different ways of looking. We can look at talk—and other movements—as physical movements or as meaningful actions, that is, we can look at an event as either res naturam or res artem. The problem with much work in social psychology (we are wary of making this claim for other social sciences) is that it looks at movements (e.g., the movement of the lever on the "shock" machine in the Milgram obedience experiments, the utterance "Line A is longer than Line B" in conformity studies) as unproblematically equivalent to their meanings, that is, as actions (e.g., obedience or conformity). There is a failure to recognize that to describe something as an action is to make an interpretation, to give it social meaning (Bavelas, 1994). In most instances, the distinction is not acknowledged; the meanings are simply taken for granted. There are some exceptions. For example, Gilbert (1995) notes:

> None of us has ever *seen* a nurse help a patient or a used-car dealer cheat a customer. What we have seen is a series of physical movements: Thigh muscles contracting and releasing ... lips flapping, and all. But nowhere in this constellation of physical motions will we find *helping* and *cheating*, because *helping* and *cheating* are not actions, but *action identifications*. (p. 115)

We have little quarrel with Gilbert's claim until the point at which he states that helping and cheating are not actions, but rather action identifications. We object to this argument because it confuses the notion of actions (what is being done, i.e., helping and cheating) and action identifications (our definitions of what is being done). (We would say that to see behavior as helping and cheating is to see it not as movement, but as action.) The problem is compounded as the argument continues. Action identifications are discussed as "inferences we draw about the meaning of the physical changes that constitute behaviour" (Gilbert, 1995, p. 115). To call such identifications "inferences," rather than, for example, interpretations or claims about meaning, sets up the most problematic notion, namely the idea that "action identification, like any other form of inference, can go wrong," an idea continued in the next paragraph: "What factors determine the accuracy of our action identifications?" (Gilbert, 1995, p. 115).

The assumption is that meaning resides in the movements—we just need to identify the meaning correctly. But movements have no inherent, essential meaning; rather, they can be given multiple meanings by different interpreters (and by the same interpreter on different occasions), meanings that can vary across situations. For example, the meeting of certain body parts of two persons (notice how difficult it is to describe any movements without interpreting) can be called sexual intercourse by one person and rape by the other. And because the meaning is not inherent, there is no ground for selecting one or the other interpretation as more correct in the conventional sense of correspondence to the state of the world, as we discussed above. We may very well get agreement on what to call something, but this means only that the interpretation is shared. So, even though Gilbert recognizes that there are two different ways of looking, he ends up treating them as if they were the same, that is, as matters of res naturam, with all of the attendant notions of correctness, causality, and so on. As we have argued previously (see Kroger & Wood, 1998), this sort of approach is endemic in social psychology. (We note parenthetically that our reading of Gilbert's work is not a discourse-analytic one; it is simply standard conventional critique.)

In sum, from the discursive perspective, all movements, including utterances, are treated as actions, that is, as meaningful, social doings. With respect to attitudes, for example, the argument is as follows. To say, "I don't like spinach" or to wrinkle up one's nose when a plate of spinach is presented both involve the action of expressing an attitude. Neither is taken as indicative of some underlying attitude in the sense of a cognitive or mental structure; rather, the attitude is constituted in its expression. More simply, the actions do not reflect the attitude—they are the attitude. Note that the argument is not that there is no mental expression of such an attitude; there may or not be (e.g., a person may think or say to her or himself, "I don't like spinach"). As Potter and Wetherell (1987) discuss, the discursive position is not antimentalistic. However, the discursive position is anticognitive, in the sense that it does not see the mental expression as the true attitude, but as simply another expression. (And if the mental expression is inaccessible to another person, it is because it is private, not because it is mental.) Nor is the mental expression privileged in the sense of being the (underlying) cause of either the vocal expression of the attitude or of some other movement or action (e.g., pushing the spinach away, refusing an offer of spinach).

We have also tried to counter the notion that the discursive approach is simply a form of linguistic behaviorism. Edwards and Potter (1992, p. 100) have offered several reasons why such an analogy is misleading, and we shall not repeat those here. They include the point we have emphasized, that the discursive perspective approaches movement as action, not as physical movement or as undifferentiated behavior. We emphasize also that regardless of whether we approach talk and other movements as physical movements or as actions, we do so almost invariably in words; that is, both physical movements and actions are themselves constituted discursively. We have been considering this sort of activity in terms of our work as researchers, and it is worth reminding ourselves reflexively that our discursive formulations of utterances and other movements as physical movements or as actions and as particular sorts of actions (obedience, sexual intercourse, rape, etc.) have consequences (see Kroger & Wood, 1998). It is also worth reminding ourselves that the sorts of activities in which we engage as researchers are also engaged in by participants. That is, participants themselves have the option of treating the utterances of themselves and others as reflecting some sort of underlying inner cognition ("That's not what I really meant") or as actions in their own right ("What I mean is what I say"). Participants also have the option of treating their own accounts as simple, impartial descriptions of movements as physical movements (by deploying various devices designed to enhance facticity, objectivity, etc.) or of drawing attention to the status of their accounts as interpretations ("Well, I think that it's a crime—but that's just my opinion"). It is precisely these sorts of activities that we study.

PRACTICAL ISSUES

The emphasis in the discursive perspective on the way in which the world is socially—that is, discursively—constructed and on the multiple and relative rather than the singular reality-reflecting status of those constructions or versions is sometimes taken to mean that discourse analysis is not of practical use, that it provides no basis for social action. A detailed consideration of this issue would take us too far afield. Rather, we wish here to point only briefly to some of the features of the discursive perspective that are relevant to practical concerns.

First, talk is action, and discourse analysis involves talk (and writing); therefore, it is a form of action. Discourse analysis can contribute to change in the way that people talk. And again, because talk is action, change in talk (e.g., from sexist to nonsexist talk) is important not as something that is associated with change in practice; it *is* a change in practice. Discourse analysis can point to the ways in which certain practices serve to obscure and therefore perpetuate what is taken for granted. For example, consider the way in which the term *nurse* has been used without modification for a female nurse, but the term is marked by *male* when the nurse is a man; it is taken for granted that nurses are—or should be—women. (See also the discussion in Sampson, 1993, of the unarticulated standards used to judge members of minority groups and other cultures.) Discourse analysis can identify conversational practices that are problematic for participants and can also identify unproblematic practices that we (as members of the culture) think should be problematic (cf. MacMartin, Wood, & Kroger, in press). More generally, discourse analysis can help to identify alternative practices, ways that things could be done differently (Tracy, 1995). And the requirement that discourse-analytic claims be grounded in participants' rather than analysts' categories means that they are by definition relevant to participants' concerns and therefore have the potential to address those concerns. Papers in journals such as *Discourse & Society* and the work of critical discourse analysts, among others, speak to a variety of political, practical, and applied issues and to the utility of discourse analysts in addressing these issues, and we encourage readers to consider the ramifications for these concerns of the discourse-analytic research that we discuss in this book.

Some reservations about the discourse-analytic perspective relate to the idea that discourse is not treated as a report of either internal or external events and that discourse analysis is therefore not helpful to those who must make judgments about whether or not such reports are accurate or true, who must select a particular version as the correct one. We would argue that both theoretically and practically there is no basis to take reports as evidence for some internal event or attitude, notwithstanding the overwhelming reliance on such reports in many areas of the social sciences, in which the problematic status of self-report is largely ignored. There is no possibility of corroboration in the strict sense; researchers have devised numerous methods for attempting to subvert the problem, although many of these simply replicate the original problem of treating talk as a route to cognition. Usually, however, such reports are simply taken on faith. But this does not suggest that we must abandon concepts such as attitude that are invoked in the making of judgments about a person's actions. The discourse perspective does include such concepts, but as we have discussed above, the discourse perspective views them as they are realized in discourse rather than as internal, hidden events or things. Thus, we can agree that a person has expressed a racist or other inappropriate attitude without having to assume that she does or does not have such an underlying orientation. The discursive approach thus allows for strong condemnation of the utterance but does not require condemnation or exoneration of the speaker; it provides a conceptual foundation for the popular injunction that we should criticize the "behavior," not the person. It is the case that questions in law sometimes require judgments about mind (e.g., the notion of the guilty mind), intention, and so on. But again, the discursive perspective does treat these issues, albeit as matters of discourse rather than cognition, and furthermore, so does the law, at least as a practical matter. And discourse analysis can help us to illuminate precisely how judgments about intention and so on are worked up by participants in the legal process.

Is it not possible to take descriptions of external events as reasonably faithful versions of those events? There are two critical issues here from the discursive perspective. The first concerns memory. As with attitudes and attributions, discourse theorists have begun to turn their attention to remembering as a social action and to the identification of what counts as an accurate memory in terms of discursive, social construction (see Edwards & Potter, 1992). Discourse analysts cannot offer opinions about whether a specific memory is accurate; they can, however, point to the ways in which such a memory and the criteria used to assess it have been constructed. We think that such a contribution is an advance over conventional perspectives on memory, in which there are also problems with reported memories as reliable versions of events (either internal or external), particularly traumatic events (MacMartin & Yarmey, 1999); to date, proponents of these conventional perspectives have been unable to move beyond disagreements about whether memories are true or false.

The second issue concerns description itself. As we discussed previously, it is possible to approach the description of events as a matter of physical movement, to justify a particular description (e.g., that a particular man had a particular kind of bodily contact with a particular child) by pointing to physical evidence, for example, tests for the presence of semen or DNA assays. And there may be no dispute about this sort of description. The problem arises when we want to describe that contact as an action, for example, as child sexual abuse; there can be no evidence that such an action took place, because action is about meaning. We have only interpretations. Sometimes this does not matter, because there is agreement not only that particular movements occurred, but also that such movements should be interpreted in particular ways. For example, there are classic child sexual abuse scenarios, such that the movements involved are invariably constituted as child sexual abuse, at least within particular communities. But such agreement is often lacking, for example, in cases of sexual harassment or adult rape. This does not mean that there is no basis for the selection of a particular version as correct. There must be, or we would be unable to designate one version as right or wrong, yet we do this every day, both informally and formally (e.g., in the legal system). Rather, the correctness involved is social; it concerns correspondence not to the physical world, but to some criterion that is socially constructed in social terms. The selection of versions as socially acceptable might also be based on questions about what "works" or on practical tests in a social sense. For example, to call certain movements child sexual abuse is not simply to offer a version of their meaning. If the interpretation is enshrined in law, there will be consequences—consequences that may reduce the likelihood of such movements.

These sorts of considerations are by no means unknown to those who must make judgments. What can the discourse analyst add? We cannot contribute directly to decisions about whether a person has been killed or has had sexual relations, nor to decisions about whether these events should count as murder or rape (although as political activists, feminists, etc., we might want to do so). What we can do is to look at how factual discourse is built and used. Potter (1996) puts it this way: "An explicit account of some of the procedures involved in that building, and the relations between the nature of the description and how it is used, might well assist a critical evaluation of what is going on in [a] setting by both participants and analysts" (p. 230). We think that an analysis of how reality is represented is no small contribution. And as we discussed above, we can look at how people (including analysts) work up claims that they are doing a particular sort of description of some event as movement or interpretation, and how they work up particular kinds of interpretations. To make something count as a particular sort of description is an accomplishment. All descriptions involve a version, even those that are ostensibly about the world as a physical matter (as we see in disputes about such descriptions, e.g., the DNA evidence in the O. J. Simpson case in the United States). We cannot presume that "for any cases where descriptions are *actually at issue,* there is a straightforward, beyond-dispute procedure for getting them right" (Edwards, 1997, p. 304).

The discourse-analytic perspective on issues of truth and reality does not mean that it must necessarily undermine the efforts of those who must make such judgments; it does not argue that judgments cannot be made meaningfully. Commitment to the idea of multiple versions does not mean that there are no criteria for selecting one over the others, nor that one can avoid such selection. Relativism does not equal a lack of political commitment; the failure to take a stand *is* to take a stand (Gill, 1995). These issues reflect larger debates about realism, relativism, and social constructionism, debates that deserve much more extensive and sophisticated consideration than we can give them here. Discussions of the larger issues may be found in Edwards (1997), Gill (1995), Hacking (1999), Parker (1998), and Potter (1996).

SUMMARY

We have discussed in this chapter some of the central conceptual and theoretical issues involved in looking at language and discourse from a discursive perspective. We have argued that the discursive perspective entails three major differences from conventional orientations: (a) an emphasis on talk as action, (b) an emphasis on talk as the event of interest, and (c) an emphasis on variability. The shifts involved here are not minor. They entail fundamental reversals not only in focus, but also in the use of concepts that have been given privileged status. Cognition as both an explained and explanatory concept has come to be seen as less than useful. However, the notion of mind is retained in the sense that mind is constituted in talk. The shifts collapse old distinctions (language vs. thought, verbal vs. nonverbal, language vs. action) and make new ones relevant (movements vs. action). They involve reversals (e.g., variability is seen as an advantage rather than as a problem) and reframing (e.g., attitudes are viewed as categories of action rather than cognition, attributions are viewed as accomplishments rather than outcomes of cognitive processes, and consensus is seen as a construction rather than as information used to make attributions; cf. Edwards & Potter, 1992). The shifts also require other moves. Categories are treated as produced in discourse rather than as preexisting. The relevant categories are those of participants, rather than those of researchers. We treat these issues in detail in subsequent chapters. We merely note here that these moves and many others are entailed in the view of talk as action. The shifts—from a concern with what people are talking about to a concern with what they are doing in and with their talk and from a concern with what happened to a concern with how events are discursively constructed—require major shifts in the specific kinds of research questions that are asked. The shifts also have parallels in methodology. For example, they require a reversal in research strategy from a focus on the elimination of variability through techniques of data reduction (statistical or qualitative) to a search for variability as a tool for understanding and as a matter of interest in itself (Potter & Wetherell, 1987). More generally, these shifts suggest that we take nothing for granted and that we question everything, including our own categories and assumptions. This orientation is a major conceptual and methodological theme of the discursive perspective. In sum, we hope to have demonstrated that discourse analysis involves much more than method, that methodological change is part of an overall perspective requiring major change in how we think about and look at the social world.

2

Varieties of
Discourse Analysis

Newcomers to discourse analysis are often disconcerted to find that there is not just one but many varieties of discourse analysis. That state of affairs is due in part to the developing nature of the field and to differences in the disciplinary origins of discourse analysis. Discourse analysis originated in branches of philosophy, sociology, linguistics, and literary theory and is currently being developed and carried out in a variety of other disciplines as well, prominently in anthropology, communication, education, and psychology (Potter & Wetherell, 1987). Discourse analysis today is both multi- and interdisciplinary. That is a source both of strength and, sometimes, of confusion, especially to the beginning analyst. It means that the various perspectives differ in many dimensions, dimensions that are foundational and methodological. These dimensions include orientations toward language as action and as topic, the definition of terms, the nature and role of theory, the nature of research questions, the sorts of data that are analyzed, the conceptualization and treatment of context, data collection, sampling, transcription, categorization, levels of analysis, quantification, the warranting of claims, and the writing of reports. Initially, there was relatively little overlap across the different varieties. That is now changing, although there will always be some multiplicity of perspectives because different varieties not only serve different investigatory purposes, they also involve incompatible assumptions.

We cannot attempt either to identify all of the different varieties of discourse analysis or to discuss in any detail how they vary. Appendix B and the Glossary will give readers some sense of the features of various versions. Rather, our concern here is to focus briefly upon those varieties that are closest to the basic assumptions we considered in Chapter 1 and to consider them with respect to some general methodological issues. Before doing so, we attend briefly to a matter with which all the varieties of discourse analysis are concerned, namely, the meaning of *discourse*.

We use the term *discourse* to cover all spoken and written forms of language use (talk and text) as social practice. This usage works for most purposes, but does require further comment, because readers will undoubtedly run into variations. For example, some analysts use the terms *discourse* and *text* interchangeably; some use *discourse* for spoken forms and *text* for written forms (although both are verbal, a point we mention explicitly only because of the common usage of *verbal* to refer to oral rather than written language use, as in, e.g., a "verbal contract"). In some work, a more basic distinction is drawn, which parallels that made by Saussure (1974) between *la langue,* language as an abstract system of signs, and *la parole,* language as it is actually used by speakers—but this distinction is not marked by consistent use of the terms *discourse* and *text*. For example, text has been viewed as an abstract, theoretical construct that is realized in discourse (see also van Dijk, 1977), but sometimes the terms are reversed, that is, discourse is treated as an abstraction and text as its specific realization. And in some cases (e.g., poststructuralist work; see Potter & Wetherell, 1987, p. 31), the term *discourse* is used to encompass both the idea of language as a system of possibilities and the notion of use.

The issue is further complicated by the use of the term *discourse* to denote both a general concept (i.e., as a noncount noun), as in the preceding case, and separable entities (or systems) that can be counted (i.e., as a count noun). For example, consider Kress's (1989) version:

> Discourses are systematically-organized sets of statements which give expression to the meanings and values of an institution. . . . A discourse provides a set of possible statements about a given area, and organizes and gives structure to the manner in which a particular topic, object, process is to be talked about. (p. 7)

Other writers use the term *discourse* rather than *interpretive repertoire* to refer to structured systems of terms, figures of speech, and metaphors (Burman & Parker, 1993).

Further, neither *discourse* nor *text* is necessarily restricted to language. For example, Fairclough (1993) and Harré (1995) would extend the term *discourse* to include semiotic practice in other semiotic modalities (e.g., visual images and nonverbal movements); Parker (1989) defines texts as "delimited tissues of meaning which may be written, spoken or reproduced in *any form* that can be given an interpretative gloss" (p. 57).

Some of the distinctions between terms that we have discussed have been described simply as differences in emphasis (e.g., Stubbs, 1983). But others involve important theoretical and methodological issues. For example, the idea that the availability or prominence of certain discourses (e.g., about rape; see Chapters 3 and 7) can both enhance and constrain social practice is a major feature of some discourse-analytic work (e.g., in feminist and critical dis-

course analysis). The inclusion of visual images and graphics in notions of text
and discourse can be essential in the analysis of media (e.g., the examination in
Lazar, 1993, of advertisements that present images of a man and woman at
work accompanied by text that serves to undermine gender equality). The different notions of discourse embedded in various perspectives are one reason
why those perspectives are sometimes seen to be incompatible. Nonetheless,
our point here is simply to alert novice analysts to possible confusions rather
than to overburden them with scholastic preoccupations (for more on these,
see, e.g., Haberland, 1999). Our own general practice is to use the term *discourse* for both the activities of speaking (conversation or talk) and writing
(text) and their material embodiment, addressing any variations if required for
clarity. As a theoretical matter, we can see some merit in a broader sense of discourse that includes potentially all movement, not only speaking, writing, and
those movements traditionally included under nonverbal behavior, in order to
avoid prejudging their implications as and for social action. As a practical matter, discourse as we consider it here will be largely verbal (along with those features with which it is inextricably intertwined, e.g., pauses and intonation).

SELECTED VARIETIES

Not all varieties of discourse analysis are suitable for addressing questions
about social practice, because some varieties are both metatheoretically and
methodologically incompatible with the basic assumptions and goals we identified in Chapter 1. So, for example, we do not draw on the discourse processes
tradition (see Glossary) because of its emphasis on discourse as a route to presumed internal cognitive states and its reliance on conventional methodology.
We sketch here very roughly and broadly the major perspectives or groups of
perspectives that we find most useful for conducting research; their themes and
analytical categories are discussed in detail in Appendix B and are also explicated in the context of specific examples of analysis throughout the book. The
variety of discourse analysis that we find most useful is that developed in social
psychology (for ease of reference, we will refer to this as discourse analysis in
social psychology [DASP]), in particular by Edwards, Potter, and Wetherell
(e.g., Edwards & Potter, 1992; Potter & Wetherell, 1987). This is in part because
of our own disciplinary background, but also because this variety encompasses a
large set of concepts and notions that are useful in a variety of research projects,
and it tends to be most accessible to researchers in a number of disciplines. The
broad utility of this approach reflects the influence of a number of perspectives
and disciplines outside of social psychology (e.g., ethnomethodology, conversation analysis, sociology of scientific knowledge, poststructuralism, communication, linguistic philosophy) along with the development of these and other
approaches (e.g., rhetoric; cf. Billig, 1996) within social psychology (Potter,
1997). Some of the central concepts and notions of DASP are interpretive reper-

toires, attitudes and attributions as discursive accomplishments, accountability, practices of fact construction, the working of descriptions, the management of stake and interest, and emotion categories. Together with other analytic notions (such as those we later identify under other perspectives), these concepts span a range of concerns from micro- to macroanalytic (roughly speaking).

Conversation analysis (CA) is arguably the most microanalytic variety of discourse analysis; its origins are in sociology, in the work of Sacks and his colleagues (e.g., Sacks, Schegloff, & Jefferson, 1978). CA is now often referred to as "talk-in-interaction" (Schegloff, 1989) to stress that conversation analysts are interested not only in casual or everyday conversation, but also in a much broader range of material (e.g., talk in institutional settings). The primary focus of CA is sometimes said to be the organization of talk; however, it is more precise to say that the object of study is the interactional organization of meaningful action (including its nonverbal features; Pomerantz & Fehr, 1997). The great achievement of CA is that the investigation of seemingly narrow organizational features of interaction (e.g., turn taking) has yielded information about a very large number of practices and thus provides a wealth of analytic resources for the analysis not only of talk-in-interaction, but also of other sorts of discourse. For example, conversation analysts have identified differences in the structure of acceptances and refusals of invitations (more generally, preference structure); forms of conversational repair and other methods of conversational alignment; devices for the categorization of persons; practices in the management of arguments; and the ways in which storytelling is accomplished interactionally.

We also draw on other approaches, although in a somewhat different and more selective fashion. Critical discourse analysis (CDA; Fairclough & Wodak, 1997) refers to a set of discourse-analytic perspectives that, overall, are of the most macroanalytical sort. The origins of these perspectives are by and large in linguistics, and the perspectives all share a concern for critical examination of social and cultural practices (often within a Marxist perspective). The emphasis is thus on the understanding of discourse in relation to social problems; to social structural variables such as race, gender, and class; and above all to power. CDA perspectives vary a good deal, and we see some as more useful than others (e.g., those that stress qualitative and detailed empirical work and do not adopt the traditional cognitive perspective). We note here as well the broad perspective of poststructuralism (PS; see Potter, 1996), a general intellectual movement developed in French cultural analysis, history, and philosophy (by, e.g., Barthes, Derrida, Foucault). As a general movement, it is particularly difficult to summarize. Briefly, it involves going beyond a concern with the structure of language to consider a wide variety of features of language use, with an emphasis on the problems of treating texts as representational. One important notion concerns the ways in which discourses construct objects and subjects. For example, medical discourse not only constitutes a variety of objects (e.g., particular diseases); it also constitutes people as doctors and patients. Attention is also given to various sorts of oppositions (e.g., speech vs. writing) and ways to deconstruct them, and additionally, to absences and to concepts of authorship. There is some overlap between some forms of PS and of CDA, for example, the concern with discourses as well as discourse, the concept of intertextuality (see Chapter 8), and the emphasis on social change. The emphasis in CDA on linguistics and the breadth and relative inaccessibility of PS writing limit to some extent their utility for novice researchers. In addition, they are less helpful than some other perspectives, because they tend to emphasize abstract discourse functions rather than concrete, situated language use; furthermore, they are less specific in the provision of concepts and methods. But they are important for issues of breadth and context and for drawing attention to social practices on a large scale.

Finally, work in pragmatics is important for both foundational notions (e.g., the way in which utterances can be interpreted to mean something more or different from their conventional or literal meanings, i.e., conversational implicature; Grice, 1975) and for its attention to a wide variety of discourse features that play a role in analysis (e.g., grammatical devices, markers). Like CDA, pragmatics takes many forms, some of which are more useful than others (e.g., those that emphasize social vs. linguistic functions and do not rely on conventional experiments or the use of discourse fragments). However, in contrast to CDA, pragmatics is an important source of specific discursive features for use in a variety of approaches.

These, then are the major perspectives that inform our view of discourse analysis (with an emphasis on DASP and CA for research methods). But we also draw selectively on work from other perspectives and by particular researchers who do not fit very clearly within a particular approach. For example, concepts from narrative approaches can be useful in a number of ways, as can the work of Tannen (1989) on linguistic strategies that appear in both literary discourse and conversation (see Chapter 7 and Glossary for these and other possibilities). Our concern here has been to present the major perspectives in broad strokes. These perspectives share a number of similarities and a number of differences (see Appendix B for references to detailed comparisons); there are also similarities and differences that cut across perspectives. We consider next very briefly the features that are most important for research activities.

First, all of the major perspectives that we have discussed share an emphasis on discourse as practice. In discussing discourse as topic rather than resource, we stressed the focus on practice, on the phenomena constructed in discourse, on the actions being accomplished. We want here to modulate this point somewhat, because there is a variety of interests and goals in discourse-analytic research such that this focus may be in the foreground or the background in any particular project. Thus, some researchers (e.g., those working in the DASP tradition) may be interested in a particular practice (e.g., conversational repair) for the way it works in an episode of marital conflict, whereas others might be interested in that practice because they are concerned to say something general about conversation (in the CA tradition). Or a researcher might study the way in which Ph.D. examining committees negotiate a decision either because they are interested in negotiation or because they are interested in academic discourse. In other words, researchers may sometimes have an interest in discourse in general, for its own sake, in addition to a (necessary) concern for the particulars of practice. Practice may also be placed in the background in another way. For example, a researcher may have a particular interest in a certain kind of resource (e.g., interpretive repertoires, vivid description, the use of constructed dialogue) or in a particular phrase or set of expressions (e.g., *well, like,* "mall speak") and so may look at their use in a wide variety of practices. There is also a great deal of variety in the sorts of social practices and topics that are of interest to researchers; they can range from conventional, substantive concerns (e.g., identity, racism) to metatheoretical issues (e.g., the reformulation of attribution as a discursive practice rather than a cognitive process). It is possible nonetheless to identify certain themes in discourse-analytic work. Some of these themes may seem to be more characteristic of particular perspectives; for example, as we have noted, issues of power and inequality are particularly likely to be addressed directly in CDA or PS work. But the issue is more that certain themes are worked up differently in different perspectives. For example, notions of self and identity might be treated in CA as matters of "membership categories" and in PS as constituted by positioning in different discourses.

Second, there are differences in the sorts of discourse with which researchers work; to some extent, these line up with different perspectives. For example, in CA, the discourse of interest is talk in (naturally occurring) interaction. In pragmatics, the focus is on spoken language use. In CDA and PS, the emphasis is on written texts, media discourse (particularly written), interviews, and fictional work of various kinds (e.g., films), although there has been some attention to talk in institutional settings and in everyday interaction. Work in DASP includes all of these possibilities. There was originally a fairly heavy reliance on interviews, but more recent work is turning away from these (Potter, 1997; see also Chapter 5). There are signs that even CA is expanding the sorts of discourse it is willing to consider (e.g., Hopper, 1999, argues for the supplementary use of film and literary texts, and Hutchby & Wooffitt, 1998, examine interview data in their recent text on CA).

Third, we note that although not all of the perspectives originated in linguistics, they are all sensitive to linguistic features. There is a grammar to social life, both in the metaphorical or model sense (in that social life has a semantics and syntax; cf. Sacks, 1984) and in the way that social meanings are grammatically encoded (e.g., the way in which the use of passive voice allows the speaker to avoid identifying the agent of an action; the way in which the modal *should* encodes obligation). Overall, the focus is on the social functions of the linguistic features, not on the linguistic features in their own right. But there are variations in the extent to and manner in which researchers from different perspectives draw on linguistic evidence to develop and support analytic claims. For example, CDA researchers such as Fairclough (1992a) are inclined to stress the linguistic features of words or phrases in accounting for their social functions, whereas DASP researchers (e.g., MacMillan & Edwards, 1999) are more likely to consider the possibility that it may be some nonlinguistic feature (e.g., the implications of particular words or phrases) that is most crucial. Some researchers also point out that the relationship between grammar and social life can work both ways, that is, studies of language use can have implications for linguistics, for ways of thinking about language, grammar, and so on (see Ochs, Schegloff, & Thompson, 1996).

Finally, we raise briefly the issue of the direction of discourse effects. Approaches to discourse differ (not always explicitly) in how these are theorized. Some approaches (e.g., PS) emphasize the ways in which "people are positioned by and *effected through* discourse" (Edley & Wetherell, 1997, p. 205). Others (e.g., CA) stress the ways in which people are the active users of language. These views are sometimes distinguished as "top-down" and "bottom-up," respectively, because the former focuses upon language use in relation to broad cultural codes (the "discourse" of PS), whereas the latter focuses upon situated utterances. The issues here are "central to ongoing debates about agency and constraint in social life; that is, the extent to which social realities and actions are products of individual initiative or are shaped by larger social forces" (Miller, 1997, p. 37). But the views are not necessarily in conflict. It is possible to look at people in both ways, as "simultaneously the products *and* the producers of discourse" (Edley & Wetherell, p. 206).

The theoretical distinction is reflected in a distinction between top-down and bottom-up analytical procedures. The former tend to focus upon issues of power and ideology and to use analytical concepts such as interpretive repertoires, cultural narratives, and discursive regimes, concepts that are relatively broad. The latter emphasize the detailed structural and functional features of discourse, deploying such concepts as turn taking, preference, and fact construction (Edley & Wetherell, 1997). Again, the two approaches are not necessarily in conflict. As Miller (1997) notes, there are studies in which "agency and constraint are not mutually exclusive issues . . . but coterminous aspects of the settings under study and appropriate topics for study in their own right" (p. 37). We agree with the arguments of Edley and Wetherell and of Miller and others that both top-down and bottom-up approaches (theoretical and methodological) are useful. However, this is not to suggest that one can simply and unproblematically combine various versions of discourse analysis. It can certainly be argued that some are indeed incompatible with one another, for example, cognitive and noncognitive perspectives; however, in line with the discursive perspective, we would suggest that incommensurability be seen as a topic or issue to be addressed rather than as a problem or incontrovertible assumption. And within the collection of those perspectives we have discussed here, there seems to be a move toward recognizing the strengths of different approaches and the possibility of drawing on more than one approach within the same project.

The question then becomes one of how to go about doing this. In our view, the most appropriate strategy is to begin with participants' concerns, with the way that they themselves work up the issues at hand, before claiming, for example, that a piece of text demonstrates a particular discourse or facework or the operation of power. For example, in an analysis of sexual coercion, Gavey (1989) claimed that the discourses of permissive sexuality and of male sexual needs could be found in particular statements made by a woman asked to describe an uncomfortable sexual experience, and that these discourses positioned the woman in particular ways (e.g., as liberated, as responsive to male needs). Widdicombe (1995) suggested that this analysis was problematic, because there was no grounding of this claim in the discourse itself, that is, no identification of "what exactly [it is] about the words or phrases . . . that substantiates the claim that they are informed by or illustrate particular discourses" (p. 109). For example, no support is given for the equating of "I didn't want to hurt someone's feelings" with the satisfaction of men's need to have sex. Widdicombe argued that the "search for abstract discourses about which political statements can be made" misses "ways that people portray the significance of their own identities" (p. 124). But is an analysis grounded in participants' concerns sufficient, rather than merely necessary? How do you bring in notions of gender, power, and so on? There are lively debates around these questions (see, e.g., Schegloff, 1998; Wetherell, 1998) that we cannot pursue here. We think that there are possibilities, such as treating such notions in a sort of second-order analysis or bringing them into the discussion of the analysis (see MacMartin et al., in press; Schegloff, 1997). We address some of the details in Chapter 8. But we stress here that despite the difficulties of drawing on multiple approaches, being overly prescriptive about the right way to do discourse analysis closes off possibilities for dialogue, richness, and creativity (see also Wieder, 1999).

METHODS OF DISCOURSE ANALYSIS

We have argued for the strengths of drawing upon different perspectives, but we are mindful of the potential pitfalls of eclecticism. With respect to methodology, we therefore do not propose a simple combination of approaches, but a strategy of drawing upon resources—notions, techniques, devices, and strategies from different perspectives as appropriate to the specific project at hand. We propose, if you like, a kind of made-to-order rather than off-the-rack discourse analysis, a bricolage, in recognition of the different concerns of researchers. (See Denzin & Lincoln, 1994, on the qualitative researcher as *bricoleur,* i.e., someone who produces "a pieced-together, close-knit set of practices that provide solutions to a problem in a concrete situation," p. 2.) This does not mean that we rely only on the resources provided by the various perspectives. Bricolage may sometimes require us to develop our own particular techniques or to identify devices, practices, or resources that have not been discussed before, and this is one important way in which the field develops. Put simply, we should aim not only to use discourse analysis, but to do discourse analysis (see Schegloff, 1999, on this point with respect to CA).

We speak of methods in the plural in part because different perspectives are associated with different methods and in part to discourage the idea of there being *a* or *the* method of discourse analysis. There are some shared notions across perspectives with respect to methods, at least as we use them. For example, the collection of discourse data assumes that if we wish to understand social events, we need to look directly at those events as they unfold, not at retrospective reports or second-hand data or other forms of "self-report" (particularly questionnaires; see Hopper, 1999, for a discussion of such reports as "cartoon data"). And data analysis requires an attention to the details of talk and text that is a far cry from conventional approaches. But we want to emphasize that there are multiple possibilities with respect to data, data collection, and, especially, analytical resources and their use. At the same time, we stress that no analysis will use every possibility. Not all will be appropriate in each case. And there are always many different ways to look at a piece of text, at multiple versions of analysis. It is very unlikely that an individual analyst or even a group of analysts would wish to work them all up, even in the unlikely event that this were feasible. So how does the novice select the sorts of analytical resources to use? Researchers can be guided by their own specific interests in particular resources and practices, as well as by the specific goals that they have for a particular project. Above all, however, they should be guided by the data. The task of selection should become clearer through our subsequent discussion and examples of analysis. Researchers will also need to make decisions about the sort of data to use and how to collect the data; we discuss the theoretical and practical issues involved in Chapters 4 and 5.

We insert here a cautionary note. Analysts do not necessarily have to embrace the discursive perspective in order to carry out work in the way we will describe. As Coupland (1988) has phrased it, "Discourse analysis does not *have* to be sustained by a committed, interpretivist, relativist epistemology" (p. 5). But we think it important for researchers to understand and accept at least provisionally the basic assumptions that we have identified. There is room for some difference of opinion; for example, we will discuss some approaches and concepts about which we have reservations (e.g., facework). But we would strongly discourage certain sorts of projects, for example, those that involve distributional analysis. For example, a researcher may be concerned to document the extent of usage of a particular device or practice or to do some sort of comparison (e.g., across cultures, of women and men) of the use of a particular linguistic feature. This sort of work is highly problematic. There are, certainly, issues of sample size (in terms of both persons and utterances) and the type of data to be collected. But more important, we do not think it appropriate to ask these sorts of questions (e.g., gender comparisons) about this sort of language usage (devices taken out of context). So, we encourage readers to familiarize themselves with discourse analysis in its many varieties and to articulate their own assumptions—metatheoretical, epistemological, and methodological. Otherwise, discourse analysis runs the risk of becoming "just another thoughtless empirical technique" (Parker, 1992, p. 122).

We present in the next chapter examples of analysis that illustrate some of the possibilities we have discussed here. We hope to give readers a direct sense of what is involved in doing analysis before we go on to discuss methods of data collection and analysis in a more systematic and necessarily abstracted fashion. But first, we make some general comments about discourse analysis as we practice it in comparison to other sorts of qualitative perspectives and to content analysis as that term is usually understood. Our experience has been that because that kind of work involves qualitative (nonnumerical) data, novice discourse analysts tend to carry over assumptions from such work that inevitably get in the way when they go about their first projects. Our discussion also provides a different context in which to consider some of the principal features of discourse analysis.

Discourse Analysis and Other Qualitative Perspectives

Methods in the social sciences lie along a continuum ranging from the wholly quantitative (e.g., the quantitative analysis of quantitative data, as in the processing of personality-test scores) to the wholly qualitative (e.g., the qualitative analysis of qualitative data, as in CA). When we talk about "other qualitative perspectives," we are referring to approaches such as grounded theory (Glaser & Strauss, 1967) and narrative analysis (Sarbin, 1986), which differ from discourse analysis on other than the quantitative-qualitative dimension. Like discourse analysis, other qualitative perspectives also involve more than methodology. The relationship between discourse analysis and other qualitative perspectives is a complex one; a full comparison would require extensive treatment of the two in relation to metatheory, methodology, and analysis. We consider here only some basic points. In comparing the analytic methods of discourse and other qualitative perspectives, we focus on qualitative analysis as it pertains specifically to the discourse of research participants (rather than, e.g., the field notes of researchers) and in which the analysis, like that in discourse analysis, is discursive (i.e., qualitative or nonnumerical; see Chapter 8 for discussion of this issue). We emphasize the second point because we find that the term *qualitative analysis* is sometimes applied by conventional researchers, inappropriately, in our view, to work in which the data are qualitative but the analysis is quantitative. Discourse-analytic methods and those of other qualitative perspectives differ sufficiently to be identified as different methods. Some forms of qualitative analysis are in the positivist mode; analysis is seen in terms of variables or conventional notions of reliability and validity. But even those approaches that are compatible with a social-constructionist orientation (see Denzin & Lincoln, 1994) tend to involve some fundamental differences in perspective from discourse analysis, differences that are reflected in analytic procedures.

Discourse analysis differs metatheoretically from other forms of qualitative analysis in its view of experience as fundamentally constituted in discourse. The two involve different assumptions about language and the use of language as a resource. In other qualitative analysis, the concern is with what the discourse might reveal—about phenomenological experience, rules or scripts, social structure, and so on. In contrast, discourse analysis focuses on the discourse itself, not on internal structures or previous events to which the discourse is seen as a route. Discourse analysis "subvert[s] appeals to inner essence, whether it is defined cognitively (mechanistically) or phenomenologically (experientially)" (Parker, 1989, p. 114). Further, discourse analysis rejects the possibility of producing one true interpretation of the discourse (as do some other forms of qualitative analysis). This stance has implications for the ways in which analyses are warranted and evaluated (Tracy, 1995). Many versions of qualitative analysis assume that there is an objective world to be known; such versions use criteria of reliability and validity for evaluation, although they may use different terms for establishing reliability and validity in comparison to quantitative research. Discourse analysis rejects the assumption that there is a world (internal or external) that can be known separately from its construction in discourse and thus takes the view that it is inappropriate to use replicability and accuracy as criteria (see Chapter 10).

Discourse analysis is concerned with the identification of social functions, whereas many qualitative approaches are concerned with the generation of a set of interrelated (and often hierarchical) categories (a set that may or may not be taken to represent some internal psychological structure). In discourse analysis, the units of analysis are variable and may range from words, phrases, and sentences to paragraphs or even larger units. In other qualitative analysis, the units tend to be both fixed and somewhat larger, for example, lines or sentences or turns. The basic analytical strategy also differs. Other qualitative analysts would be likely to classify each unit under some category that captures the content of the talk—what is said; in contrast, a discourse analyst would also attempt to identify what is done and how it is done, that is, to identify the function of the talk not only by considering its content, but also by taking it apart to see how it is structured and organized. Discourse analysis places greater emphasis on variability (both within and between persons) than do other methods of qualitative analysis; for example, the latter are more concerned to work up a category scheme that will apply to all members of a group or subgroup, whereas discourse analysis is concerned to account for the discourse.

We contrast the two approaches to data analysis in terms of synthesis versus analysis. In the synthetic approach (conventional qualitative analysis), one first reduces the data by grouping it into categories (at which point analysis usually stops) and then proceeds to look for relationships among the categories. In the analytic (discourse-analytic) approach, one essentially expands the data by breaking it down and examining relationships among the components in order to identify function. (Even in grounded theory, which is sometimes described as a process of breaking down and then putting together the data, analysis seems often to consist of progressively more abstract categorization vs. analysis in the sense used in discourse analysis.) The difference is analogous to that in biology between anabolic and catabolic processes or that in algebra between the reduction and expansion of equations.

Discourse analysis and other forms of qualitative analysis do share a number of features, for example, the notion that discourse can have multiple functions or meanings. Additionally, any analysis must involve interpretive work of some sort along with categorization; for example, to identify a segment of talk as "overlapping speech" requires a decision about what counts as overlapping—about whether this instance fits that category. But in discourse analysis, categorization is more closely grounded in the specific discourse at hand. Discourse analysis also involves a different sort of categorization: what is categorized are the utterances of participants as movements (e.g., talking at the same time; see Chapter 1) rather than as actions (e.g., interruption) or as instances of some abstract category referring to internal experience, such as anxiety or impatience. Discourse analysis does make a move to treating utterances in terms of actions, but the critical point is that this sort of categorization must be shown to be an activity of participants; it cannot simply be the interpretation of the analyst.

There are additional differences in the conceptualization and treatment of "categories." Most critical is the emphasis in discourse analysis on the socially constructed nature of categories; categories and category construction should be constantly questioned rather than being taken for granted. For example, the category of "family" does not refer to a set of particular individuals, but to a way of interpreting, representing, and ordering social relations (Gubrium & Holstein, 1990). The straightforward application of the analyst's categories is seen by discourse analysts more as an imposition than an application, in that it ignores the participants' constructions. Categories are not simply a resource of the analyst. They are an important resource for participants, who construct and use them in a variety of ways for a variety of purposes. For example, categories make available various kinds of inferences; for example, the categorization of oneself as an "old person" can be used to suggest certain incapacities (e.g., memory failure). Thus, the task of discourse analysis is not to apply categories to participants' talk, but rather to identify the ways in which participants themselves actively construct and employ categories in their talk. Further, all categorization is provisional; analysis requires constant, reflexive attention to the process of categorization of both the participant and the analyst.

Our discussion to this point has been very abstract, so we present here one brief example of analysis to show the way in which discourse analysis treats categorization as a matter for participants and to contrast this treatment with that offered by one type of conventional qualitative approach, namely, grounded theory (Glaser & Strauss, 1967). The following excerpt is from an interview with a woman whose father is a resident in a long-term care facility (Dupuis, 1997):

> I would call it a fact of life, I guess. It is just part of my life. I think it is still trying to keep him as part of the family. I think that is it. I don't want to exclude him, that is the word that I am looking for. I don't want to exclude my father from anything. (p. 124)

We might begin our analysis by noting the use of the conditional *would* in the first sentence and its appearance in the phrase "I would call." The conditional frames the utterance as a response to a question from the interviewer (the implicit "If asked" or "Since you ask"); the phrase constructs what she is doing as naming her experience and doing so for the first time. (Consider possible alternative phrasings, such as "I call it a fact of life" or "It is a fact of life.") This interpretation is supported by the use of *I guess,* which, along with other modal expressions (*I think*), also serves to render the speaker's constructions as somewhat uncertain or at least hedged (weakened in force). There are also four uses of dummy *it,* that is, of a deictic whose reference is not identifiable (is ambiguous, nonexistent, or too broad; see Penelope, 1990). The first two uses could have multiple referents (e.g., her father's condition, his residence in the institution, her contacts with him). The third use seems to refer to her visits with her father, suggesting that this is likely also the referent for the first two uses. However, the fourth use ("I think that is it") involves a different referent and one that is quite ambiguous; the phrasing is a classic dummy *it* phrasing (as in "Coke is it"), although one could possibly read in something like "the reason for my visiting." So the discourse is marked by a kind of vagueness not only about the speaker's views, but also about the object or topic of those views.

The speaker also refers to a desire ("want") that in light of her prior utterances could be seen to construct a motive or goal for her actions. But this motive is constructed in negative terms (what she does not want to do) and further, it is one that she indicates is difficult to identify ("that is the word that I am looking for"—and note the formality of this expression in contrast to the phrasing that we might expect to see in this sort of conversation, i.e., "that's the word I'm looking for"). Further, formulating her wish as not wanting to exclude versus wanting to include reinforces the positioning of her father (as someone who until now has been included) that was done in the previous utterance ("keep him as part of the family"). In the last line, this wish is extended beyond the family via the extreme case formulation "anything" (Pomerantz, 1986).

For the next step in the analysis, we might want to recycle back to the beginning of the excerpt and ratchet the level of analysis up a notch to consider more directly the lexical content of the utterances. The speaker constructs *it* as a "fact of life," a categorization that is usually deployed to suggest that no further discussion or consideration is required. More specifically, we can see "a fact of life" as an idiomatic usage that resists challenge through its generality and taken-for-granted nature (recall our discussion in Chapter 1). (And as we noted previously, the speaker presents her answer in a way that suggests that this is the first time that any categorization has been called for.) The next sentence, "It is just part of my life," not only suggests that no categorization is required; it also frames *it* in a way that downplays any activities of the speaker (assuming that this is the referent for *it*) and thus implies that there is nothing to take credit for (an interpretation supported by the subsequent framing of the speaker's activities in terms of what she is not doing (does not want to do).

Our brief workup does not exhaust the possibilities for analysis of this excerpt, and the analysis would need to be considered in the context of the rest of the interview and its analysis. But we think that it is sufficient to show where this sort of finely detailed analysis is going. Our point is that it can be used to work up and ground a claim that the overall function of the speaker's talk in this excerpt is to construct a view of her activities as "taken for granted," both in the sense that it is assumed that she will do what she does and that this assumption is not identified explicitly. The import of this claim can be illustrated by comparing the analysis to that of Dupuis (1997), who used grounded theory in the study from which the excerpt was taken. Dupuis analyzed this excerpt as an example of one way in which adult daughters attempt to maintain normalcy, namely by maintaining the parent as part of the family unit. Maintaining normalcy was seen in turn as one of the purposes of regular visiting as described by adult daughters. We see here a good example of the contrast between grounded theory approaches and discourse analysis. The grounded theory analysis emphasizes a hierarchical, categorical approach in which discourse is seen as representing some underlying thematic structure, whereas our analysis has stressed the details of the discourse, the way in which the discourse itself involves the working up of a category and the functions of the discourse. The two analyses also differ substantively. In contrast to Dupuis's analysis, in which daughters are presented as deliberately pursuing a course of action in order to attain particular goals, our analysis suggests that at least for one daughter, there has been no clear formulation of her activities, that such a formulation is difficult to make, and that it is worked up on the spot, as it were. And these activities are not presented as specifically or identifiably motivated, but as something that she just does (in response to the possibility that her father might not be kept as part of the family, might be excluded from everything).

We note finally that differences between the implications of these two analyses are not trivial, although they may not be apparent from our brief discussion. But on the basis of our reading of other literature and of current developments in social policy, we would suggest that the naming, articulation, and specification of people's activities vis-à-vis their older family members is both part of and contributes to the trend toward the formalization of care. For example, the formulation of visiting your mother, taking her shopping and so on as "care giving" is the sort of discourse practice that can facilitate the off-loading of social services onto family members—for good or ill, depending upon how it is done. We cannot pursue this question here except to point out that it would take us in the direction of some form of critical discourse analysis.

In sum, the critical difference, in our view, between discourse analysis and other sorts of qualitative analysis is that discourse analysts do not view analysis in terms of or as equivalent to categorization; furthermore, discourse analysts are particularly wary of premature categorization. As Schegloff (1993) has argued, it is inappropriate to categorize before one has done the analysis that would warrant the use of that category.

Discourse Analysis and Content Analysis

Content analysis is often classified as a qualitative approach. However, we see it as quantitative, because although it deals with qualitative data, the analysis is quantitative. Conventional content analysis involves the coding of a text into mutually exclusive categories, the counting of category occurrences, and their statistical analysis. A frequently cited example is McClelland's (1961) work on achievement motivation, in which books from different cultures were analyzed for themes of achievement, and the achievement content of the books was taken as an index of cultural emphasis on achievement. The units of discourse that are coded may be words, phrases, sentences, themes, or units specific to the type of material that is analyzed (e.g., for newspapers, headlines or column inches). The content that is coded is limited to the representational, referential, or propositional meaning of the unit. Depending on the categories that are used, the coding may involve varying degrees of interpretation, but both the categories and the way that material is to be interpreted and coded are predetermined, that is, they are not guided by the discourse. Further, there is usually a check on the reliability of the coding via some sort of quantitative assessment of the degree of agreement among coders.

There are two major issues in the comparison of content analysis and discourse analysis. The first concerns content itself. In discourse analysis, the conception of content is much broader than it is in content analysis. As we discussed in Chapter 1, discourse analysts are interested in semantic or representational content, but this is not their only or primary concern. The second issue concerns the type of analysis involved. Discourse analysis does not involve coding into exclusive categories, because discourse can have multiple functions or meanings (and strictly speaking, discourse analysis does not involve coding into categories at all, as we discussed in the previous section). It also does not involve the use of predetermined categories or interpretations, the calculation of quantitative assessments of coding reliability, or the statistical analysis of relationships. Discourse analysis involves much more than coding and the assessment of relationships between coding categories. In sum, discourse analysis and content analysis are two very different species. Content analysis involves a much more mechanical process of categorization, neglects the possibility of multiple categorization, and aims to quantify the relationship between coding categories. It cannot provide the sort of sensitive, penetrating analysis provided by discourse analysis.

3

Examples of
Discourse Analysis

The spirit of discourse-analytic research is inductive; that is, it involves moving from the concrete to the abstract, from the particular to the general. In keeping with that spirit, we present in this chapter some examples of discourse-analytic research from which we hope readers will develop a sense of the activities involved before going on to the more abstract discussion of methods and analysis provided in Chapters 4 to 8. The best way to develop that sense is to carry out one's own analysis. The analysis of discourse data is partly a craft, in that it requires skills that cannot be wholly specified in cookbook fashion (take ½ cup of preference structure and fold into 2 cups of interpretive repertoires; mix well). But the analyst still requires an acquaintance with examples of discourse-analytic research in addition to a grasp of the general principles of discursive psychology and of the various methodological strategies and resources. Such familiarity is not a substitute for experience; it is a prerequisite. Research examples not only provide models for analysis; they also yield information about concepts, devices, practices, and strategies that can be used in analysis.

Accordingly, we present here a number of examples of discourse-analytic research drawn from published articles. We shall of necessity simplify the published analyses, reframing them as necessary for the purpose of illustrating particular points. (See Appendix A for an explanation of the transcription conventions and symbols used throughout the book.) We hope readers will be encouraged to consult the original works for the fuller presentations. We selected these examples for multiple reasons: to give readers some idea of how this type of research is done, to illustrate the different sorts of interests that we mentioned in Chapter 2, to show the use of different sorts of material in a variety of settings, to introduce some useful devices and strategies, to demonstrate the sort of work done within different perspectives, and to identify some of the issues in analysis. But we also selected the examples here because we found them to be intrinsically interesting, surprising, or both when we first came across them.

RESPONDING TO BEING TEASED

We begin with a study by Drew (1987), who used a conversation-analytic approach to investigate the phenomenon of serious or humorless responses to teasing in a large corpus of recordings of telephone and face-to-face conversations in arguably informal circumstances between people who are closely acquainted (as family members, classmates, etc.).

Excerpt 1 [p. 221]

```
      Dot:      Do we have two forks 'cause we're on television?
 →    Mother:   ⌈No we---
      Angie:    ⌊huh huh ⌈huh hh    ⌈h ( )
      Father:   ⌊Yeahah          ⌊h hah .hh=
      Mother:                       uh huh ⌈huh huh
      Angie:                              ⌊heh heh heh
      Father:                             ⌊ =Right yeh
                pro    ⌈bably the answer right (the - ⌈re)
      Angie:          ⌊eh hah hah                     |
 →    Mother:                                       ⌊.hhh You have pie
 →    Mother:   You have pie:: tonight
```

Mother responds to the tease with the beginning of a serious response, which she abandons when Angie starts to laugh. She joins that laughter shortly after Father does, but she eventually goes on to complete her serious correction with her explanation for setting two forks, which is that pie will be served. So what we have is a display of recognition of the tease (laughter) plus a serious response (rejection of the proposal in the tease). This combination occurs in various forms, that is, laughter that is prompted, simultaneous with or prior to the serious response, together with the serious response. (In only 3 cases out of approximately 50 is there laughter without a serious response; that is, the person being teased goes along with it.) Drew argues that the laughter displays recognition of the tease (and therefore requires such a recognition), but the serious response in itself does not display such recognition (although the person may have done so in prior or subsequent laughter). This means that a serious response cannot be explained simply as a failure of the person to recognize the tease.

But a display of recognition (usually by laughter) does not occur in all cases of a tease (although some displays may have been missed, e.g., if they involved

smiling or some other gesture rather than laughing that was not recorded because the interaction was not videotaped).

Excerpt 2 [Del is caller; p. 226]

```
Del:     What are you doing at ho:me.
              (1.7)
Paul:    Sitting down watching the tu: ⌈be,
Del:                                    ⌊khnhhh:: ih-huh .hhh
Del:     Wa:tching n-hghn .h you-nghn (0.4) watching dayti:me stories uh?
              (.)

→ Paul:  No I was just watching this: uh:m: (0.7) .h.khh you know one of
         them ga:me shows.
```

In this case, as in some others, there is no display of recognition of the tease (that
Paul is watching soap operas or junk), only a serious response (that he was
watching a game show).

Finally there are some instances in which a tease is ignored; that is, there is
neither an obvious display of recognition nor a serious response.

Excerpt 3 [p. 228]

```
Mary:    Well I know him from sight I u-he doesn't know me.
Al:      Oh.
              (.)
Al:      He'll get to know you (won't ⌈he). ihh

→ Mary:                              ⌊He seems like he's
         rilly a nice person. =
Al:      =Yeh he's okay.
```

In this excerpt, Al has invited Mary to a party. They are discussing another guest,
a member of a rock band, some of whose members Mary has dated from time to
time. Rather than responding to Al's tease, she produces a serious response of
what Drew calls innocent interest. Drew argues that although there is no obvious
display of recognition of the remark as a tease, as something not serious, ignoring the remark can be taken as such recognition. That is, the person treats the
remark as something not serious by ignoring it; she returns to what the teaser had
been talking about before the tease.

In general, then, recipients treat a tease as requiring a serious response, even
when they indicate their understanding that it is not serious. Before attempting
to account for this phenomenon, Drew addresses the issue of how we can iden-

tify something as a tease (given that participants may not display their recognition). He argues that teases are constructed in various ways to make it very clear that they are humorous and not to be taken seriously. The most striking feature is that of very obvious exaggeration; for example, in the excerpts above, being videorecorded by a friend is depicted as being "on television," "daytime stories" is an extreme version of soap operas and so forth (compare with bedtime stories as a children's activity), and "getting to know" someone is an understatement for sexual contact. Teases may instead or in addition be marked as teases through contrastiveness; that is, they contrast with something that both speakers know or that one has just told the other.

How can we account for serious responses to teasing even though the teases are apparently not sincere and are often recognized and responded to as not serious? In keeping with the conversation-analytic approach, Drew (1987) examines the "sequential environment for teasing" (p. 233); that is, he looks at where teases occur. He finds that they do not appear just anywhere, but rather, they are seconds (that is, turns that follow and therefore appear as responses) to some prior utterance of the person who is being teased. For example, in the second excerpt above, Del's tease follows Paul's admission to what Drew calls an offense of laziness: He is at home (vs. work, etc.), he is sitting down, and he is watching the "tube" (vs. a specific program). Drew found that all of the teases that he examined exploited their prior turns in some way, for example, by satirizing, trivializing, or doubting materials in the prior turn or turns—and the prior turns involved are always those of the person being teased (or turns in which that person is implicated in some way). Further, there is something about the prior turns that makes them particularly vulnerable to being exploited in a tease. To put it simply, they all have the property of being overdone in some way, because they involve excessive complaining, bragging, and so on. Thus, when we look at teases sequentially, we can see that a tease challenges some prior utterance of the person being teased—and that in responding seriously to the tease, the recipient reasserts their original version of some person, event, or other subject.

The close examination of the way teases are built and the places they appear also permits Drew (1987) to identify more specifically the functions of teases. Briefly, they serve to display skepticism of the teased person's claims, reports, assessments, and so on. They also function to attribute some kind of deviant activity or category to the teased person. For example, in the first excerpt, the deviance attributed to the Mother is that of being phony or pretentious (by setting two forks in the presence of nonintimates). As Drew points out, the activity or identity involved (i.e., the setting of forks, etc.) is not itself in dispute. This means that the deviant ascription may also conceivably apply. That is, it is close enough to reality to have a hostile element or at least to occasion a response by the teased person that will set the record straight.

Drew's (1987) analysis makes a number of points that have implications for discourse-analytic work more generally. First, it emphasizes that although we might be able to distinguish analytically between recognition (as a private matter) and the display of recognition, we can as a practical matter see only the latter—and we see the former only in the latter. The analysis thus highlights the necessity to focus strictly on what is done in interaction, including the constitution therein of what are conventionally treated as cognitive phenomena. It shows the use of laughter as a way of displaying an orientation (in this case, recognition) to the utterance of another participant (and points to the importance of having video recordings of face-to-face interaction for some analyses). The analysis also shows us that even something that is seemingly insignificant, such as a tease, is potentially a serious matter for participants, implicating as it does at least partially or possibly a negative evaluation of the tease recipient's identity or claims. Along this line, we would add that teases could also be treated in terms of their rhetorical function. That is, in displaying skepticism, teases are oriented to the possibility of an alternative version and can serve to undermine another's formulation of events, identity claims, and so on.

According to Hutchby and Wooffitt (1998), the phenomenon of interest in Drew's study—responses to teasing—is a particular one. That is, the responses do not have any generalized form; they have no defining characteristics in themselves, but rather, they are seen in terms of what they are responses *to* (p. 110). We turn next to a study in which the phenomenon of interest is a more general one, specifically, a conversational structure that can be used to dismiss any sort of rival claim.

MAKING CONCESSIONS

Antaki and Wetherell (1999) examined a phenomenon that they identify as "show" concessions, that is, a conversational structure in which a speaker not only concedes (i.e., agrees to a position on an issue after previously disagreeing), but also makes a show of conceding. Their data consisted of about 160 such structures that were drawn from five different sorts of transcribed material, including interviews of various sorts (e.g., with cancer patients), marriage guidance counseling sessions (see Chapter 9), and the London-Lund corpus of conversation (Svartvik & Quirk, 1980).

In this first excerpt, "the speaker 'makes a show' of their concession by proposing something, conceding counter-evidence, and then restating the original proposition" (Antaki & Wetherell, 1999, p. 9).

Excerpt 1 [Excerpt includes additional markings by Antaki & Wetherell to indicate propositions and reprise (in italics), to indicate concession and contrast markers (in bold), and to provide a "gloss" or interpretation (on right); p. 9.]

```
 1  A      you can really get used to the home
 2         brew (.)      ⌈no additives just sugar
 3  B                    ⌊( )
 4  A      and malt (.) and hops (.)
 5         the only thing I ever vary(.)
 6         you can vary is really              [proposition]
 7         well you can vary anything          [concession]
 8         but the only thing I'm (.) the thing
 9         that you really vary is (th-) hops  [reprise]
10         (.) you know and instead of putting
11         two ounces which is what they do in
12         these kits I put three to four
```

Note here the rhetorical effect. The speaker first makes a proposition in the form of an extreme case formulation (Pomerantz, 1986) ("the only thing"), which is very easy to disconfirm. The speaker then moves to defend against the danger of being challenged on this claim by making an explicit show of conceding (Line 7) and then reprising the original proposition. This draws attention to his awareness of the problem and easily rebuts it. His original proposition then sounds stronger—but it is exactly the same as the one that is reprised. Antaki and Wetherell argue that the three-part structure serves to undo any conceding that the concession alone can achieve. That is, "making a show of conceding fireproofs something in the speaker's own position, making it less liable to challenge, upset or rebuttal" (p. 11).

Antaki and Wetherell (1999) go on to compare the rhetorical effects of the three-part structure to ways of conceding that do not make a show of it. For example, a speaker can simply reply to a challenge from another party by agreeing after having disagreed. In contrast to the use of the three-part structure, simply conceding that you are wrong will not serve as a defense of your argument. Antaki and Wetherell secure this point by comparing an excerpt in which the speaker simply concedes to a challenge to a fictionalized (by the authors) version of the excerpt in which the speaker uses the three-part strategy. As the authors point out, we can hear the concession in this latter version as attending to and disarming the challenge. To save space, we will not reproduce that evidence here. Rather, we want to draw attention to the details of making a show.

Antaki and Wetherell (1999) propose that the outline of the three-part structure is as follows:

1. material that could reasonably be cast as being a challengeable proposition;
2. *okay, allright, of course, you know,* or other concessionary marker, plus material countable as evidence against the challengeable proposition or its implications;

3. *but, nevertheless,* or other contrastive conjunction plus (some recognizable version of) the original proposition. (p. 13)

Antaki and Wetherell identify two types of evidence that show that it is the participants themselves who display and orient to the three-part structure. The first is the speaker's use of specific markers. Concession markers usually concede evidence in some way; in addition to those identified above, speakers may also use markers such as *granted* or *fair enough.* There are also other expressions that can work as concession markers (e.g., *you know,* modals such as *can* or *could*), and there are combinations (as in the next Excerpt). The most obvious reprise or contrast marker is *but;* other possibilities include *nevertheless, whereas,* and *anyway.*

Excerpt 2 [pp. 14-15]

1	Resp	. . . and *it was the viciousness of it* [proposition]
2		that con ⌈cerned me. It wasn't (.2)
3	Int	⌊yeah
4	Resp	they **could** march a::ll day, >you know. [concession]
5		that was I-, **you know fair enough,**
6		they had that (.2) °and good°. **But**
7		*it was the viciousness of it* [reprise]

Antaki and Wetherell propose that concessionary markers have three functions. The first two are retrospective; markers (here, **could, you know fair enough**) frame what has gone before (the viciousness) as something that is disputable and as the source of the subsequently reprised proposition. The third function is prospective; the marker introduces what is to come as material offered to counter the proposition. We can also see here two functions of reprise or contrast markers. The contrast marker **but** signals that the concessionary material is finished and that what comes next is in opposition to what has been said previously. Antaki and Wetherell also emphasize that what follows the reprise marker "has to be a recognizable reprise of the original proposition, or the structure might not achieve hearable closure" (p. 14). To be recognizable, the reprise cannot be too different or distant from the original proposition; the closer it is, the more powerful the effect. In the previous excerpt, the reprise is very close and repeats the original proposition exactly (which Antaki & Wetherell suggest gives "the feel of deliberate rhetoric," p. 15).

The second type of evidence involves the way participants together coordinate the action. For example, the device may be realized in the utterances of more than one person; that is, the same person does not do all three parts of the structure. Antaki and Wetherell (1999) argue that this can only happen if there are expectable slots for the different parts, that is, if the three-part structure is indeed available as a resource for speakers to use. They give an example in which one speaker contributes the proposition (we're the envy of the world because we have the royal family) and concession (there are other royalty elsewhere—various and sundry kings), but another speaker does the reprise ("**but** *they're not like our Queen*," p. 16), which the first speaker then elaborates (by referring to a tradition of royalty).

To this point, Antaki and Wetherell (1999) have established that there is a three-part structure to which participants orient; this structure serves to bolster the speaker's position and, by implication, to weaken the countercase. These rhetorical effects are not available through contrasting ways of doing concession. But Antaki and Wetherell argue that the structure can also be used to attack an opponent's position as well as to defend one's own; that is, it can work as offensive as well as defensive rhetoric (see "Discourse Analysis in Social Psychology" in Appendix B). Antaki and Wetherell identify three ways in which the structure can be used offensively. In the absence of space to present the evidence provided by Antaki and Wetherell, we simply list them here: (a) Trojan horses (which incorporate a caricature of the other side's case), (b) stings in the tail (which reprise the original proposition as a reversal of the conceded material), and (c) cheapeners (whereby making something a concession serves to devalue the opposing case).

We summarize the features of the Antaki and Wetherell (1999) work that are noteworthy for the doing of discourse-analytic research by comparing their work to the study by Drew. Both studies draw on a range of data sources, particularly the Antaki and Wetherell work, which includes data of different sorts (e.g., from interviews). Like Drew, Antaki and Wetherell take a conversation-analytic approach, in that they are concerned with issues of structure and sequential organization. Unlike Drew, they deploy an analytical strategy that involves their own working up of a fictional version of a data excerpt in order to illustrate and support their claim that the structure they have identified works differently from others with which it can be contrasted. In both articles, there is a concern with issues that are broader than the particular discursive practices under analysis. Drew is concerned to make the point that identities and possible tensions relevant to teasing cannot be predicted but instead are occasioned in sequences of talk as resources for interactional use by speakers. Antaki and Wetherell are concerned to make their work a contribution to the discursive psychology of cognitive phenomena in talk. Along this line, we draw attention to an apparent parallel between the two studies, namely that Drew distinguishes between recognizing and displaying recognition, whereas Antaki and Wetherell distinguish between conceding and making a show of conceding. There is a difference, however. In the Drew study, recognizing remains a private matter. However, in the Antaki and Wetherell work, we can see in the data both the concession (e.g., "well you can vary anything") and the display of concession (via the three-part structure). That is, awareness of other positions is an interactional rather than a cognitive matter.

The Antaki and Wetherell work differs from that of Drew in that it draws not only on CA, but also on DASP, for example, in its attention to matters of stake and interest that are involved in the making of claims and to issues of rhetoric. It is more general in that it situates the "show concession" structure in a group of discursive devices that attend to similar concerns of stake and interest, and in that the structure itself is a general one, which can be used to dismiss rival claims of any sort. That generality is illustrated in the "glosses" that identify what is going on in abstract terms: proposition, concession, reprise. Such abstractions underline the importance and broad applicability of the structure; at the same time, their relevance to specific substantive topics or issues may not be readily apparent (although Antaki and Wetherell do briefly discuss racist talk in terms of the structure). We turn now to research in which a serious social issue was in the foreground of analysis.

LEGAL CONSTRUCTIONS OF SEXUAL ASSAULT

Coates, Bavelas, and Gibson (1994) analyzed trial judgments in cases of sexual assault. The impetus for their research was an idea that one reason for the failure of the criminal justice system in Canada to deal adequately with assault and sexual assault is that the language used in cases of assault fails to recognize such cases sufficiently as serious crimes. They analyzed a sample of 12 judgments by 10 different judges; all of the judgments included descriptions of the assaults with the judges' reasons and decisions. In 6 cases, the complainants were women; in the other 6 cases, they were children. All of the accused were men. There were 2 cases of acquittal; the remainder were convictions or guilty pleas.

Coates et al. (1994) identified a number of themes in the judgments that were anomalous in that the language used created unexpected meanings and implications. They report on five of these themes. The first was the erotic-affectionate characterization of sexual assault. Trial judgments might be expected to include a description of the assault in neutral or negative terms. Although this was the case in some judgments in which the accused was found or pleaded guilty, a number of the judgments used vocabulary that was better suited to consensual sexual acts than to assault. For example, the term *intercourse* (sometimes accompanied by *with*) was used to describe rape, even though the term intercourse is usually used to describe consensual sexual acts, not violence done to another person. Details of the assaults were described in sexual terms, for example, *fondling*. Assaults were often attributed to sexual, not violent sources (e.g., to the accused's sexual appetite rather than to his difficulty in controlling violent impulses). Coates et al. argue that this sort of language (of which they identify numerous other instances) is inappropriate and inaccurate and creates a misleading description of events.

The second theme was a distinction between sexual assault and violence. That is, the judges' references to the assault (in nonacquittals) referred to the lack of violence or of external violence, or they suggested that the violence was of a lesser degree. For example, a judge stated that one of the counts of assault for which a man was sentenced involved "less in the way of an actual physical assault" (Coates et al., 1994, p. 194). Such characterizations were used in some cases to mitigate the length of the sentence that was imposed. The descriptions of sexual assault as violent were infrequent and usually occurred in cases involving children.

The third theme involved the issue of appropriate resistance. For example, in one case of acquittal, the judge stated that "the complainant did not seize the opportunity to push the accused off her . . . [although] she had been able to do so earlier with her back and her legs" (Coates et al., 1994, p. 195). Coates et al. argued that "the clear implication is that she should have continued with actions that had not worked" (p. 195). Further, they suggest that the notion of appropriate resistance applies to combat between men who are equals and is not suited to asymmetrical situations in which there is a high likelihood of physical harm. In support of this argument, they note that children who did not resist were never criticized.

The fourth theme concerned the character of the offender. Coates et al. (1994) present a number of examples to show that, although in sentencing decisions the act was characterized negatively, the convicted defendant was often described in positive terms (e.g., impeccable or exceptional character). Finally, the last theme was the avoidance of agency for the assault. Judges frequently nominalized the acts, failing to identify either the agent or the victim (e.g., "there was an abuse of this trust," "they were both forced acts of buggery," p. 196). As Coates et al. point out, there are alternative ways of phrasing these statements that would assign responsibility. For example, they note that in one case, the judge stated that "Ms [X] sustained some bruises and a temporary limp" (p. 197). They suggest that in view of the defendant's conviction for the assault, this statement could well have read, "The accused hit Ms [X] hard enough to inflict some bruises and a temporary limp" (p. 197).

Coates et al. (1994) argue that the themes, that is, the patterns of language usage that they identified, are anomalous because they are inconsistent with both the law and the experience of the victims. But they are not "oddities" in the judgments; rather, they are "well integrated in the texts in which they occur" (p. 197). To explicate both the meaning of and basis for this claim, they draw on the notion of interpretive repertoires. Interpretive repertoires are general discursive resources that can be used by speakers and writers to construct versions of events, actions, persons, internal processes, and so on and to perform a variety of other actions (e.g., the justification of particular practices such as discrimination). Such repertoires have been defined in a variety of ways, for example, "systematically related sets of terms, often used with stylistic and grammatical coherence, and often organized around one or more central metaphors" (Potter, 1996, p. 116). Coates et al. suggest that there are only two repertoires that are available for describing sexual assault: stranger rape and consensual sex. (We describe these in detail in Chapter 8 in our discussion of Wood & Rennie, 1994.) These repertoires are alternatives; that is, in describing assault, one must draw on one or the other. The problem is that neither fits the majority of cases of sexual assaults, which are committed by assailants who are familiar to and often trusted by the victim. Coates et al. argue that the language used to describe assault adopts by default the consensual sex repertoire.

In order to illustrate and support their claim, Coates et al. (1994) present the first half of one of the sentencing judgments in the sample and provide a detailed analysis of the material in terms of the themes and the repertoires. We cannot report all of their points here; we focus instead on some of those that have not been covered above. Coates et al. note first that the unsuitability of the stranger rape repertoire is suggested in the judgment itself: "The circumstances surrounding the offence and the parties themselves are somewhat unusual" (p. 198). The judgment then adopts the default repertoire—a misunderstanding about consensual sex. Coates et al. argue that the events are presented in the form of an affectionate, romantic story, a claim that is supported by their re-presentation of the text with fictitious first names substituted for the words *complainant* and *accused* and with some parts elided. In this form, the story looks much like a romance novel in style, terms, and tropes. For example, "while she maintained that she was 'pinioned' in this position [sitting on the couch with her legs up across his lap] for up to two hours, she nevertheless admitted that she was even then generally enjoying the evening, the company, and the discussion" (p. 199). Further, a large portion of the judgment is devoted to this story, with relatively little attention to the issue of violence; details of the assault itself are vague, equivocal, or missing altogether. One paragraph lists specific acts of violence in which the offender did *not* engage; another discounts physical evidence of violence.

Coates et al. (1994) also point to the way in which the theme of the impeccable character of the offender is given prominence in the judgment. The 2nd, 3rd, and much of the 11th (last) paragraph are given to a detailed and positive description of the offender's immigration, work, and family history. Further, the complainant's character is not supposed to be at issue in Canadian law. Nonetheless, the judgment includes arguably gratuitous references to her education (identifying her as a Native Indian), to her marital status (divorced), and to her child (who lives with the other parent), all of which have negative implications. Coates et al. also focus in detail on three grammatical choices that avoid the offender's agency: (a) using passive or other indirect phrasing (e.g., "guilty of having committed" vs. "the accused committed"), (b) discursively constructing the complainant and the accused as a couple (e.g., "they" vs. "he and she"), and (c) diminishing the negative actions in which he is clearly the agent (e.g., by presenting them as her version).

Coates et al. (1994) present a strong case for their claim that the judgments illustrate and draw upon two limited repertoires. Studies of interpretive repertoires tend to emphasize their functions at a macro level, for example, in terms of their particular ideological effects, but their analysis nonetheless requires attention to the particulars through which such effects are created. Coates et al. identify various elements of the repertoires and show how they work and work together. For example, they consider alternative phrasings that would do different sorts of work; they also take into account the relative attention given to different matters, for example, the sexual versus violent nature of assaults and the character of the offender. The focus on repertoires locates this work within the DASP approach. We think that this sort of work would be enhanced by more detailed attention to other features of that approach. For example, we would stress the sort of work done by various descriptions of assault (rather than focusing, as Coates et al. do, on their accuracy, although we recognize the critical political function of framing the descriptions in this way), particularly with respect to the sorts of attributions that they do.

We would also recommend that researchers give some attention to the sort of discourse that they are analyzing—in this case, to the conventions of legal discourse (cf. MacMartin, 1999). For example, the use of neutral language to describe an offense reflects to some extent the requirement in writing legal judgments to demonstrate impartiality. The attention given to the character of the offender can be seen as a demonstration of the need to consider character in sentencing decisions. And the grammatical devices by which agency is avoided can be understood at least partially in terms of the requirement to focus specifically on particular elements of the crime. These considerations do not necessarily detract from an understanding of the judgments in terms of the repertoires identified by Coates et al. (1994). For example, it is important to note that not all judges adopt the language of neutrality and avoidance of agency. Rather, the point is that we need to situate our analysis in an understanding of legal conventions, to consider the ways in which general features of legal discourse can serve to support specific sorts of repertoires and particular versions of events in relation to particular sorts of offenses.

METAPHOR AND REMINISCENCE

One of the defining features of interpretive repertoires is metaphor. The analysis of metaphor is a feature of many different forms of research and has been used for a variety of purposes (e.g., to understand information processing, describe cognitive structures, etc.). We consider here a study in the DASP tradition that demonstrates a discourse-analytic approach to metaphor. Buchanan and Middleton (1993) examined the ways in which careworkers construct different versions of the value of reminiscence that relate to their different practices in us-

ing reminiscence in interactions with older persons. They analyzed extended excerpts from interviews with three workers, with a particular focus on the
metaphors, analogies, and figures of speech employed to characterize reminiscence and old age. For example, Mary presents reminiscence as a sort of time
travel: "it's alright to go back now and again," "taking them back (.) to war days,"
"sometimes they'll take theirselves back" (pp. 60-61). She contrasts reminiscence with the positive activity of keeping up to date (e.g., "but . . . I think's a
good thing to keep them up with the everyday goings on," p. 61). Without doing
so directly, she suggests that reminiscence might be problematic in that it dis-
places people from the present; furthermore, people might not only go back
(which in itself suggests a kind of regression) but stay back. Her use of metaphor
thus contributes to an argument for her relative avoidance of reminiscence.

Mary also uses a variety of other resources to construct this argument, many
of which serve to qualify her account. For example, she particularizes her argument by restricting it to the specific group with whom she works ("I don't like
to keep these [the "mentally alert"] away from today," p. 61). She also cuts
short her statement that "it's best to keep 'em- (.)" to offer first a qualification
("it's alright . . . now and then") and then a more moderate expression of her
original view, "a good thing" (pp. 60-61).

Buchanan and Middleton (1993) also draw on CA to give a finer reading of
what is accomplished in the workers' accounts and of the specific conversational devices by which this is achieved. For example, as we noted above,
Mary's talking about the present as a "good thing" implies that reminiscence
may not be positive without stating so directly. Buchanan and Middleton suggest that such indirectness can be viewed as marking a "dispreferred" version,
that is, a view that reminiscence is not as valuable as it is often assumed to be.

Jane uses a different metaphor to describe reminiscence and thus produces a
different version of its value: Older people are "walking encyclopedias" (Buchanan & Middleton, 1993, p. 69). Reminiscence is thus valuable because it involves the transmission of knowledge. But Jane's position on reminiscence is
not that simple; like Mary, she qualifies her view. Reminiscence is an inadequate token of exchange ("all they've got to give is their memories," p. 69; in
this statement, *all* = "only" or "just" memories) that is nonetheless valuable,
simply because it allows older people to reciprocate ("that's all they've got to
give to say thank you," p. 69). And Jane also talks in detail about how she attempts to keep clients up to date, and how this "stimulates their thinking"
(p. 68).

Neither Mary's nor Jane's position on reminiscence is simple; each displays
variability. But they are not equivalent; that is, there is also variability between
them. We could say that Mary and Jane take two different positions, except that
this would not do justice to the complexity of their accounts. For example,
Buchanan and Middleton (1993) argue that Mary does not simply defend her
unorthodox position. Rather, she makes her argument plausible by including
the opposite position, but she includes it as an extreme case formulation

(Pomerantz, 1986), which permits her to discount it. For example, in discussing whether it is good to talk about the past, she states, "not *all* the time no (.) not all the time" (p. 61). Few would agree with doing reminiscence all the time; rejection of this extreme view effectively serves to support Mary's position. But in constructing her argument as a kind of dialogue between two positions, Mary also recognizes some truth in other positions, a recognition that in itself renders her own position reasonable.

Like Mary, Jane also acknowledges that there are other views of reminiscence. However, she presents these in a different way, through the use of reported speech (e.g., "you'll hear people say (.) ooh he's telling me that story about when he was in the war," Buchanan & Middleton, 1993, p. 70). This sort of presentation allows Jane to discount such negative views of reminiscence by attributing them to others. As Buchanan and Middleton point out, we can also see reported speech as a way of presenting positions indirectly; such indirectness can serve to suggest that the position is "dispreferred," as we discussed above. We would add however, that although the position may be presented indirectly, the reported speech is itself direct; that is, the reporter (ostensibly) provides direct quotations rather than indirect quotations (or speech), which involves paraphrasing another's speech. Tannen (1989) has argued that direct reported speech makes accounts more vivid, more involving. Jane's use of this device thus permits her to emphasize the negative view of reminiscence while at the same time undermining that view. In sum, Buchanan and Middleton show that all three careworkers' accounts (including Anne's, which we did not discuss here) are constructed in such a way as to support a particular sort of activity (doing or not doing reminiscence work), but they do not involve simplistic versions. Rather, they entail complex arguments presented in dialogic form, and they draw on a wide variety of conversational devices, among them the use of metaphor. The study is a good example of the way in which the analysis of interview material can draw on a range of devices and strategies from the DASP tradition to elucidate the rhetorical organization of accounts of practices and the functions it serves. Buchanan and Middleton did not invoke here specifically the concept of interpretive repertoire, although their work suggests that it might be worthwhile to consider different views of reminiscence in terms of repertoires and to examine the use of such repertoires in different contexts and discourses, including the scholarly literature. They do include notions from CA, although they are less specifically concerned with issues of sequential organization, issues that are less likely to be in the foreground in the analysis of interviews or other material in which there are very long turns by one participant.

We mention briefly one other study in which attention is given to metaphor. Coupland, Coupland, and Robinson (1992) analyzed the responses of older participants to "How are you?" (HAY), which was the first question asked in interviews on experiences of health care. They were interested in the extent to which the question was treated as phatic (conventional) or nonphatic (genuine request for health-relevant information) and in the ways in which participants managed transitions from phatic questions to nonphatic talk about health. They found that most responses were neither strictly phatic nor nonphatic but instead were qualified or hedged. One common way of hedging was through the use of a verticality metaphor (e.g., "well (.) up and down like you know," p. 223). Coupland et al. note that this metaphor is used extensively in English to indicate goodness-badness, health-infirmity, and so forth; the Lakoff and Johnson (1980) work in which this is demonstrated is an excellent source of analyses of a variety of metaphors that figure in everyday discourse. Coupland et al. also identified a number of other sorts of hedged responses: filled pauses, qualified initial negative appraisals (e.g., "not too bad," p. 223), explicitly relativized appraisals (e.g., "a (.) few aches and pains like everybody else," p. 224), and laughter. Their study is a good example of work that focuses on a very narrow segment of an interaction but that nonetheless is relevant to a range of broader issues. The study is limited in that it does not track participants' initial responses across the remainder of the interview.

DOING FACE AND POLITENESS

We conclude with an example of analysis that uses the concepts of face and politeness. There are a number of different approaches to these concepts. We focus here on the one that has received the most attention, that of Brown and Levinson (1987). Briefly, Brown and Levinson argue that interactants are concerned to protect both their own face and that of others. Face, the public self-image that every member wants to claim for him or herself, consists "in two related aspects: (a) negative face: the basic claim to . . . freedom of action and freedom from imposition; (b) positive face: the positive consistent self-image . . . claimed by interactants" (p. 61). Social life requires us to carry out a variety of acts that threaten face (face-threatening acts, or FTAs), for example, making requests, asking for information, criticizing, making offers, expressing disagreement, and so on. In order to accomplish such acts with the least damage to face, interactants employ a variety of politeness strategies, which consist largely of a wide variety of ways of using language (lexical, syntactical, grammatical, prosodic). Strategies for carrying out FTAs are grouped as follows: on-record actions (communicative intention is clear) without redress to face; on-record actions with redressive action directed to positive face; on-record actions with redressive action directed to negative face; off-record actions (the meaning is to some extent negotiable, as in metaphor, hints, etc.); and not carrying out the act.

Research on politeness and facework has tended to focus on the analysis of spoken interaction. In contrast, Myers (1989) examined politeness in scientific articles; his work is a good example of the analysis of written material and of the use of many distinctions and concepts from the Brown and Levinson theory. Myers considered two kinds of FTAs: claims and denials of claims. Like criticisms, such acts may threaten both positive and negative face (in the sense that they both question the worth of other researchers' contributions and constrain the possibilities for future research). Myers focused his analysis largely on threats to the face(s) of the audience, although he does identify some of the ways in which the use of certain positive politeness devices (e.g., praise) may threaten the face of both the audience and the writer. Further, he focused specifically on some positive politeness strategies that emphasize solidarity (although one could argue that all positive politeness strategies do this) and on some negative politeness strategies involving various kinds of hedging (or ways of weakening claims). We have space here to give only a few examples (italics added by Myers; see Myers for source of quotations; page numbers refer to Myers article). Our first excerpt from Myers's examples is, "Although *we* may thus view genes and DNA as essentially 'selfish,' *most of us are*" (p. 7). In this excerpt, the authors mitigate the criticism of others' ideas by using pronouns that stress solidarity, specifically by including themselves in the group being criticized. But writers also use other devices to indicate common ground, for example, including one's own articles among studies that are criticized; showing "emotional" responses that indicate identification with a common goal (e.g., satisfaction: "one *pleasing* feature," p. 8; disappointment: "Unfortunately," p. 8); and joking (e.g., through new terms and titles: "the wobble hypothesis," p. 10).

The hedging of a claim is a negative politeness strategy insofar as it marks the statement as provisional in some way; it awaits acceptance by the readers and thus does not impose upon them. Hedging can be done in a variety of ways: the use of conditionals ("*might* be attached," "*could* be involved"); modifiers (adverbs; "*probably* spliced"); or articles (propose "*a*" vs. "*the*" structure) and the expression of personal viewpoints ("We believe," "I would like to argue"; examples from Myers, 1989, pp. 13, 15). All of these hedging words suggest that there are alternatives to the claim or claims being made. As Myers points out, such hedging of claims is very common in scientific texts. Some of the devices used (particularly the negative strategies) coincide with those that can be seen as required by a particular scientific attitude (e.g., hedging, impersonalization to convey objectivity); that is, they are not just oriented to the relation between writer and reader. However, others do not coincide with such conventions (and may seem contradictory to the scientific attitude by inserting personal beliefs, viewpoints, etc.). Myers therefore claims that there are many stylistic features of scientific discourse that can only be accounted for in terms of facework strategies.

Myers (1989) presents many more specific instances of the use of politeness strategies. We focus here on some more general features of his analysis. One of Myers's findings is that claims and denials of claims are usually redressed through the use of some sort of device that makes them more polite. He argues further that "these politeness strategies indicate the impositions inherent in these acts. That is, the texts themselves show that the authors are aware of the

FTAs" (p. 6; i.e., the texts orient to the face threat). Myers also considers exceptions to the general pattern, that is, cases in which claims are not redressed, and he shows that these can be accounted for in a way that is consistent with his interpretation of cases of redress, that is, that writers are orienting to face. It can be shown that for many of the claims made without redress, the benefit to the readers outweighs the threat (e.g., announcing a revolutionary technique), so that there is no need for redress. (Similarly, when describing methods, writers freely use imperatives, although these are usually considered to be quite face threatening and to call for mitigation.) For other cases, there are demands of efficiency that are accepted as outweighing the threat (e.g., in abstracts). Myers also considers cases in which mitigation is accomplished through the use of off-record or indirect strategies, for example, a violation of Gricean maxims that thereby implicates some sort of face threat. (See Appendix B for discussion of Gricean maxims.) For example, to state that "An understanding of . . . will be advanced only by rigorous testing of hypotheses" (Myers, 1989, p. 23) is to state something that should not require stating (because readers would all agree) and therefore implies (without saying so directly) that some researchers are not carrying out such testing.

Readers may have noticed that although there are a number of similarities between Myers's (1989) work and the studies that we have described above (e.g., some of the specific devices), the Myers work is different in that it relies on a specific single theory, a theory that requires explication before one can appreciate the analysis. This feature is related to the problem that we see in Myers's work, namely that there is insufficient support for the interpretation of the various features identified as doing facework. That is, the interpretations are not grounded in the orientations of the writers and readers of the articles, but rely instead on pretheorized categories of analysts. Myers's argument, at least in part, is that the interpretation of the discourse in terms of facework is supported by default; that is, many of the practices that he identifies cannot otherwise be accounted for. We would suggest however, that there are other possibilities, namely that most of these practices can also be seen as situated rhetoric, that is, as pointing to the possibility of other versions or claims in ways that serve to strengthen the author's own case. We have elsewhere discussed this and other interpretations that do not rely on facework (see MacMartin et al., in press). More generally, we think that Myers assumes that the conventions of scientific discourse are of a particular sort, that scientists will draw on what Gilbert and Mulkay (1984) identified as the empiricist repertoire. Very briefly, in this repertoire, priority is given to the data, and no mention is made of personal and social commitments. The use of devices such as impersonalization to do objectivity fits well with this repertoire. However, as Gilbert and Mulkay have shown, scientists also draw on a contingent repertoire, in which professional actions and beliefs are influenced by factors outside the realm of physical phenomena, such as personal characteristics and social ties (see Chapter 7). In using off-record or indirect strategies of the sort that Myers describes, writers can be seen to draw upon and orient to this repertoire, for example, by implying that there is some personal factor involved in the failure of some researchers to carry out rigorous testing. Similarly, the use of devices (e.g., those stressing common ground) that Myers describes as doing positive politeness can be understood in terms of a scientific repertoire in which the importance of social ties is recognized, without resorting to an interpretation that involves the positive face of readers.

Readers may wonder why we have included the Myers work in view of our reservations about the analysis. First, the use of theories and concepts of politeness and facework is common in certain sorts of discourse-analytic research (e.g., that of Tracy & Tracy, 1998), so analysts should have some familiarity with such work. Second, theories of politeness such as that of Brown and Levinson (1987) draw our attention to numerous and varied discourse devices, and we can see some of this richness in Myers's work. Further, the concepts themselves are intriguing, and despite the emerging controversies over their use in analysis as in the Myers work, there may still be a place for them in discourse-analytic work. We discuss these possibilities in Chapter 8 in the context of a more general consideration of participants' and analysts' concepts (see also MacMartin et al., in press). Finally, in addition to seeing the Myers work as a way to introduce some of the issues of interpretation that we take up later on, we also think that it is intrinsically interesting. In part, this is because of its focus on formal, written texts. More specifically, it illustrates a certain kind of reflexivity; that is, it is an example of using discourse-analytic methods to examine our own sort of activities, that is, academic work. We discuss other discourse-analytic work on scientific discourse in Chapter 7 (e.g., Potter, 1984) and Chapter 9 (Tracy & Carjuzáa, 1993; see also Tracy, 1997a).

Our discussion of these examples is intended to help readers develop a feel for the process of carrying out discourse-analytic research and to encourage them to carry out their own work. But you may still be wondering precisely how researchers go about generating their interpretations of and claims about discourse. We take up this matter in Chapters 7 and 8, following our discussion of issues of data and data collection.

PART II

METHOD

Discourse and Data

The focus in the previous chapter was on the broad spectrum of issues in discourse analysis. The emphasis here is on the question of what counts as discourse, as data in discourse analysis. In our experience, researchers new to discourse analysis tend to rely much too heavily on interviews. We want to encourage a much broader approach that reflects the view of discourse as including all forms of talk and text. Nonetheless, this does not mean that any discourse will do. We first address some issues to be considered in decisions about suitable discourse, and then discuss the variety of sources of discourse data, both in general and in the form of a list of examples.

ISSUES

Recordings and Records Versus Reports

The discourse that is the focus of analysis in discourse analysis does not refer to language in the abstract, but to language in use. That is, discourse refers to the words that were spoken, to the text that was written. But what we work with—the data—are audio or video recordings (for spoken discourse) and records, that is, written discourse itself. Spoken discourse is material but ephemeral, so we need to have a reproduction of that discourse that can be examined repeatedly. That reproduction must be a recording; we cannot rely on a recollection or report by researchers or other observers of what was said. Such reports are not the same as recordings or records that incorporate reported speech as part of a participant's discourse, for example, where the participant says, "Then John said, 'You must be wrong' and I almost exploded." These are not excluded because the focus is on the reported speech as part of what the current participant says, not as an utterance of the person whose speech is reported.

This methodological requirement is theoretically driven in that it reflects a theory of discourse, in particular the idea that the verbal (and nonverbal) details are critical and furthermore that a reporter's recollections necessarily entail an interpretation of what was said, not simply a description. It is therefore insufficient to work with a report of discourse, even if this is made in writing simultaneously with or immediately following the observation of the discourse, because even the most experienced researcher cannot possibly attend to and include all of the details that may be important, and the report will invariably embody potentially problematic formulations of the events. The report will be inadequate even if the reporter attempts to include verbatim speech rather than a summary, because speech occurs far too rapidly to be taken down completely and without misquotation. The reporter's recollections are not only ephemeral, they are also inaccessible and unavailable for analysis. Only a recording can allow the multiple listenings that are required for analysis.

There can be one exception to the requirement for recording, namely the use of court transcripts. Court reporters are skilled, and the transcripts are made with the aid of either a mechanical device, a shorthand system that permits rapid on-line note taking, or both; further, the formality and turn-taking system of courtroom proceedings make them somewhat easier to take down than everyday conversation. But such transcripts should be used with reservations and only if there is no other way to obtain that kind of important discourse.

Fidelity

The recording of spoken discourse must be of high fidelity; that is, it must correspond as closely as possible to the discourse. The making of a transcript also raises issues of fidelity, of preserving various features of the recording. We consider these in our discussion of the details of transcription in Chapter 6. For written discourse, concerns about fidelity only arise when the discourse and the record are not one and the same. For example, the written discourse may be altered or interpreted in some way in the preparation of the record. Such changes depend a good deal on the nature of the original written text. As Brown and Yule (1983) point out, interpretive work of some sort is likely to be required in cases in which the original text is literary (e.g., plays that appear in several different editions) or handwritten (e.g., letters; prescriptions; shopping lists; essays that present problems of legibility, spelling, etc.). There are also cases in which the written discourse cannot be copied or taken away, for example, when it appears in certain advertisements, graffiti, posted notices, and so on; a record will need to be produced in the form of a photograph or video recording. Although we aim for the highest fidelity that can reasonably be achieved, we must recognize that there is always some sort of intervention, interpretation, or transformation of the discourse by the researcher before the stage of analysis (see also Silverman, 1993, p. 208).

Naturalness

The term *natural* can be problematic. It is sometimes used to refer to discourse that is unplanned or spontaneous. There may be differences between planned and unplanned discourse (e.g., in linguistic features; Stubbs, 1983). But the distinction is difficult to make in practice and cuts across most forms of discourse. For example, written discourse may be planned or unplanned (e.g., e-mail), as may be spoken discourse (interviews or everyday conversation). Sometimes the term *planned* is used interchangeably with *constructed,* but all discourse is constructed, whether it is planned or not. Furthermore, it is all constructed from more or less the same materials, that is, the language that is available. Recommendations about the use of natural discourse refer therefore to the circumstances under which the discourse is produced. The concern is for discourse that is "naturally occurring," that is, discourse that is not produced through the instigation of the researcher (as it is, e.g., in interviews and, especially, laboratory studies; Psathas, 1995). The preference for naturally occurring talk is not because such talk is somehow more natural or more genuine. Language in the laboratory is natural in the sense that it is not out of place in that setting; as Potter and Wetherell (1995b) note, interaction in a research setting is "genuine": "it is genuine interaction in a laboratory" (p. 217). The same can be said about interviews. In any case, "any interactional phenomenon can be *naturalized* by *treating it* as natural" (Edwards, 1997, p. 89; see also Potter, 1997).

There are nonetheless concerns about the use of nonnaturally occurring talk. One problem is that language produced in the laboratory is not usually of interest in itself, but it also cannot be taken as a representation of (or substitute for) some discourse of interest that *is* naturally occurring, for example, everyday conversation. Discourse that is produced in interviews is less problematic in that it is not taken to represent naturally occurring discourse. But interview discourse is still restricted in that it is affected by the interests and formulations of the researcher (Potter, 1997; see also Edwards, 1997, p. 89).

We are in general agreement that discourse analysis should focus upon naturally occurring discourse, but we note some qualifications. First, the distinction between naturally occurring discourse and discourse produced at the instigation of the researcher is not always clear-cut. Consider, for example, work in which a researcher tapes a dinner conversation in her own home (e.g., Tannen's, 1984a, analysis of a Thanksgiving dinner); in such a case, the discourse is produced at the instigation of the person who is the researcher, but not primarily (or only) in her role as a researcher. Further, if a research participant were unaware of being a participant (e.g., if telephoned by someone who does not present him or herself as a researcher), the discourse produced would not be researcher instigated from that participant's point of view, although any contributions of the researcher (and the discourse overall) would not be naturally occurring. In part, the question here is whether you have a reason to analyze discourse that you (or some other researcher) are responsible for producing. A related issue concerns invented discourse, by which we mean discourse that is made up by the researcher (in some cases drawing on reported speech) to criticize previous research, to make a theoretical point or argument, to assist in analysis, or to supplement an empirical claim. (We exclude discourse invented for the purpose of data collection, e.g., as part of a scenario, because we would not treat such discourse as data.) Invented discourse can be helpful for analyzing other discourse (e.g., conversations), for example, when one substitutes a different utterance or adds an utterance in order to assess the function of the discourse at hand (see Chapter 7; see also Jackson, 1986).

Fictional discourse (e.g., novels, plays, films) deserves attention, because it is naturally occurring in that its production is not instigated by the researcher. Nonetheless, its specialized nature and its presentation as imaginary means that, like the discourse produced in laboratory studies, it will be of limited interest in its own right. But although fiction cannot be treated as representative of anything other than itself, there are interesting parallels between fictional works and everyday conversation (Tannen, 1989). And there are a number of special uses for fictional discourse (which includes both great works of art and works in the vulgar tongue, as in the ubiquitous TV sitcom). For example, fictional discourse can be analyzed for the ways in which it provides interpretive repertoires (see Chapters 3 and 7) on which other discourse users draw. It can thus play an important role in intertextual analysis (see Chapter 8). In addition to analyzing fictional work, discourse analysts can draw upon the variety of devices that have been identified by literary theorists and film analysts. Invented and fictional discourses are constructed for different purposes, but they are similar in many respects. Thus, fictional discourse can also be used to make a theoretical point or argument (see, e.g., Potter, 1996, who draws on the film *True Stories* to demonstrate some points about postmodernism) or to corroborate naturally occurring discourse (see, e.g., Hopper, 1999). And both invented and fictional discourse may be useful for planning research (see Chapter 12).

Discourse Recording

The requirement that we work with a recording of discourse raises concerns that the discourse might be affected by the process of recording it, in which case it is no longer naturally occurring and may thus be unrepresentative. First, we need to ask whether it is usual practice to record the discourse of interest, for example, in the case of the broadcast and recording of television debates. If so, representativeness would not be affected by the procedure of recording. Second, we need to address the basis for the concerns. Discourse is likely to be affected by the recording process only if speakers are aware that their discourse is being taped. But how can awareness be assessed? We need at least to separate the issue of awareness from the issue of whether or not speakers were informed that their discourse would be recorded. Some speakers may become aware that a tape is being made, although they were not so informed; others may have been informed, but they are not aware of or largely disregard the fact of recording. Further, the orientation of speakers to the process of recording may vary in degree, may change across time, may vary across interactants, and may depend on the topic of discourse and the nature of the situation. Some researchers have suggested that under some circumstances, participants forget that their discourse is being taped, for example, when they are highly involved in the activities taking place during the taping and when the recording takes place over a relatively long period of time. Lee and Peck (1995) analyzed discourse from a television series in which a network camera crew filmed family interactions in a home setting. They argue that the time period was sufficiently long for participants to become accustomed to the presence of the camera, and further, that "the interactional norms operating in groups where members know each other well often override the constraints of the recording situation" (p. 32). Grimshaw (1992) has made similar observations in the context of research on international negotiations. However, he notes that there is likely to be a long period of monitoring in such circumstances because of the greater stakes involved and because of concerns about the uses of records. He also suggests that monitoring could be reduced if recording were made routine. More generally, this practice is likely to be helpful because it allows both speakers and analysts to treat recording as a normal or familiar aspect of context rather than as something exotic or threatening. Ultimately, however, we need to accept that there is no clear way to eliminate or assess the effects of recording on discourse.

Nonverbal Data

Beginners and critics alike often ask, "(But) what about the nonverbal aspects of interaction?" Their concern is legitimate, but it also reflects a tendency that we see in both everyday and some social science discourse to give undue emphasis to the nonverbal, to see it as more important, as more deserving of attention than the verbal. We consider this issue here briefly in the course of setting out our view of the appropriate treatment of nonverbal data.

There are numerous reasons for this sort of emphasis on the nonverbal: the privileging of action over talk; the ideas that communication involves the transmission of messages (e.g., beliefs, attitudes, feelings, information), that there is only one underlying meaning, and that the best (most accurate) sign of that meaning is something that is nonverbal. The last notion assumes that the nonverbal channels are more trustworthy than the verbal, because they are less controllable (or more "leaky" of the true meaning) (see Brown, 1986). Research in the social sciences, particularly psychology, seemingly provides support for claims about the primacy of the nonverbal channels, especially in relation to the communication of attitudes and emotions.

There are multiple problems here: the failure to acknowledge the importance of language as action; the conduit metaphor; the assumption that apparent inconsistency is best addressed through an attempt to reduce action to one
message; the failure to recognize that language alone can perform multiple
complex functions, creating the appearance of contradiction. (And from a discourse-analytic perspective, we must question the very notion of contradiction: What we have at most is variability. What counts as a contradiction or as
inconsistency is disputable, worked up to accomplish particular effects.) We
can question claims about control and leakiness. We may monitor our posture, but our words may leak, and many of us, at least some of the time, appear
to exercise very little control over our speech. Further, the nonverbal aspects of
action are not necessarily inherently uncontrollable (Bavelas, 1994). If we had
as much instruction and experience in the control of the nonverbal aspects
as we have had in the control of the verbal (through formal education, literacy training, etc.), they might well be more controllable. (The emergence of
courses and books on the use of body language, etc., suggests that such a shift
is more than hypothetical, at least in North America). Problems also infect the
research on nonverbal communication. Brown (1986) has argued forcefully
that research showing the superiority of the nonverbal is able to do so only by
restricting or eliminating the verbal altogether (see also Beattie, 1983).

It may be the case that people pay more attention to nonverbal than to verbal
features (and argue that they are more important) in part because it is easier to
do so. The nonverbal features tend to be more visible (or audible) and tend to be
slower and easier to process (e.g., a particular gaze or tone of voice is usually
maintained across a stretch of speech). But people's reports of what they attend
to may not identify what they actually do attend to, nor do such reports show
unequivocally how people respond to the utterances of another person. Nonverbal features may also draw the attention of the analyst; transcripts are thus
particularly important for keeping our focus on the verbal as well as on the nonverbal.

Our comments have concerned whether particular claims about the nonverbal are supportable. As discourse analysts, we also want to examine those
claims in terms of their functions. We think that they can be viewed as situated
pieces of rhetoric designed to challenge or even dismiss work on language and
discourse. For example, the question "What about the nonverbal?" in response
to a description of discourse analysis suggests that discourse analysis neglects
an important aspect of social interaction. When prefaced by *but,* the question
works to set up the nonverbal in opposition to the verbal and to give the former
greater weight. But discourse analysts do not reject the nonverbal; rather, they
reject the blanket opposing of the verbal and the nonverbal.

We see the relationship of verbal and nonverbal features of interaction as
much more complex than is portrayed in the question "What about the nonverbal?" We do think that there are differences between the verbal and the nonverbal, and that it is important to note the "enormous range and flexibility of

verbal language" (Beattie, 1983, p. 6). And, as Brown (1986) has stated, "language is a universal medium that can express anything that can be thought or felt" (p. 500), whereas the nonverbal medium is much more limited in scope. But we would also stress the similarities. Language can be used in ways that are sometimes attributed only to the nonverbal system. For example, as we noted in Chapter 1, language can do style as well as content (or "how" as well as "what"). Compare "'Come in, Miss Jones. Do take a seat. I want to discuss with you why you've been absent for the past three days' and 'Hi Lesley, where've you been?'" (Beattie, 1983, p. 10). Ambiguity and indirectness can be achieved both verbally and nonverbally. Both language and the nonverbal system are indeterminate, in that the meaning of the signs within them is arbitrary (i.e., conventional, not given by nature), and ambiguous, in that they are inextricably tied to the context of use. But the picture is yet more complicated.

What Is Meant by "Nonverbal"?

There is a good deal of confusion about how language works, not only in popular discourse but also in the social sciences. For example, one undergraduate text contains the following statement: "It has been clearly established that teachers can convey their expectations to students *nonverbally,* [italics added] by their intonation, *words,* [italics added] and indications of their emotions" (Oskamp, 1997, p. 323). The statement locates what is done with words outside the verbal system. We see here the same sort of problem that Brown (1986) identified with respect to experimental studies: contributions of the verbal system are eliminated, and it is then argued that the nonverbal system predominates.

The classification of words as nonverbal is not a problem in the research literature on nonverbal behavior, but there are a number of other confusions or at least disagreements in that work. For example, Beattie (1983) has suggested that social psychologists tend to include "the vocal accompaniments of language (stress, tone, patterns of hesitation, etc.)" (pp. 9-10) in the nonverbal channel. Beattie continues, "Most linguists would, however, like to make a distinction between some of these elements—paralanguage (pauses, hesitations, etc.) and prosody (intonation and stress)" and would "include prosody as an essential element of language" (p. 10).

Beattie's (1983) arguments can be elaborated. Not all linguists would necessarily include or classify features in the same way. For example, Crystal (1987) includes timbre or voice quality (e.g., whispers, husky tone) under vocal paralanguage; more generally, he defines paralanguage as "features of speech or body language [body movement and appearance] considered to be marginal to language" (p. 427). Brown (1986) includes avoidance of eye contact, not smiling, and postural shifts along with high vocal pitch in the nonverbal channels, whereas he considers longer pauses and slips of the tongue along with slow rate under speech. There are other variations in what is or can be included in the channels, for example, whether the nonverbal channel should include appearance, dress, touch, gaze, personal space, posture, and so on or be restricted to certain bodily movements. There are also differences across languages in whether important distinctions are achieved semantically, grammatically, or through prosody or voice tone.

The notion of silence requires special attention. First, we need to distinguish between those cases in which a person has spoken, but we have no information about what the person said (e.g., we cannot hear them) and those cases in which a person did not speak, that is, was silent. The former are not cases of speakers working without the verbal system; it is only other interactants or analysts who are doing so (e.g., as in research in which participants are not permitted to hear what was said). But silence is not just an absence; rather, it is an absence that is unexpected and inappropriate. In conversation, such silences are the dispreferred response (see discussion of CA in Appendix B). We can probably all recall conversations in which one person says to another, "I'm upset because you're not talking to me"; in such a case, not talking is an action. Silence is the discourse analyst's version of mathematical zero. Its meaning is complicated and depends on where it occurs, as conversation analysts have shown (Sacks et al., 1978; Schegloff, 1995; see CA, Appendix B). On these grounds, silence could be assigned at least as well to the verbal as to the nonverbal channel.

Finally, we should also consider that written texts contain features that can be seen as equivalent to the nonverbal aspects of spoken language. These include the nature of the marks that are used to present the words, for example, lower- or uppercase letters (e.g., for flaming in e-mail), italics, bold type; their arrangement, patterning, or organization (e.g., as headings, in paragraphs); punctuation; nonverbal symbols, graphics, or images; and spacing (perhaps rarely, but possibly, a form of silence).

Implications

It is clear that discourse analysis does not neglect the nonverbal. We can ignore certain nonverbal components under some circumstances (e.g., gestures, eye contact, posture in telephone conversations), but we need to consider at least some nonverbal aspects, because the verbal system requires a physical (nonverbal) medium of delivery. We cannot utter words aloud without making a sound. This argument also applies to written language. The words as meaningful units are conveyed via marks on the page, and the organization of written work is conveyed not only by the words themselves, but also by the ways that their marks are patterned (e.g., in paragraphs). But the recognition of the importance of the nonverbal goes beyond this. The great emphasis placed on working with recordings of spoken discourse reflects the concern for preserving all of the details of interaction, both verbal and nonverbal. Similarly, the transcripts with which discourse analysts work include both the words and the nonverbal aspects (to varying degrees; see Chapter 6).

The inclusion of both verbal and nonverbal features reflects the view that not only are they both important, they are also interrelated and cannot be separated. As Beattie (1983) has argued, we should "not treat the verbal and nonverbal systems as separate and separable but as connected and connectable" (p. 11; see also Brown, 1986). We should consider them as going together, "as part of a precisely integrated whole" (Bavelas, 1990, p. 5). As a demonstration of this point, consider how we can look at the words on a transcript (or other piece of writing, e.g., an advertisement) and readily imagine what they sound like (although we cannot so easily hear sounds or observe other movements and imagine the words that are spoken). And after you have worked with a lot of transcripts, you notice that the verbal does tend to sound like it looks; if you read it aloud or to yourself and then compare this to the audiotape, you often (although not always) find that the versions sound very similar to each other. We are able to imagine the nonverbal features partly because the way in which the words are spoken is constrained by both social convention and physiology.

Thus, we do not think it fruitful to categorize various signs or signals as verbal, linguistic, paralinguistic, and so on. Rather, we should consider everything that might be important and view the whole as a semiotic system; that is, we should think of discourse in the broadest sense. This involves recognizing the multiple facets and functions of the system and attending to how its features can be seen to work together. Essentially, we use the same procedures of analysis for all features (see Chapters 7 and 8, which discusses an analysis in which the focus was laughter), treating each sign (including those identified by some as nonverbal, along with graphics, pictures, etc., as appropriate) as we do any other sign. We emphasize that this is not a question of the interaction of variables; the features cannot be treated in isolation as variables in the usual way, because their meaning is constantly shifting with the context. We need to analyze as many of these as are feasible and necessary for the project at hand.

This picture of semiotic harmony does not mean that the features will always work together cooperatively. It does mean that we cannot simply discount some features; if there appears to be a contradiction (between or within verbal and nonverbal features), we need to view it as we noted above, as a construction by participants, as an accomplishment of the discourse as a whole. We will certainly see what seems to be a sort of "good cop-bad cop" routine or something parallel to the "disagreement" between a salesperson and his or her partner or sales manager. But instead of assuming that one cop is nice and the other nasty, that the salesperson is being contradicted by the manager, we need to look at everything that is being done and ask what is accomplished through these packagings (to obtain a confession or to close a sale). To do so, we will need to give careful and thorough attention to the words that are spoken or written and to the form in which they appear.

Summary

In considering what can count as discourse data in discourse analysis, we have emphasized the need to work with recordings and records (not reports) of verbal and nonverbal aspects of discourse. We have also discussed the circumstances of discourse production and recording. We extend this discussion briefly and conclude with our own views of what is most appropriate for discourse analysis (views that we think are relatively common among discourse analysts, at least in their broad strokes).

The general discourse-analytic principle is that we do not go behind the text to look for a prior reality—events in the world or internal cognitions. Discourse is not a route to something outside the discourse, including other discourse. Discourse is situated and must be viewed in its own context. "Language is always observed within a social context of some kind; the concept of an unobserved, uncontaminated speech style is in fact an idealization" (Lee & Peck, 1995, p. 32). The discourse that we analyze can only be taken to represent itself; it cannot be treated as representative of discourse in another context. In conventional laboratory studies, this problem is discounted because of the assumption that researchers are gaining access to internal, stable characteristics of persons (cognitions, traits) that transcend situations (an assumption that also applies to conventional interviews). Theoretical challenges to the assumption of situational independence have not been extended to method; that is, such work fails to consider the situation in which assumptions are examined and to question the fundamental cognitive perspective on which it is based. In contrast, discourse analysis both challenges that perspective and realizes that challenge in method. It recognizes the theory-method link.

So, representativeness is not an issue as long as we study the discourse in which we are interested. We recognize that researchers may sometimes be interested in laboratory discourse, for example, if their questions concern research methods or where they judge laboratory talk to be as good as—though not a substitute for—any other kind and to have certain practical advantages. If the researcher's interests involve interpretive repertoires, the researcher may wish to study talk in (researcher-instigated) interview discourse. Researchers may be interested in how novelists portray particular features of speech (e.g., adjacency pairs) or have other specific uses for fictional or invented discourse, as we noted above. But we expect that most of the time, researchers will be interested in discourse as it occurs outside the laboratory or fiction—and therefore should be looking for discourse that is not produced through the instigation of the researcher and that is not explicitly fictional.

We must also recognize that we may not always be able to look directly at discourse in which we are interested because of ethical and practical concerns that require the modification of ideal practices. For example, there may be technical difficulties in recording discourse (e.g., outdoor conversations), and there are often ethical constraints on recording without informing participants.

We may sometimes want to draw on certain kinds of discourse (e.g., invented, fictional) because they are easy to produce or obtain and do not present problems of recording. But we should be careful not to fall back on these kinds simply because they are available or involve usual practice (e.g., laboratory studies, researcher interviews). Nonetheless, the study of certain topics (e.g., those involving actions, particularly by the powerful, that are considered to be private, secret, nonnormative) may be impossible unless we are willing to examine nonnaturally occurring talk or naturally occurring talk of a different kind. For example, it is extremely difficult to obtain recordings of naturally occurring interactions that involve child sexual abuse, so one must rely upon interviews, policy documents, courtroom proceedings, and so on and frame one's questions accordingly. Still, we recommend that in the first instance, researchers make their best effort to obtain naturally occurring discourse.

SOURCES OF DISCOURSE DATA

We assume that most readers will begin their work with an interest in some particular research question or phenomenon and will search for discourse data suited to this interest. However, we also suggest that work should begin whenever a researcher comes across or happens to have discourse that looks interesting (Sacks, 1984, p. 27). In any case, our main concern here is to emphasize that there are many possibilities for suitable data that researchers might not think of initially. One useful way to begin is to try to imagine all of the activities in which discourse related to the questions of interest might occur. For example, if the research question concerns identity construction in academic discourse, one could think of a variety of relevant activities: giving lectures or seminar presentations, meeting with students during office hours, submitting articles for journal publication, presenting a paper at a conference, participating in a thesis examination, asking questions of a colloquium speaker, conversing with faculty or students at lunch, requesting and writing letters of reference, and so on (e.g., see Tracy & Carjuzáa, 1993). And we can consider different ways of carrying out such activities. For example, if the research question concerns how people go about making a complaint, the researcher could examine written discourse (e.g., letters) or spoken discourse (e.g., telephone or face-to-face conversation). Even when one begins with an interest in a specific type of discourse (e.g., courtroom discourse), there are many details to be considered (e.g., the type of case, the presence of a jury, the type of exchange—direct or cross—and the like). We encourage the contemplation of a wide variety of possibilities and particulars in part because it is useful for opening up the research question, but also because the collection of discourse data can be very time consuming—and the analysis certainly will be. So if the researcher is constrained by a particular question, there is a need to be quite careful and selective in choosing data.

The selection of discourse also depends in part on the researcher's prefer-ences. Some researchers exclude written texts. Some researchers focus on written texts, and others include all sorts of spoken or written texts. Our own preferences are eclectic, and we provide suggestions for a variety of spoken and written texts. But we first address briefly some broader issues related to the selection of discourse data. First, there is the notion of the primacy of every-day, casual, or mundane conversation, by which is meant that talk in which the order and length of turns are not preassigned, in which the participants can choose the topics, and in which the topics are often personal (and perhaps, to outsiders, trivial; Edwards, 1997). The idea is that such talk is the basic form from which all other forms are derived and against which other forms can be seen as variations or deviations. This does not mean that our focus should be exclusively or largely on such talk. As Edwards points out, there may be no pure examples of mundane talk, and the idea that it is foundational may require qualification.

More generally, it is difficult to specify forms of discourse in any unambigu-ous way. We can probably agree on the specifications for gross categorizations, for example, written versus spoken discourse or telephone versus face-to-face talk, and we have no trouble identifying a particular instance of discourse as a member of such a category. We might also agree that interviews can be distin-guished from (other) conversations in terms of structural features of turn tak-ing, the use of pauses, and so on (Schegloff, 1993). But to call an interaction an interview involves more than a reference to such features. Such an appellation assumes differential power controlling the agenda and a unidirectional flow of information. As discussed above, we may wish to conceptualize research inter-views simply as interactions (which would be in line with the origin of the term: *inter*: between, and *videre*: to see). Similarly, the difference between conversations, interrogations, debates, and arguments can be seen as a matter not of structure but of orientation to power and purpose. For example, what is seen by one spouse as a conversation might be perceived by the other spouse as an interrogation. The distinction between monologue and dialogue is unsus-tainable if we recognize the dialogic properties of all discourse (Bakhtin, 1981). Nor does it help to distinguish forms of discourse in terms of particular properties. For example, everyday conversation is often described as spontane-ous and relatively unmonitored. But it is not necessarily the only form of discourse that is spontaneous, nor is conversation necessarily spontaneous. For example, a person's utterances in a casual conversation with a neighbor may have been carefully scripted and rehearsed, as when the person makes a complaint about the neighbor's noisy dog. Furthermore, conversations may vary a good deal in this regard, for example, across different settings (e.g., home vs. work; Potter & Wetherell, 1995b). Similarly, we cannot clearly class-ify some forms of discourse as literary (e.g., works of fiction) and others (e.g., everyday conversation) as not literary, given that all discourse may draw variously on a wide variety of literary devices (e.g., listing, repetition; see Tannen, 1989).

In sum, we cannot make statements about forms of discourse in general in terms of some set of essential properties. Rather, we must look at the forms as ways that people orient to discourse of a particular sort and further, at the way in which people do so on particular occasions. It is not that we cannot talk about formality, literary features, and so on; rather, we can only talk about them as distinctions made by participants themselves. We cannot specify ahead of time that the discourse we look at will be of a particular kind, because the features in which we are interested are matters of orientation rather than essence. The best we can do is to select material that may bear on our questions and to guard against taking its features for granted. More generally, we should be prepared to find that the material turns out to be a more interesting example of issues other than those with which we may have started (see Sacks, 1984, p. 27).

The reluctance to give an a priori identification to discourse creates some difficulty, because we need to identify what we are talking about in order to talk about it. It is awkward to refer simply to "what we are talking about," and it is perhaps also disingenuous, because we do have some shared understanding of terms such as *conversation* and *interview* that is adequate for many purposes. And we rely on these understandings here simply to discuss possibilities for selecting discourse data; however, we simply cannot do so for analysis (see Edwards, 1997, p. 63, on the notion of ethnomethodological indifference). We cannot provide an exhaustive list of the possibilities. As Psathas (1995) puts it, "All manner of interactional phenomena that a researcher may be able to come upon and record are potential data sources" (p. 45). But the very ubiquity of discourse means that the novice researcher may need some help in identifying sources. Table 4.1 presents a number of examples that we hope will stimulate readers to generate their own suggestions. The examples are organized largely around locations and format as physical or material categories in order to avoid as much as possible pretheorizing about the nature of the discourse and the persons involved. In the next chapter, we discuss how to go about collecting data from these sources.

TABLE 4.1 Sources of Discourse Data

Spoken Discourse: Face to face

Locations

Home (including residential institutions); school; offices or work sites; medical settings (hospitals, clinics, physicians' offices, nursing homes); legal settings (police stations, courthouses, prisons); playgrounds (athletic clubs, tennis courts, golf courses); museums; theaters; cinemas; stores; restaurants; street settings

Activities

Household chores, recreational interactions, parties; meetings, meals, coffee breaks, joint task, simulations or training exercises; medical interviews (discussions, meetings, question-and-answer sessions, interviews, and other exchanges); classroom or seminar discussions, job talks, book clubs, focus groups; faculty meetings, community meetings, conferences, conventions; ordering and purchasing merchandise, trading at the stock exchange, auctions, talk at information-return-complaint counters; therapy sessions, medical consultations; talk show interviews or conversations; political debates; door-to-door campaigning, selling, soliciting of donations; colloquia, oral examinations; parliamentary question period, Senate hearings, press conferences, courtroom and quasi-judicial proceedings (e.g., by professional associations); speeches, lectures, conference presentations; advertisements; opening and closing statements in courts of law; picketing; political demonstrations

Spoken Discourse: Telephone

Conference calls; calls to information, complaint, reservation, order (services, merchandise) lines; interviews; surveys; polling; emergency (911) calls; telephone answering machine messages

Spoken Discourse: Mediated or other

Television, film, documentaries; audio- or videotaped correspondence; messages

Written Discourse: Correspondence

Letters; memoranda; messages; e-mail (including "chat" groups); questionnaires and written responses; requests for feedback (e.g., by stores, airlines) and responses

Written Discourse: Publications

Articles in magazines, newspapers, and journals (e.g., academic articles); books, book chapters; court judgments, statutes; contracts; policy documents; advertisements, notices, signs, announcements; minutes of meetings; files (e.g., for job candidates, graduate school applicants, and patients, including case notes made following examinations, interviews, etc.); graffiti; calendars; brochures; manuals; letters to the editor; fictional work, namely novels, plays, short stories, television and film scripts, librettos, and poems

Written Discourse: Unpublished

Diaries, shopping lists, memos, notes; works of fiction

NOTE: Most written discourse will be found in paper or computer files (including the Internet) or on library shelves, but we should not overlook the wide variety of surfaces on which written discourse may be found, both indoors and outdoors (e.g., bulletin boards, walls, construction boardings, telephone poles, washroom cubicles).

Data Collection

We assume that our readers have experience in conducting research, and so we focus on issues that require special attention in discourse analysis. On the one hand, the emphasis on the situatedness of discourse suggests that particular care be taken to note the following sorts of information: the circumstances under which the discourse was produced and recorded; date, time, and place; the conditions under which documents (written texts) were produced (e.g., anonymity, confidentiality); and the ways in which they were preserved, stored, and made available to the researcher. Researchers will also invariably make observations about the characteristics of participants in the interaction (e.g., gender, age). On the other hand, all of this information can be problematic. People and situations can be described in multiple ways; descriptions are inevitably selective and may not capture those features that turn out to be relevant to participants. We return to this issue in our discussion of sampling below and in Chapter 8.

We first consider procedures for obtaining data (making recordings, finding records and recordings, interviews, and experiments) and then discuss issues of sample selection and size.

DATA COLLECTION PROCEDURES

Discourse Recordings

We consider here the major nontheoretical issues involved in making audio and video recordings of discourse. The process can be more complicated if the production of discourse is not instigated by the researcher, both because of the particular sorts of legal and ethical constraints involved and also because of technical constraints. For example, the researcher may have less control over the setting in which the discourse is recorded. There can also be a problem in making recordings from radio or television broadcasts.

If the broadcasts are not aired live, the broadcast tape may have been edited, and we end up with a recording of a recording that is not a sufficiently faithful reproduction of the original discourse.

There are a number of ethical issues to be addressed in making recordings of discourse, issues concerning permission (from participants and other parties), privacy, and potential consequences, among others. We do not discuss these in any detail here only because they are not unique to discourse analysis. We nonetheless stress that they deserve considered attention; it would be anti-thetical to the spirit of discourse analysis to assume that research objectives override the necessity to obtain informed consent whenever this is appropriate from an ethical (and not simply a legal) standpoint. But there can be creative solutions. For example, in some cases (e.g., recording a conversation of one's roommates or a seminar discussion), participants may be content to give a gen-eral permission for recording without the need to be informed in advance about the particular occasion on which it will take place, or they may consent to rou-tine recording without requiring that they be informed about the particular sec-tions that will be used for analysis.

There are a variety of technical issues to be considered. Except for research involving telephone calls, it must be decided whether the recording will in-clude both audio and video channels. The choice will depend in the first in-stance on the research question and on the extent to which the analysis needs to consider information that would be excluded from an audiotape. A videotape is clearly required if one is concerned with the coordination of discourse with other activities, for example, with the performance of a (nonverbal) task or with features that are only available on video (e.g., facial expression). Other cases are less obvious. It could be argued that the analyst can never be sure that a particular sort of information is not relevant, and some researchers (e.g., Bavelas, 1990) have urged that researchers routinely collect both auditory and visual information. We agree in principle but suggest that the advantages of video recordings need to be weighed against the substantially greater technical difficulties involved. The additional information available from a videotape may not be necessary to the extent that it is redundant with the discourse and the paralinguistic information available on an audiotape.

Readers are urged to consult the more detailed discussions of specifications and procedures that are available elsewhere. For example, work on interview-ing often includes a discussion of procedures for recording, as do discussions of the analysis of conversation. Kendon (1979; see also Heath, 1997) has con-sidered a number of aspects of the use of film and videotape. A number of chap-ters in Roger and Bull (1989) address various issues in audio and video recording. More recently, Goodwin (1993) has contributed a detailed account focused on the use of video, sound, and computer equipment. The sort of equipment available (as well as its cost) changes rapidly, so it is helpful to dis-cuss the possibilities with suppliers and also with other researchers who have recently done similar sorts of work.

Archives

The term *archives* is used here in a broad sense. We focus on public archives, but note that researchers may also maintain or have access to personal archives (e.g., videotapes of family occasions such as weddings, letters in written or audiotaped form, etc.). Public and university libraries are obvious places to look for magazines, newspapers, journals, books, and so on, but they may also have collections of films, including documentaries. Documentaries are useful because they often contain different types of discourse pertaining to the same topic, for example, interviews, speeches, and conversations. Libraries also include collections of letters as well as documents from various government departments. The libraries maintained by radio and television stations may include documentaries and recordings of drama, comedy, news, public affairs, and talk shows, and they may thus provide access to debates, question-and-answer sessions, quasi-everyday conversations, and so forth. Such libraries may also include records in the form of scripts and documents. Government departments are an obvious source of written documents (policy, legal statutes, etc.), but they may also provide recordings of conversations (e.g., emergency calls, telephone inquiries). Private companies and organizations (e.g., Better Business Bureau, telephone companies, consumer organizations, airlines, disute resolution services) may be willing to make available copies of correspondence or of audiotapes of telephone calls, because the work of a discourse analyst can supplement their own analyses and may potentially improve their procedures in various ways (e.g., see Firth, 1995). Audiotapes of training procedures in various educational institutions, government programs, and private industries may also be available for research purposes (e.g., simulations of physician-patient interactions, the training of customer service representatives, therapy conducted by apprentice clinicians). As in most research, serendipity is important; it helps to be alert for unexpected opportunities. For example, the chance remark of a colleague that he was on his way to a celebration of another colleague's successful appeal of a tenure decision led us to the collection of a sample of letters, because the comment suggested an opportunity to replicate and extend a previous study (Wood & Kroger, 1994).

There are also benefits to working with material from secondary sources. As a first step, a researcher might wish to consider whether any of the data that have been formally preserved in archive form would be suitable. For example, there is the University of Texas Conversation Library (see Hopper, 1992) and the data from the Child Language Data Exchange System (CHILDES) project (MacWhinney, 1991). Transcripts of various sorts have also been published; for example, see Crystal (1987, p. 411) for information about various computer corpora. More often, a researcher will be made aware of possible material either through publications or informal contacts (e.g., at conferences) and will attempt to obtain the material directly from the original researcher.

Researchers who are involved in some sort of service delivery (e.g., therapy, counseling, consulting) may be good sources, because such work may be recorded in conjunction with research activities as well as for training or consultation purposes. We should also consider the possibilities from disciplines that are not usually thought of in connection with discourse analysis; for example, historians can sometimes provide useful records (e.g., letters), as can social geographers (e.g., recordings or minutes of community meetings).

Researcher-Instigated Discourse

Interviews

Discourse-analytic work relies less on interviews today than it did initially, at least in DASP (Potter, 1997). But as we noted in Chapter 4, interviews still have a place, so it is worth mentioning briefly some of the important differences between interviews in discourse analysis and those with which readers are already familiar. The differences are both theoretical and procedural. Interviewing in discourse analysis is similar to interviewing in other forms of qualitative research in that both types are relatively unstructured; that is, the questions asked are open ended and cannot be entirely specified in advance. Both also employ a variety of probes or follow-up questions. But there are some differences in interviewing strategy based on differences in fundamental assumptions. In discourse analysis, encouraging participants to speak fully means encouraging them to display the sort of variability that is seen as a major feature of discourse and that is employed as an analytical tool. It is not assumed that there is a single, correct answer to a question and that the interviewer's task is to ensure that the participant transmit that information completely and accurately. Rather, what is produced is one possible version. From this point of view, the usual requirement that interviewers be neutral and uninvolved is problematic (Potter & Wetherell, 1995a). What is required is an "active" interview in which the interviewer and interviewee are viewed as equal partners in coconstructing meaning (Holstein & Gubrium, 1995). Answers that are produced in the interaction are not simply "there," waiting to be elicited; they may never have been produced before that moment.

In discourse analysis, then, interviews are both viewed and carried out as conversational encounters. Potter and Wetherell (1987) emphasize an interventionist approach; the interviewer "should try to generate interpretative contexts in the interview in such a way that the connections between the interviewee's accounting practices and variations in functional context become clear" (p. 164). The term *interventionist* is a good one; it means that the researcher is neither neutral nor indifferently supportive. It does not mean that we challenge the participant (in the sense of criticizing their contributions) but that we make the interview challenging by providing opportunities for the participant to produce the fullest account. It means taking the person seriously by responding to contributions in a way that permits him or her to consider possibilities and alternatives.

There are several ways in which this can be done. The same issue should be considered several times in different contexts (Potter & Wetherell, 1987), which will allow for the exploration of different formulations of events, the refining and reworking of categories (Widdicombe & Wooffitt, 1995), and the examination of ways in which answers to one question are related to answers to another. Discourse-analytic interviews require follow-up questions that involve or invite comparisons or the identification of limits (e.g., via extreme case formulations; see Appendix B) in addition to standard follow-up probes such as pauses, requests to say a little more about the topic, and so forth (see Spradley, 1979, for suggestions on different kinds of contrast questions). Discourse analysts also deal differently with the issue of seemingly irrelevant or overly discursive or rambling contributions by participants. Whereas other types of interviewing involve attempts to get the participant "back on track" or assume that relevance will emerge in the analysis, discourse-analytic interviews require pursuit of the relevance of the contribution with the participant at the time of the interview, an activity that requires not only careful listening but also ongoing interpretive work.

There is a good deal of material available on how to plan open-ended interviews (e.g., questions, probes; see Potter & Wetherell, 1987). In our view, one problem that has received insufficient attention is that we often seem to be asking participants to do our job rather than to speak in relation to their own experience. That is, we ask them to employ our abstractions and categories and to attend to the issues of interpretation that we think are important. (Such questions could be described as leading in a nonobvious way, in that they do not indicate the expected answer, but constrain its framing. This may render such questions even more restrictive than obviously leading questions; this fact points more generally to the problematic notion of the leading question.) DeVault's (1990) discussion of feminist strategies for interviewing emphasizes ways of asking questions that make sense to participants because they refer to participants' categories (e.g., what is involved in feeding a family, in keeping safe; how women spend time at home vs. a previously defined concept of housework; recall also the discussion of caregiving in Chapter 2). DeVault also conceptualizes an interview as an active conversation in which meanings are constructed together, and her model can be usefully extended to work with all participants. Questions that make sense to participants are often those to which participants can and will respond with a story of some sort.

Spradley (1979) suggests that we should not ask about the meaning of a term, but about the ways it is used. He also frames the interviewer's task as finding questions as well as answers; in order to understand participants'

answers, we need to understand the questions for which they see their responses as being answers. This does not necessarily mean that we avoid using
categories or asking questions that are not those of participants, but it does
mean that we do so for a specific purpose and recognize what we are doing.
Further, we also make such categories and questions open to discussion rather
than taking them for granted. For example, asking a person to identify the most
serious problems faced by seniors (e.g., as in some surveys) may help us to
identify prevailing cultural discourses about age and social problems (e.g.,
loneliness); it will not necessarily tell us whether or how categories of age and
of problems are relevant in that person's own constructions of identity and so
on. In sum, interviews in discourse analysis are viewed as a type of interaction,
as an unfolding sequence of coconstruction (Jacoby & Ochs, 1995).

Experiments

Experiments may be useful in some cases and with certain restrictions. By
experiments, we mean the instigation of discourse production by a researcher
who is not an interviewer or other sort of interactant. Such intervention is experimental in the broad sense of "to test or try"; it may also be experimental in a
more narrow sense; that is, it may involve some sort of systematic variation
(e.g., in the conditions under which data are produced or in the information
given to participants). As we discussed in Chapter 4, experiments are only appropriate for certain limited kinds of projects. We would add that they should
only be used if there is no alternative and that they should not involve deception, a convoluted practice that in our view entails so many ethical, methodological, and conceptual problems that the data are rendered uninterpretable.
We would also discourage experiments in which participants are assigned to
different conditions, because such experiments tend to involve inappropriate
comparisons and quantitative analyses and to obscure variability both between
and within participants. Nonetheless, there might be occasions on which a researcher wishes systematically to have participants produce data under different circumstances, for example, where carrying out all of the tasks might be too
much for one person. We describe next some examples of tasks or techniques
that can be used appropriately to generate discourse data.

Researchers may wish to bring participants together to discuss a particular
topic or to carry out a specific task; the interaction may be dyadic or in the form
of a focus or discussion group. For example, Bavelas, Chovil, Lawrie, and
Wade (1992) asked participants to tell each other about incidents they had experienced that involved a close call or near miss (e.g., an accident). Coupland,
Coupland, and Grainger (1991; see Chapter 9) recruited 20 older women from
Day Centres and 20 younger women through a newspaper advertisement. Each
woman was paired once with a same-age partner and once with a different-age
partner. The pairs were seated in a video studio and asked to "get to know one
another." Another example is the task developed by Blakar (1973) in which one

person is asked to describe two routes on a map. For the simple route, the maps used by each person are compatible. For the conflict route, the maps are incompatible and thus create problems for communication.

Cathers (1995) asked eight couples (each consisting of a man and a woman who had lived together for at least 5 years) to discuss eight scenarios describing everyday situations involving talk in close relationships; the scenarios were drawn from Tannen's (1990) work on gender and communication style. We note that some discourse analysts (e.g., Potter & Wetherell, 1987) discourage the use of scenarios. We would also reject the use of a conventional scenario methodology, that is, one in which the scenarios are viewed as experimentally manipulated stimuli for the delivery of independent variables, in which the scenarios are assumed to replicate the situation they describe, and in which participants' responses are taken as a stand-in for their response to that situation. But scenarios can be acceptable if viewed as detailed formulations of questions or if used to pose alternative or problematic views (as in discourse-analytic interviews). Similarly, techniques such as questionnaires and discourse completion tasks (i.e., asking participants how they would respond) are not helpful when used in conventional fashion because of the assumptions made about representation and because of the ways in which such techniques constrain discourse production (Turnbull & Saxton, 1997). But a conventional questionnaire (e.g., concerning racist attitudes or sexual behavior) might provide an interesting starting point for certain kinds of discussion (which could also generate material for a discourse-analytic critique of that methodology). Finally, participants can be asked to carry out a task that involves nonverbal activity (e.g., preparing a meal or wrapping a pram; Steiner, cited in Cranach & Kalbermatten, 1982).

Turnbull (see Turnbull & Saxton, 1997) has developed a technique for producing conversational data involving the refusal of requests. Students who signed up for a volunteer subject pool were telephoned by a research assistant who requested the student's participation in an experiment that was to take place on a Saturday morning; if asked about the purpose of the study, the caller said that it involved reactions to electric shock. The students were not informed initially that they were participating in an experiment nor that their conversations were being taped. The ethical concerns thus raised were addressed by informing the students immediately at the conclusion of the conversation about the taping and the experiment, by guaranteeing them anonymity, and by obtaining their permission to use the tape.

This technique avoids the difficulties that arise when participants are informed in advance that an experiment is to be conducted, but it is not clear how useful it would be for studying aspects of conversation other than refusals of requests or conversations that involve topics other than participation in an experiment. And these cases may raise yet more serious ethical concerns. At best, this sort of procedure should be reserved for those cases in which there is no alternative.

SAMPLE SELECTION AND SAMPLE SIZE

Issues

From the perspective of more conventional research, the samples involved in discourse-analytic research are often viewed as problematic, largely because they are thought to be too small to permit generalization of results beyond the sample. But discourse analysts do give careful attention to questions of sample identification, sample size, and generalizability. However, they consider these in relation to a set of very different goals, assumptions, and criteria for the warranting of research. There is a long story to be told about sampling, but we shall not do so here. We assume that readers are primarily interested in how to respond to the question "What about generalizability?" and in how to select the appropriate sample for discourse-analytic work. We comment briefly on the first concern and then focus our discussion on the second.

The simplest answer to the question is that discourse-analytic claims are as generalizable as those generated in other forms of research, particularly in experimental social psychology. There are differences in the nature of the claims that are made and in the way that they are justified, and these have implications for the role of sample size. In conventional research, claims involve statements about statistical relationships between quantified variables. For example, it has been found (Janoff-Bulman, 1979) that the more likely women are to blame their being raped on their own behavior, the more likely they are to believe that they can avoid rape in the future. In contrast, discourse-analytic claims are not about variables, and they are framed discursively. For example, Wood and Rennie (1994) found that the accounts of eight women who had been raped were characterized by complex discourse strategies involving both blame of various sorts and the absence of blame. These strategies were used to negotiate both victim and nonvictim identities (see Chapter 8 for details). The difference between the two approaches might be described as a difference between an external and an internal emphasis. The first approach tells us only that there is an association; the second tells us exactly how various versions of blame are worked up by participants in various ways to achieve different sorts of functions. We might say that it involves looking inside the correlation.

The nature of discourse-analytic claims reflects the stress of the discursive perspective on the problems entailed in premature abstraction and its emphasis on the necessity to ground analysis in particular concrete instances of discourse, understood as occasioned and contextualized. Discourse analysts try to avoid the "fallacy of abstractionism, that is, the fallacy of believing that you can know in a more abstract form what you do not know in the particular form" (Douglas, 1970, p. 11). (This is not to say that the statistical identification of relationships is a pointless task; we discuss its role in Chapter 8.)

The difference between the nature of discourse-analytic and conventional claims means that there are also different procedures for warranting claims in discourse analysis (see Chapter 10 for details). In conventional work, the validity of a claim depends upon the use of the appropriate statistical test, which both supports and depends upon the adequacy of the sample size. In discourse analysis, warranting procedures do not depend on statistical tests. This reflects in part the discursive nature of claims; it also reflects the requirement in discourse analysis that claims must not simply apply to the sample as a whole, but must also account for every instance relevant to the claim (via accounting for exceptions; see Chapters 8 and 10). The absence of statistical tests means that there is no test for the adequacy of the sample size, but the requirement of accounting for exceptions means that no such test is needed.

To some extent, the issue of small sample size in discourse-analytic work is moot, because the samples in discourse-analytic work are usually quite large in terms of language instances, as we discuss below. But sample size is not the only concern in relation to generalizability. We note that according to Rosenthal and Rosnow (1991, p. 205), the lack of random sampling in most experiments is not an issue, because in contrast to surveys, experiments are not intended to provide estimates of population values. The same applies to discourse analysis. Rosenthal and Rosnow argue that a greater problem in experiments is the overreliance on college students, who are likely to be unrepresentative even of other college students. This problem can be seen as one of generality (i.e., a discipline or field that relies largely on such studies is limited to claims about college students) or generalizability (i.e., the inferences made about the larger population on the basis of the study are inappropriate). From our point of view, the crucial issue is not the generalizability of a particular study but the generality of claims that can be made within a particular study and across studies. Given their emphasis on situatedness and fine detail and their reluctance to make unsupported inferences, discourse analysts tend to make few assumptions about generalizability and to take a piecemeal approach. But there is a good deal of variability both within and across different discourse-analytic approaches with respect to the generality of claims. For example, conversation analysts are often concerned to develop formal accounts of sequential patterns (e.g., the way in which refusals of invitations are structurally different from acceptances). But the concern does not stop there. Schegloff (1999), for example, emphasizes that we should "take the observations one makes in a particular context and ask how that serves to confirm and specify what has seemed to be the case with that phenomenon in other data, or how it mandates a change in our understanding of the phenomenon" (p. 146). This approach has worked to identify generalities of structure for a whole range of actions. What comes to mind readily is the robust phenomenon of preference structure. This phenomenon is remarkable for its generality across multiple situations and sorts of interaction—and it is based on very large samples of data. It is also general in that it is abstracted not only from specific wordings but also from specific actions. Other CA work is somewhat more restricted, in that it focuses on a particular device and on the social-interactional work the device is being used to do (e.g., the tease; Drew, 1987). Similarly, other sorts of discourse-analytic work also vary with respect to their generality. For example, Coupland and Coupland (1997) examined all national newspapers and the 23 most popular magazines in the United Kingdom over a period of 2 weeks in an analysis of environmental discourse, whereas the Wood and Rennie (1994) analysis of eight interviews was relatively circumscribed. Although the Wood and Rennie study identified some of the devices that are available for negotiating identity, it did not tell us about the range of circumstances in or experiences for which people might draw on these devices.

In sum, the first aim of analysis is to make statements about the sample that account for every instance of the particulars. We also want to make general statements that transcend individual episodes. But we want to support the general statements through actual demonstrations, not through sweeping attempts at generalization, such as those often found in experimental studies where the responses of undergraduates are shamelessly, if implicitly, extrapolated to all of humankind. We want to wait until the possibilities suggested by the analysis of those episodes are confirmed by the analysis of other episodes. We think it best to avoid general, a priori judgments about the generalizability of different types of research; rather, we should examine each project individually for what it claims and assess whether any inferences made are reasonable.

Nature of Sample

Decisions about the sort of sample to be selected in discourse analysis are similar to those in other research, in that the sample should be relevant to or representative of the phenomenon of interest. However, there are some additional considerations; the challenges of sample selection involve more than size. As Potter and Wetherell (1987) point out, the interest in discourse analysis is in language use rather than language users; the units of analysis are texts or parts of texts rather than participants. If one is interested in a particular aspect of discourse (e.g., identity construction by rape victims), one needs to identify types of text that are likely to contain instances of such discourse (e.g., interviews with rape victims). We do need to identify persons (or dyads or groups) or sources that are likely to provide the discourse of interest, but we need to keep our attention on the type of discourse, not on the person who produces it. For example, if the aim of an analysis is to examine fact construction in scientific journals, the sample could be selected to represent different sorts of journals, historical periods, and so on. The person who produces that discourse is by definition doing so as a scientist. The problem arises when the discourse is produced by persons who occupy multiple membership categories, any one of which might be relevant to discourse production, and we make unwarranted assumptions about those categories. We give just two brief examples.

Imagine that you want to study intergenerational discourse; you thus select a sample of conversations between persons of different ages. But age differences may or may not be necessary and are even more likely not to be sufficient for the production of intergenerational discourse. Any dyad that is potentially intergenerational can also be characterized in many other ways (e.g., by gender, similarity of interests), and it is these other ways that may be relevant to the participants (see Schegloff, 1997). Similar concerns arise with respect to other standard categories, such as gender and race. Our second example relates to categories of experience rather than to persons per se. A student wanted to interview a sample of women who had each resolved her grief over the death of her mother and a sample of women who had not in order to understand the two experiences. The difficulty with the proposal was that until she had actually interviewed the women, she could not really say much about whether or how they had "resolved their grief," and so she could not select her participants on this basis (without falling back upon questionnaires in which the dimensions of experience were predefined for participants, effectively preempting analysis).

The two examples illustrate somewhat different sorts of problems: which category to use as a basis for selection and how to know whether a particular person is a member of a category. But the examples are similar in that in both cases, the sample is not well defined until after the analysis is done; indeed, this can be seen as one of the purposes of analysis. Selection is thus provisional, but it is not haphazard, as long as it permits the inclusion of discourses that are relevant to the phenomenon of interest. The important point is to avoid unwarranted assumptions about the persons who generate the discourse.

Discourse analysis also differs from other approaches in its emphasis on variability, and thus on heterogeneity. For example, researchers using grounded theory may develop their analysis with a small group of participants who are relatively similar on some dimension and then check the analysis with a different group. In contrast, discourse analysts might want to begin with participants who, although similar in some sense, are different enough that they might give different versions. For example, in Levinas's (1995) study of sexual harassment, all the participants were members of a particular academic community, but some were men, some were women, some were faculty, and some were students. The aim was not to compare these groups but to ensure that potentially relevant groups were represented. As noted above, however, the relevance of any particular membership categories is disputable—and one could argue that any text or person who speaks to the issue at hand will do as well as any other. Still, as long as we are being selective, we might as well attempt to keep some dimensions homogeneous.

There may be benefits to analyzing discourse that we believe is unlikely or unrepresentative or discourse that is produced by atypical persons ("outliers") or groups; this may be a particular use for literary or invented discourse. In identifying the functions and effects of such discourse, we may also identify possibilities for the use of talk that have gone unrecognized. For example, such analysis could focus upon conversations that do not unfold in the way that conversation analysts have described (e.g., the conversations of people said to be suffering from schizophrenia).

Size of Sample

The labor-intensive, time-consuming nature of discourse transcription and analysis usually requires that sample size in the traditional sense of number of participants be relatively limited. The need for interviews to be conducted by researchers themselves can also limit the number of participants. However, because the focus of discourse analysis is language use rather than language users, the critical issue concerns the size of the sample of discourse (rather than the number of people) to be analyzed. For example, if the researcher is examining the structure of turn taking, a single conversation might be sufficient in that it would yield a large number of instances of turn taking (Potter & Wetherell, 1987, p. 161). In some instances, a single text might suffice, for example, when that particular text is the focus of interest and the effect described is important, interesting, or potentially consequential (Potter & Wetherell); in such instances, the sample is equivalent to the population. The most likely problem for the analyst is that the sample is too large rather than too small.

The specific research question or questions to be addressed and the type of analysis that is anticipated are obvious guides to sample size (although, as we discuss in Chapters 6 and 7, these may well be modified during initial reading and analysis). For example, if one is interested in the structure of a particular text, the sample will be that text. If one is interested in a particular aspect of discourse (e.g., identity construction by rape victims), one needs to obtain sufficient texts (e.g., interviews with rape victims) to yield numerous instances of such discourse. The (manageable) number required can usually be estimated fairly well based on the length and content of the interviews, on previous work, on experience and logic, and, if necessary, on one or two pilot interviews. One might need relatively more discourse for a coarse-grained analysis (e.g., of interpretive repertoires) than for a fine-grained analysis (e.g., of turn taking), and the amount of text necessary from each person or source will depend on the degree of emphasis in the analysis on sequential features and the scope of those sequences.

A preliminary reading of the texts selected may suggest a modification of the sample or sample size. Further modifications might be required after analysis is under way. If there appears to be a great deal of variability across participants in the discourse of interest, one might wish to collect more texts (or to narrow the focus of analysis); if there appears to be a good deal of overlap, the number of texts to be analyzed might be decreased. Such decisions will also depend on the extent of variability within texts—if it is large, there may be sufficient analytical leverage with a relatively small sample. Selection does become easier with experience. It depends in part on how well one can recognize important features and patterns in advance (Potter & Wetherell, 1987). For example, if the research questions concern a particular type of discourse with which the researcher is familiar (e.g., academic presentations), she or he will have some sense of the structures and functions that are likely to be critical and of their relative occurrence in a particular number of texts. Thus, although sample selection is provisional, experience and familiarity with a variety of published discourse analyses usually allow the analyst to make selections that turn out to be appropriate.

One notion on which qualitative researchers sometimes draw in deciding upon sample size is that of saturation, which in grounded theory means the analysis of additional protocols until one obtains no new categories, properties, or relationships among them, which often happens after the analysis of 5 to 10 protocols. However, in discourse analysis, the analyst works with many different kinds of units, treats categories differently, and is not necessarily interested in comprehensiveness. The concern is not so much with exhausting categories as with identifying some of the ways that people use language and working through these in detail. So the notion of saturation in discourse analysis is much more elastic: The endpoint is not that one stops finding anything new with further cases, but that the analysis of the cases considered to date has been thorough. The researcher must judge whether there are sufficient data to make an (interesting) argument and to warrant or justify that argument, for example, to provide the exceptions that can be used to assess claims. That is, the question about number comes down to having a sufficient number of arguments of sufficient quality and having sufficient data for those arguments to be well grounded. We would emphasize that discourse analysts have no need to apologize for small numbers of participants or texts—bigger is not necessarily better.

Preparation for Analysis

TRANSCRIPTION

Transcription refers to the transformation of spoken discourse into a written form that is fully amenable to analysis and available for inclusion in the report of the research. Researchers who are new to discourse analysis are sometimes surprised to learn that it requires the transcription of recordings. They are further dismayed to find that transcription is complicated and very time consuming. Transcripts are not the data (except for the very rare cases in which only a transcript is available). Rather, the data are the recordings themselves (Hutchby & Wooffitt, 1998), because regardless of how thorough and careful the analyst is in representing the features that are included, there are limits: A literal rendering is impossible. But the transcript makes analysis possible. Transcription is essential because it is not possible to keep the features of discourse in mind sufficiently while listening (recall the discussion of nonverbal data); we need to slow down the discourse so that the details can be identified. Transcription is also required so that a record of the data can be made available to others for checking the analysis and also for reanalysis (Hutchby & Wooffitt, p. 92).

Further, transcription must be comprehensive (verbatim), both because it is impossible to specify in advance which features might turn out to be important and because the details of discourse are critical for the preservation of variability and for interpretation. If the details are skipped, the analyst will be working with oversimplifications, idealizations, and unacknowledged interpretations (Heritage, 1984). Bavelas (1990) argues for including all features (particularly the nonverbal) in order to preserve context (but see O'Connell & Kowal, 1994, for a contrasting view). We do need to recognize that it is impossible to capture every feature of the original interaction or its recording and that the context of the original version is different from that in which analysis takes place (Tannen, 1989). Nonetheless, we agree with Bavelas (1990) that "we must maintain the integrity of the message" (p. 6). Although we may not be interested in certain features (e.g., pauses) and their functions, we should still include them, because they can assist us in the generation and justification of our interpretations and because they allow the reader to make a better assessment of our claims. And if sufficient detail is included, the transcript will be readily reusable for a different type of analysis. (Our focus here is on transcription of spoken discourse, because records of written discourse are usually unproblematic. But we note that even when working with written texts, care should be taken to include all of their features, not just the individual words; see Chapter 4 on nonverbal data.)

A major issue in transcription concerns the way in which discourse features are represented. The standard *orthographic* approach uses conventional spelling for words ("Well sir now I'm going to tell you something. I'm running a garage sale here.") and tends to use a verbal description for other signs (e.g., "laughs"). But this approach does not reproduce the sound of discourse very well. A *phonological* approach modifies the standard orthography by presenting words and other signs through a combination of words, quasi-words, and other symbols. For example, we might see, "Well sir now I' gon'tell yih sum'n. I'm runnin a g'rage sale here .hh" (from Schegloff, 1980, p. 137) or "heh heh heh" for laughter, brackets to indicate overlap, and so on. The most well-known system of this sort was developed principally by Jefferson (see Atkinson & Heritage, 1984); it is associated with CA but has been increasingly adopted by researchers who use other varieties of discourse analysis. Kelly and Local (1989) have criticized this system for producing transcriptions that are inconsistent and arbitrary in reflecting, for example, "features of tempo, pitch, loudness, vowel quality and voice quality" (p. 204), although they approve its treatment of other details, for example, "pausal phenomena, audible respiratory activity [and] the points at which overlapping talk began and ended" (p. 204). They argue for the use of a *phonetic* approach, which can provide a more precise specification of speech sounds, and they show that attention to phonetic detail may reveal some regularities that are not apparent in some transcriptions provided to them by Jefferson. However, they also express concern about the suitability of established phonetic notation systems for the study of conversation. Furthermore, phonetic approaches exceed the capacities of most nonlinguists and require specialized symbols, not all of which are readily available. Nonetheless, the discourse-analytic emphasis on detail and completeness means that transcription should use some system that enables the representation of sound beyond that given by the standard orthography.

One complaint about such systems is that they generate transcripts that are difficult for researchers from other disciplines or orientations to read. A related issue is that people (including researchers) frequently look at a transcript of their own discourse and find it difficult to recognize (or acknowledge) their own speech; it appears disfluent, full of grammatical errors, mispronunciations, and so on. They may say that they "don't sound like *that*," that talk when

you hear it does not sound like it looks on the page. This claim seems to contradict the argument we made in Chapter 4 that the transcripts do tend to sound
like they look. The trick is that one has to sound out the discourse, to read the
transcript aloud or at least to oneself. This makes the transcript easier to read; it
also makes the problems less noticeable and the discourse more recognizable
when it is one's own. The process is similar to what happens when you try to
read a foreign language that you have learned orally, through conversation,
television, and so forth. This may be possible only if you sound out the text.
When the issue is approached this way, we can say that the talk does indeed
sound like it looks on the transcript.

We have given this point some attention because researchers sometimes
wish to show the transcript to a participant (e.g., to obtain permission to quote).
The participant may not sound out the discourse and may find the inclusion of
seeming errors and irrelevancies patronizing or stigmatizing. So before showing a transcript, we may need first to explain why it looks like it does, to point
out that the everyday conversation of most people is ungrammatical, and so on,
and then to explain that it does not sound that way—which could be demonstrated by having the participant read a transcript aloud (perhaps of discourse
other than his or her own).

In sum, the most important point about transcription is that it is not simply a
technical issue of producing a record on paper of auditory and visual information, but a theoretical and analytical activity (cf. Kitzinger, 1998). Transcription involves theories—of language, method, and topic—and there is an
overlap between transcription and analysis. "The practice of transcription and
production of a transcript represents a distinctive stage in the process of data
analysis itself" (Hutchby & Wooffitt, 1998, p. 73).

Suggestions for Transcribing

We recommend the Jefferson system and have provided a version in Appendix A that includes most of the standard symbols. (It does not attend to visual
aspects of interaction, such as gaze, although some versions do, e.g., Atkinson
& Heritage, 1984.) Some version of the system is usually included in books on
CA and DA; the presentations vary somewhat because of the particular word-
processing systems used by different authors, because of authors' particular
preferences, and also because the system has been evolving (Hutchby &
Wooffitt, 1998). However, they all include attention to phenomena that are
central to the organization of conversation, for example, turns, speech onset,
overlaps, intonation, and so on. Hutchby and Wooffitt provide a useful discussion of how the Jefferson transcription conventions attend to the features of
conversation that are analytically significant in CA. But these features are also
relevant to issues other than the organization of conversation, so despite its
origins, the Jefferson system has turned out to be suitable for a wide variety of

interests and has been adopted by discourse analysts working within other perspectives. And although there have been critiques of the system, such as those we noted above, we think that it will be more than adequate for most purposes. The issue is partly one of accessibility (see Hutchby & Wooffitt), but it also reflects an emphasis on transcription as an aid to the analysis of recordings and not as a substitute for them. Further, both the process and the product of using the Jefferson system can be helpful in suggesting additional analyses. Like all systems, it has both advantages and disadvantages: "There cannot be a single ideal transcription" (O'Connell & Kowal, 1994, p. 104). (Readers are encouraged to see Hutchby & Wooffitt for a detailed comparison of the Jefferson and standard orthographic systems.)

Beginners might wish to start with a simplified version (e.g., Potter & Wetherell, 1987). But we encourage them to try to use a version of the full system, even for interview data (see Potter & Wetherell, 1995a). The system can be learned in a few hours of supervised practice (Hopper, 1989), although it takes somewhat longer to become at all fluent. Still, we recognize that the full Jefferson system may not always be the most suitable. In some cases, there may be practical issues, for example, with respect to the quality of the recording. There may be special challenges in both the transcription and translation of languages other than the one in which the analyst is working (often English, at least for the report) and also in the transcription of English spoken by those whose first language is not English (Jefferson, 1996). Or the analyst may need to adapt the system, for example, to develop additional symbols for features of the data that are not included. It may be helpful to read further about other systems that have been developed (e.g., O'Connell & Kowal, 1994). In addition, careful attention to discussions in research articles of the transcription system that was employed and especially to transcription as it appears in excerpts may yield additional symbols or ways of using existing symbols that analysts can add to their own developing collection of transcription possibilities (e.g., the use of "(.)" for brief pauses between words to capture "controlled enunciation"; see Tracy & Tracy, 1998).

Regardless of which system is used, there are some common requirements for making and using transcriptions after data have been collected. A thorough transcription of all speakers' contributions is required, including the questions and comments of an interviewer or researcher. The latter must be included as context for the answers. Some writers suggest that there should be repeated listenings before the transcription proper begins (even if one has decided provisionally what or how to transcribe). For example, Kendon (1979) proposes running through films a number of times and making rough charts of certain units such as waves or handshakes. The charts will gradually be revised and differentiated and are one of the outcomes of the research. But as we have stressed, the production of a transcript does not obviate the need for repeated listenings. Although we may agree that the discourse in general will tend to sound like it looks, this must always be checked in the particular case; further-more, we must be mindful that we can never record all nuances of sound on the transcript.

On the other hand, the emphasis on listening is no reason to be less than thor-ough in transcribing. For example, we may think that because we are going to be listening to the tape as well as working with the transcript, we can mark the transcript later if we notice anything on tape (especially nonverbal or para-linguistic features) that we want to include. But we may notice some features marked on the page that might be missed when listening. We also recommend the inclusion on the transcript of notations of events that were not picked up by the tape, for example, if there are interruptions (e.g., a person comes into the room, the doorbell rings, the cat jumps out, etc.). If the analyst is working with audio but has visual access, it is useful to make notes simultaneously on ges-tures, posture, and so on. And if you are reviewing tapes or transcripts with participants, they may point out events that occurred but are missed on the tape. The process of analysis then involves both continuous relistening and re-reading.

We have omitted one important point: Who makes the transcript? Atkinson (1984; see also Hutchby & Wooffitt, 1998) has argued that although the pro-duction of transcripts is very time consuming and requires intense concentra-tion, it should not be relegated to an audiotypist or research assistant. The close listening required for transcription helps the analyst to notice recurring details, ask what they are doing, and so on. We agree in principle, but in practice have found that it saves a good deal of time to have someone make a basic, rough transcript and then to go through it ourselves to produce the working transcript. Research assistants who are involved in the project can contribute at both stages; as Atkinson notes, there are advantages to listening or watching tapes with others both for producing the transcript and for analysis.

We recognize the temptation of working with transcripts that have been pro-duced by others, for example, transcripts of radio or television broadcasts or of court proceedings. But these can be problematic (unless obtained from a trust-worthy source, e.g., CA archives, as discussed in Chapter 5). The transcripts provided may have been cleaned up in some way (e.g., the correction of gram-matical errors and erasure of overlapping talk in courtroom transcripts; see Walker, 1986). In any case, transcription by others is unlikely to give sufficient attention to various nonverbal features, timing, and many other important de-tails. More generally, the use of transcripts produced by others gives insuffi-cient recognition to transcription as a theoretical and analytical activity. So we must be very careful in using them even as a starting point. It is essential to go back to the recording and produce one's own transcript.

We must make a final note. We have stressed that transcription should be complete, consistent, and accurate. The concern for accuracy extends to quota-tions of data, both our own and those of others. Kitzinger (1998) has argued that pervasive misquotation in discourse work is a general problem that has not received attention. Misquotation rides roughshod over the principle that even the smallest details may be important, and it has implications for the warranting of analyses in which the presentation of discourse excerpts in quotation is central (see Chapter 10).

INITIAL READING

Researchers may or may not have a clear idea of the phenomenon of interest in their data. Further, although there may be some instances in which the researcher wishes to carry out analysis on all of the discourse data that have been collected in a particular study, it is often the case that analysis will be restricted to only some portions of the data. The aim of initial reading (which includes listening) is to identify (or confirm) the specific focus and appropriate sections for analysis. (Potter and Wetherell, 1987, refer to this stage as coding, but we think it wise to avoid this term, given that it is often used in conventional work to identify the central activity of analysis, as we discussed in Chapter 2.) Although, like transcription, the initial reading does involve theoretical, interpretive, or analytical activity, its point is to make the data manageable for formal analysis. So, like transcription, the initial reading is both part of and necessary for analysis.

The analyst begins by listening to (watching) the data (for spoken discourse) and reading over the transcript several times, by getting a feel for what is there. The number and closeness of the readings may vary depending upon the purpose of the research, the type of data involved, the amount of discourse to be analyzed, and the type and extent of analysis that has been planned ahead of time. For example, if you are interested in identifying discourse on a particular topic at a relatively macro level (e.g., interpretive repertoires about consensual sex; Coates et al., 1994) or are concerned with the use of a specific expression (e.g., "well," "like"), the readings may be relatively few and quick. But this step is always necessary. There are so many aspects to discourse that even when you think you know what you want to look at, you must be prepared to change your mind when you hear or see the data. In some instances, you may change the planned analysis altogether, for example, where some feature of the discourse was unanticipated but appears to be central to the broad research question (as in Wood & Rennie, 1994, in which the plan had been to focus on identity issues, but the plan was changed when the initial reading suggested the importance of defining an event as rape). At the least, the initial reading will confirm your preliminary plans.

Novice analysts often fear that they will review the discourse several times—and still not know how to begin, particularly if their concern is to examine a particular type or sample of data rather than to consider a particular device or function. This occurs less frequently than expected, but it does happen. For example, imagine that you read over the transcript of a conversation and feel that the only thing you can say about it is that it is boring. It is at this point that you should deploy one of the most effective strategies available to the analyst, what we might call a *strategy of reversal*—or turning a problem into a topic. In this example, you would ask, what is it about the conversation that makes it boring? Is it the topics of the conversation? The ways in which participants respond or fail to respond to each other's utterances? This technique will usually give you enough of a hook or angle to get started (and it will probably not be too long before you decide that the conversation is not boring at all, at least to you as the analyst). This strategy also works well when you look at the individual segments in the analysis proper. Another approach at both levels (i.e., the discourse as a whole and the individual parts) is to consider systematically the suggestions we give in the next chapter for adopting the analytic orientation.

Once an initial approach to the data has been formulated, the analyst does a preliminary identification of the segments of discourse suitable for analysis (e.g., marking all segments in which the topic of conversation is "boring"— e.g., the weather—or marking segments in which participants are considering whether they were really raped). Both of these activities, that is, identifying the focus of analysis and the segments to be analyzed, may be repeated several times over the course of a project. For example, as analysis proceeds, it may be necessary to refine the focus, to select new segments, or both, or the analyst may wish to carry out a second or third analysis of a different topic or feature after the first one is more or less complete. Like Potter and Wetherell (1987), we stress that the identification of segments should be comprehensive in order to include all possible instances (because their relevance may not be apparent until analysis is done and because it is often the marginal cases that are most important). All segments relevant to a particular topic or concern are then pulled together in a single file and formal analysis can begin. (This requires making a judgment about how much of the surrounding discourse [context] to include, a judgment that is necessarily provisional in order to avoid foreclosing the analysis and that should be reassessed as analysis proceeds.)

There are a number of variations on this procedure. For example, if you are interested in a specific sort of discourse (e.g., academic discourse), you might wish to examine all aspects of the discourse, to consider all devices, functions, and so forth. But this will be impossible to do unless the text is quite brief; if not, you will still need to identify a particular section for analysis (e.g., the introductory phase of an academic exchange). Or if you are interested in a set of devices (e.g., for doing fact construction) that recur frequently throughout the discourse, you might need to restrict the analysis to specific sections (e.g., according to the subject of discussion). So although it is important to be comprehensive and to include everything that may be relevant to a specific goal, it is also crucial to avoid being overly ambitious (a fate that can befall both novices and experienced analysts). If you are faced with too much material, you are less likely to do a close and careful analysis, and you are perhaps also more likely to be overly general. It is better to tackle and finish a modest analysis and then to begin a second round; you can then consider how to merge the analyses.

PART III

ANALYSIS

Analysis I

Strategies of Interpretation

ADOPTING THE DISCOURSE-ANALYTIC ORIENTATION

Discourse analysis requires a particular orientation to texts, a particular frame of mind. We think it is important to develop a sense of what is involved before one even looks at the data. This may be particularly important for those trained in more conventional methods. For example, we suggest the potential importance of absence, of "what is not there," in both selected discourse excerpts and the discourse as a whole. Paying attention to absences opens up a variety of possibilities for the discourse analyst, whereas a more conventional analyst might be inclined to abandon the data set as irrelevant. In contrast to some accounts of discourse analysis as loose and undisciplined, most presentations, including ours, emphasize the necessity of careful and systematic work. However, in our experience, the problem faced by novice analysts is that they often feel constrained by the imperatives taught in conventional courses on research methodology. The first task is to recognize that discourse analysis requires the ability to examine discourse creatively in all of its multifarious aspects and an open-mindedness to entertain multiple possibilities. We therefore begin with a number of suggestions that are intended as sensitizing devices before offering more specific and ordered guidelines. (Readers may find it helpful to consider these and the other suggestions in the chapter in relation to some discourse data of their own.) We then provide an overview of the analytic process, followed by a discussion of specific concepts and strategies for interpretation.

1. As you read through a text, ask yourself how you are reading it and why you are reading it this way. That is, consider your reaction (does the text raise hackles? make you bristle? make you smile?) and try to identify the features of the text, the devices that are employed that would produce your reading. (e.g., if an utterance strikes you as insulting, is it because of the specific

91

words or phrases that are used (e.g., form of address)? because the content is inappropriate to the relationship? If a speaker seems "defensive," is it because of the use of excuses, justifications, disclaimers?) You will find yourself doing this for segments (words, phrases, sentences, etc.) of the text; look also at the overall conversation, interview, document, and so on. For example, you may react to the overall conversation in a particular way: Why? Go back and look for particular items, patterns, and so on. A cautionary note: Your reaction should be taken as alerting you to the possibility that something interesting is going on, rather than as an indication of what that might be. That an utterance raises your hackles does not necessarily mean that it should be interpreted as performing a negative function, for example, insulting the person to whom it is directed. The goal here and throughout the analysis is to identify the meaning to and for the participants.

2. Do not ignore the obvious; it may be important, or it may at least provide a place to start. For example, an initial reading of a conversation might suggest that participants are "having an argument." Rather than assuming that this cannot be a reasonable reading (because it would reduce discourse analysis to [re]stating the obvious), ask yourself if this makes sense from the participants' point of view. You can then go on to examine the basis for such a claim, identify how the argument is worked up, consider departures from the reading, and so on. The point of discourse analysis is not to generate esoteric accounts of inter-action, documents, and so on, but to show precisely how the features of the discourse make particular readings or reactions possible, plausible, and under-standable. Discourse analysis might be said to go beyond the obvious in the same way that theater critics do not simply describe their reactions to a play— anyone can react—but they know and can explain the reasons for their reactions. But given the emphasis on participants' meanings, we would be concerned if dis-course-analytic readings did not resonate in some way with those of everyday folk.

3. Assume that a focus on the literal meaning of an utterance or text may be the least helpful analytic strategy; concentrate on what the speaker or writer is doing, how that segment is related to other segments, and so on; consider also the possibilities of irony. This does not mean the complete neglect of literal mean-ing; rather, we need to ask how the literal meaning is used to do something, how it is related to what is done, and so on. (We discussed some examples of this idea in Chapter 3, for example, in relation to teases and metaphor.)

4. It is important (although often difficult) to consider what is *not* there (in terms of both "content" and form). For example, a greeting or apology may be "missing"; a researcher does not include a justification for selecting a particular method (e.g., see Tracy's, 1988, comparison of four discourse-analytic studies). Both the Drew (1987) and the Coates et al. (1994) studies in Chapter 3 drew on the observation of something that was not there (the recognition of a tease and a repertoire for acquaintance rape, respectively). Analysts using semiotics, de-

construction, and, to some extent, Gricean pragmatics (see Appendix B) rely on this sort of strategy and can provide some ideas on how to employ it. Conversation analysts have given particular attention to the notion of silence, to the idea that the absence of talk is not nothing, but something. They have shown that there are different sorts of silence, depending on where they occur (e.g., in the middle of a speaker's turn, between turns) and that these are taken up in various ways (e.g., with respect to the speaker to whom the silence belongs), with different consequences for interaction (Sacks et al., 1978; Schegloff, 1995).

5. Similarly, consider whether the critical issue is *that* something is included, not what it is (its particular content, etc.). For example, it may be telling that a researcher includes a justification for the selection of a particular method, but the justification and the method themselves may be less important. Does the inclusion imply the opposite of what is said (a case of irony or sarcasm, e.g., when a restaurant reviewer comments that there is "no need to add salt to anything")? Again, Gricean pragmatics (specifically, implicature) can be helpful here.

6. Play with the text. Ask how it would read if a particular item (word, phrase, etc.) were omitted, phrased differently (i.e., consider substitutions), or combined with some other item. (As we noted in Chapter 3, this was a strategy adopted in both the Antaki & Wetherell, 1999, and the Coates et al., 1994, studies.) Ask how it would read if it were produced by a different speaker or writer, in a different context, and so on. Similarly, consider syntax: How would the text read if the sequence of two items were reversed (e.g., a compliment comes after rather than before a request)? These strategies can help the analyst to form hypotheses about what is being done in various parts of the text.

7. Look carefully at how the text is structured, shaped, and ordered in both individual segments and overall, because structures are ways of achieving both content and function. The Antaki and Wetherell (1999) study discussed in Chapter 3 is a good example of this strategy. Think also of the way in which the organization of an academic paper, through various levels of headings and so forth, gives priority to particular topics without the author having to say so explicitly.

8. Be alert for multiple functions of discourse, which may or may not have been picked up through multiple markings of topic, content, structure, and so on in the initial reading. For example, you may have decided in that reading that a particular segment is relevant to two issues (e.g., identity, solidarity), but your analysis may identify several functions of the discourse in relation to each of these (e.g., constructing a victim identity, attributing blame, excusing inactivity; social comparison, constructing similarity, categorization).

9. It can sometimes be helpful to forget temporarily that you are doing data analysis and imagine instead that you are writing an essay for a course in English literature (an experience that many analysts have had at one time or another). This is just a way of getting started—there are differences in the two activities; for example, the discourse analyst will use psychological rather than literary

concepts and will warrant the analysis differently. But there are also similarities; for example, the concepts often overlap (e.g., narrative; and see Tannen, 1989), and both activities draw on linguistic features.

10. You will probably find that there are not always appropriate terms available for describing discourse and naming its functions. You may need to develop new terms or new concepts for discourse devices and functions; as we noted in Chapter 2, this is one of the ways in which the field develops. (This process is not different from any other field, except perhaps that the possibilities are so extensive [see Item 14]. One of the problems for the novice—and even for the experienced researcher—is that it is difficult to know whether a device has already been described elsewhere; this is another reason why it is desirable to both consult and work with other researchers.)

11. Categorization is not only an activity of the analyst; rather, participants themselves construct and use categories for various purposes. Part of the analyst's task is to describe and analyze the ways in which participants treat categories. Similarly, comparison is not only an essential activity of the analyst (e.g., comparing a participant's formulations of an event in different contexts); it is also a device used by participants (e.g., a participant employs a comparison as justification for a particular judgment).

12. In addition to focusing on variation and adopting a comparative stance, adopt a questioning stance, that is, take nothing for granted. Do this as actively as possible; reverse the taken-for-granted. For example, ask whether a particular sense or reading of a particular word, phrase, or larger segment of text relies on an assumption about gender (or about methodology; see Item 4). (For example, think of the riddles that are only riddles if one assumes, e.g., that a surgeon is male, or the way in which a description of a person's concerns and precautions about safety—e.g., not walking alone at night—are taken up quite differently depending on whether the description is taken to be about a man, a woman, a child, an older person, etc. The difficulty of identifying assumptions, of seeing the taken-for-granted, is that they are by definition not explicit. The strategy given in Item 6 can help to identify these.) More generally, adopt a strategy of reversal: Treat problems as solutions (e.g., the "boring" text in the previous chapter), solutions as problems, strengths as weaknesses. Collapse and expand dichotomies; imagine other versions (and again, note that participants also use these devices and strategies).

13. The more familiar you are with the language and how it is used, the more sensitive will be the analysis that you can do. You do not need to be a linguist or grammarian, and your goal is not to identify linguistic or grammatical features. However, grammar is important to the social workings of discourse, and attention to grammatical features can help to identify those workings. For example, we discussed in Chapter 3 the way in which Coates et al. (1994) looked at grammatical devices for avoiding agency and also Myers's (1989) discussion of devices for hedging. The emphasis is on the social implications of grammatical

features, for example, to compare the likely effects of the use of modals *have* versus *want* in an excuse for refusing an invitation to dinner: "I have to be elsewhere that evening" versus "I want to be elsewhere that evening."

14. In a sense, all of the ideas that you can muster will constitute your analytical resources. It is important to remember that you come to discourse analysis as a member of the culture, as a speaker-hearer and writer-reader of the language. This raises some dangers, but it also means that you can draw on your own knowledge. Discourse analysis is not like studying rocks. Rocks do not change under the gaze of the investigator in the way that people do under the scrutiny of a social scientist. As elsewhere, the critical feature is not how you come up with patterns, interpretations, and so forth, but how you justify your identification of patterns, how you ground your interpretations. The latter issue concerns questions of the "validity" (see Chapter 10) of what you have done.

15. Finally, give yourself permission to be an analyst, that is, to do the sort of interpretive work that is involved in analysis, in *generating* "results" (vs. more conventional approaches, in which interpretation is allegedly suspended until the results are in).

Novice discourse analysts sometimes ask whether it would be useful to look at other versions of qualitative analysis (e.g., general accounts such as that of Huberman & Miles, 1994, or specific approaches such as grounded theory, e.g., Glaser & Strauss, 1967). Some of this work includes suggestions that overlap with those we have made above; for example, among Huberman and Miles's set of 13 tactics for generating meaning, there are several that could be helpful (e.g., noting patterns and themes, seeing plausibility, clustering, making metaphors, making contrasts and assumptions). But we would not recommend consulting other qualitative work as a way of learning to do discourse analysis. We think that the differences are too great (see Chapter 2) and that time would be better spent reading examples of discourse analysis.

ANALYTICAL PROCESS

The overall goal of the analysis is to explain what is being done in the discourse and how this is accomplished, that is, how the discourse is structured or organized to perform various functions and achieve various effects or consequences. It requires the identification and interpretation of patterns in the discourse, that is, of systematic variability or similarity in content and structure, and the formation and checking of claims (conventionally, hypotheses) about functions and effects through a search for evidence in the discourse (Potter & Wetherell, 1987). Analysis essentially consists of a detailed and repeated reading of the discourse against the background of the discourse-analytic perspective.

We are reluctant to identify specific steps (as overly restrictive and prescriptive); analytic activities can be ordered roughly as basic interpretation and pattern analysis, but each consists of a host of possible activities or elements, and all of the activities involve a cycle that will need to be repeated many times in whole or in part. There have been a number of discussions of discourse-analytic steps or activities, for example, by Potter and Wetherell (1987, 1994) in the tradition of DASP, by Hutchby and Wooffitt (1998) and Pomerantz and Fehr (1997) in the tradition of CA, and by Fairclough (1995) in the tradition of CDA; we encourage readers to look at these discussions. The account that we shall give shortly draws on these and a number of others. For now, we emphasize, as do many authors, that there is no necessary sequence of activities, no standard or required way of carrying them out. In part, this is because the techniques that researchers use "rely as much on what Schenkein (1978) described as the 'conversation analytic mentality' [or more generally, the discourse-analytic orientation] as on any formal rules of research method" (Hutchby & Wooffitt, p. 93). Additionally, because analysis involves recycling and iteration, there is no necessity to begin analysis at the beginning of the data set, to consider any or all of the smaller segments before examining larger sections or even the discourse as a whole, to carry out all of the activities for units of any particular size, or to focus the analysis on any particular level. Regardless of one's theoretical position on the relationship between higher and lower levels (i.e., top-down vs. bottom-up relation) and of the focus of discourse analysis on function rather than on linguistic features for their own sake, the analysis will go up and down across different levels and back and forth from smaller to larger units. On some occasions, you may begin with a focus on grammar; on others, your initial concern may be with the functions served by drawing on an interpretive repertoire. Recycling across different sizes of units and different levels of analysis while carrying out different analytic activities ensures that regardless of how you begin the analysis, you will eventually attend appropriately to detail and at the same time address the large picture in relation to overall patterns and functions. There is actually a double recycling: through the discourse and through your analysis of the discourse. How does recycling work?

Scaffolding

Analysis involves simultaneous examination of utterances and their context, with the recognition that utterances both reflect and construct context, that one utterance can be analyzed for itself and be treated as context for others. There is a kind of scaffolding or bootstrapping involved that reflects and replicates what participants themselves do (see Heritage & Atkinson, 1984). This sort of work is not easy. One often needs to secure one point temporarily, build on it, and then return to it. The recursive or iterative nature of analysis in part reflects the way in which meanings at different levels are mutually determinate (or indeterminate). Analysis is provisional until a fairly late stage (though it is ultimately always provisional). The interpretation of a particular utterance will often need to be changed after one moves further into analysis. For example, one could identify "Why aren't you using quantification?" as a question, and the next utterance by a different speaker (e.g., "Because quantification destroys phenomenal authenticity") as an answer. But after one proceeds to further analysis (e.g., looking at other patterns—the structure of other exchanges, the overall segment), you may decide that this pair is better analyzed as "Criticism" and "Defense." The recursive, cyclical nature of the work of analysis is also an essential feature with respect to issues of reliability and validity (to use the conventional terms). Note that the interpretation is not checked via agreement (i.e., against the coding of another researcher, as in conventional notions of interrater reliability), but rather it is checked via using it in further analysis. This is one reason for the difference between discourse analysis and other work, including some forms of other qualitative work.

It may be helpful to consider the sort of scaffolding with which readers are already familiar, namely the process of writing a paper. For most of us, this involves writing, rewriting, rearranging, rephrasing, rereading (your own text and others), reinterpreting texts about which you are writing, and so on. These activities are all involved in discourse analysis, not just in the report of that analysis. Doing analysis is also like writing a paper in that although we sometimes follow the order of the final paper—writing the introduction, then the body, then the conclusions—we may also start in the middle, and regardless of where we begin, we expect that we will return to and revise that section after we have written the others. Analysis can involve the same sorts of struggles as writing a paper. We may have difficulty writing a particular section—or constructing an interpretation—and may put that bit aside for the moment. As in writing a review when the studies appear disconnected, unrelated to each other—just as the different segments of discourse data may seem unrelated—we need to organize the material so as to make it related or at least to show the ways in which it is not. And as in writing a paper, it is not always easy to decide when to stop and go with what you have, to subject it to the comments of reviewers—and, in the case of discourse analysis, to the discipline of writing the report. Analysis usually continues until the analyst is satisfied that the research questions have been addressed and that a reasonable reading of the discourse (i.e., one that will meet the warranting criteria discussed in Chapter 10) can be offered. (Put more bluntly, one keeps going until the analysis or the analyst is exhausted, at least for the moment.) Another analogy that some find helpful is to the grading of essay exams, in which you read a few answers, develop a rough key (here a set of interpretations), read a few more, refine the key, read a few more, adjust the key further, go back to the beginning and read all of the answers again, and so on.

An important difference between discourse analysis and writing a paper is that analysis is inclusive, whereas the writing of a paper is selective. In doing analysis, you do not omit parts because they are redundant, but instead, you pull them together. In writing a paper, you may find in reading over three different sections that you have made the same point in each, and so you rewrite to make the point only once. In contrast, for analysis, you would retain all three versions and consider the differences between them in terms of their precise expression, the context, and so on, as well as the way in which they might be seen to constitute a pattern.

In sum, it may be helpful to approach analysis in the same way that you would approach organizing any set of notes (here, the discourse) and your notes about those (your provisional interpretations of the discourse). The idea is to end up with a set of claims, along with all of the excerpts from which they were derived and your documentation of how the claims are supported. You can then select from this material to write up your report of the research and the analysis (see Chapter 11).

Getting Started

Although we have suggested that the starting point for analysis is somewhat arbitrary, it is reassuring to have a plan, so we suggest the following. Once you have carried out your initial reading of the discourse, that is, once you have decided which parts are to be analyzed, start at the beginning and work through a basic interpretation for each unit (where a unit is the smallest workable chunk, i.e., the smallest that you can do something with). There is no necessary place (beginning or end), level (grammar or function), or component (word or phrase) at which to start. But you can be guided by the purpose of the research, the extent to which it is focused on a particular issue (vs. a type of data), the nature of the data (e.g., conversations vs. interviews), and the initial reading of the data. For example, a researcher might be interested in "compliments," and after selecting all of the segments in which the notion of compliment might be relevant, the researcher would analyze each in terms of the specific content of the putative compliment, structure, place in the sequence, and so on. Or, an initial reading of interviews on a topic (e.g., Potter & Reicher, 1987) might suggest that participants draw upon a limited set of interpretive repertoires (sets of terms, metaphors, etc.; see Chapter 3) in relation to a particular issue or concept (e.g., the notion of "community"). The researcher would then focus on the detailed identification and analysis of the repertoires within each of the segments in which they appear. At this stage, the focus is on interpreting components within the segments in terms of their content, structure, function, and possible consequences. In the next stage, the analysis would consider patterns and then recycle as we discussed above.

Two points that probably cannot be overemphasized are the necessity for listening to or viewing tapes (along with transcripts) multiple times or doing multiple readings of written texts, as well as the importance of working with relatively brief, manageable segments. The basic activity of analysis—the continual listening or reading and interpretation—is painstaking. As Potter (1994) commented in discussing the work of Harvey Sacks:

> One of the striking features of reading Sacks's lectures, particularly when following through a whole series, is the way he struggles with a passage or even just a fragment of talk. He proposes ways of reading it, considers similar utterances, or how that utterance would sound in another context or uttered by another person. He will often move to a whole new topic simply to bring to bear a novel consideration on part of an utterance. (p. 409)

The stress here is on the struggle; good analytical work takes time. Even the most skilled analysts must do a great deal of work; in some ways, the better the analyst and the more experience he or she has, the more work is required. It is unfortunately not the case that one can simply look at a piece of text, generate an interpretation, and move on.

DOING INTERPRETATION

It is highly unlikely that an interested, focused listener-reader will fail over the course of multiple readings to generate numerous possible interpretations of what is going on. Nonetheless, there are a number of guidelines for interpretation that can help to ensure generativity, systematicity, and, ultimately, a disciplined and well-supported analysis. These guidelines involve a variety of concepts and a number of specific strategies. To some extent, they overlap with our previous suggestions and with each other. We repeat some of our suggestions here to drive home the point.

Analytical Concepts

The focus of discourse analysis on participants' meanings, together with the recognition that our own concepts construct the way that we see the world means that analytic activity involves an interplay between the data and our notions about it. We thus need to attend to these notions without being overly constrained by them, so we view the concepts that we deploy as sensitizing concepts (Hoonaard, 1997), not as categories to be applied mechanically to discourse. Analytical concepts can suggest what to look for and help us to interpret what we see. Concepts may be of a wide variety of types and levels; they may relate to content (e.g., accounts); features (e.g., intensifiers, etc.); form (direct, indirect; simple, elaborate); structure (hierarchical, e.g., movements-actions; sequential, e.g., turn taking, adjacency pairs); or function (e.g., constructing a motive).

Discourse-Analytic Perspectives

The major sources of concepts and devices are the varieties of discourse analysis that we identified in Chapter 2. The possibilities are too extensive to present adequately here. We have therefore included them in Appendix B. This permits us not only to identify them in detail but also to consider them in the context of the overall perspective in which they have been developed. We emphasize that the presentation of these notions in Appendix B should not be viewed as a matter of relegating them to an inferior position; rather, it reflects the view that they are so important that they deserve separate treatment and consideration. Traditions that are less central or less extensive can also be a resource; these are identified briefly in the Glossary.

There are also a number of useful concepts or sets of ideas that are associated with other discourse-analytic or related traditions or that transcend any particular tradition. We say a little here about some of these because they are not necessarily treated elsewhere in the book or are mentioned only in passing.

Positioning

Social-constructionist perspectives in general and discourse-analytic perspectives in particular stress the notion of selves as multiple and shifting, in contrast to the conventional views embodied in trait, role, and humanist theories (cf. Potter & Wetherell, 1987). Davies and Harré (1990; see also Harré & van Langenhove, 1991) offered the notion of position as a replacement for traditional concepts such as role. Positioning refers to the constitution of speakers and hearers in particular ways through discursive practices, practices that are at the same time resources through which speakers and hearers can negotiate new positions. "A subject position is a possibility in known forms of talk; position is what is created in and through talk as the speakers and hearers take themselves up as persons" (Davies & Harré, p. 62). For example, the discourse of romantic love makes available two complementary positions: the male hero and the female heroine. One example of the use of the concepts of position and positioning is a study by Tannock (1997) of the classroom discourse of a literacy program run by a company and a union at a canning factory. Tannock was concerned to show the way in which certain discursive practices of the instructor moved the employee-students into subject positions that were acceptable to the company. For example, students were asked to rewrite the company mission statement in their own words. This required them to adopt the perspective of the company, a perspective in which employees are not considered to be part of the company. Differences in the position of company and employees were not open for discussion, and the one paraphrase in which the author did not adopt the company perspective was treated (i.e., through humor) as unacceptable. In contrast, a union statement that students were asked to paraphrase was treated by the instructor in a more critical fashion and was framed as the opinion of one individual. In sum, the discourse available to the students was one in which they were positioned as uncritical supporters of the company.

Notions of positioning and subject positions are central to a good deal of work in the poststructuralist orientation, and they are also drawn on by those who situate their work within DASP (e.g., Wetherell, 1998). Conversation analysts also attend to the discursive construction of identities and selves, but with greater attention to the details of interaction and without relying upon notions of cultural narratives or discourses (see Chapter 9 for examples). Positioning is an important concept in considerations of the way in which people are both producers of and produced by discourse, an issue that we discussed briefly in Chapter 2.

Agent-Patient Distinction

The agent-patient distinction is fundamental. It is intimately bound up with the distinction we just mentioned, namely that between what is done *by* a person and what is done *to* a person. An agent is someone who is seen to make choices, follow plans, and orient to rules (Peters, 1960). A patient is someone who is seen to suffer the consequences of external forces or internal compulsions of the sort described so extensively by Freud. The distinction is central to accounts of human actions, accounts given both about others and about ourselves. We stress that it involves a way of seeing people, not a claim about whether they actually are agents or patients. As discourse analysts, our concern is with how the distinctions between agent and patient and between action and occurrence are worked up and deployed by people in everyday life. How are they put to use discursively for social purposes? If a person is constructed or positioned as an agent, he or she can be assigned responsibility, blame, or credit for his or her actions. If the person is constructed as a patient, responsibility can be deflected. The deployment of the distinction is seen most dramatically in judicial proceedings. A person who causes the death of another person may be convicted of homicide if she is seen to have acted as an agent, whereas she may be acquitted (e.g., by reason of insanity or mental defect) if she is seen as a patient, who as such cannot be held responsible.

There is a large variety of discursive devices for positioning self and others as agents or patients. The distinction can be grammatically encoded in numerous ways. For example, first-person pronoun usage can be seen as one way of doing agency; the speaker is at least responsible for her or his utterances (see also discussion of Sabat & Harré, 1992, in Chapter 9). Modals (see Pragmatics in Appendix B) can be used to construct necessity: To say that one must or has to do something is a way of saying that one is not an agent, does not choose the action, and therefore is not responsible. The designation of a person as the object of a verb (action) rather than as the subject (i.e., the agent of the action) can serve to position the person as dependent, as a patient. For example, consider Jenny's comment to May in the Coupland et al. (1991) study (see Chapter 9): "They let you go there," a statement that also gains some of its impact from the particular verb that is used, a verb that designates permission. One of the most important devices for obscuring issues of agency is the passive voice, particularly when used in the form of the agentless passive. A number of writers have examined the way in which these and related devices have been used in descriptions of violence against women, descriptions made by women, men, and the authors of journal articles. For example, Lamb (1991) found that articles on the abuse of women by men contained numerous examples of failure to assign responsibility to the men who battered (e.g., "Wives in America have been raped," which contains an agentless passive; "the violence," which is a nominalization, i.e., turning the verb into a noun). There are numerous other discursive devices and strategies for working up agent or patient status; for example, it can be done semantically ("I had no choice" or "It just happened") as well as grammatically.

Agency is very much tied up with issues of power, so it is not surprising to see particular attention to aspects of agency by those who work within the perspective of CDA, particularly feminist researchers. (See also Penelope, 1990, who has identified a number of linguistic features that have implications for relations of dominance and submission.) In DASP, the focus tends to be on the discursive practices associated with notions of agency, that is, practices involving attributions of accountability and responsibility.

Footing

Footing was originally formulated by Goffman (1981) to distinguish the basis on which accounts are offered and received. For example, speakers may present themselves as responsible for their words or as merely passing on a report of the experience of others; hearers may be addressed or merely present. Note that for discourse analysts, footing categories are not viewed as distinguishing whether a speaker has genuinely composed the words uttered or is merely expressing the ideas of another. Rather, such categories are distinctions that speakers themselves deploy to do interactional work. (In other words, they are participants' rather than analysts' categories.) And like other similar categories, they can be worked up in different ways. One can report an event in a way that suggests a particular footing, for example, direct experience. Conversely, claiming a certain footing, for example, that one is only passing on information from another person, can serve to distance oneself from the reported events—and from responsibility for them. Footing is an important notion in relation to accountability; the latter is a central concern in DASP, and we discuss it further in that section of Appendix B. (See Potter, 1996, for detailed discussion of footing.)

Reported Speech

Reported speech is speech that is attributed by a current speaker to another speaker. The following excerpt is from Holt (1996, p. 220):

> Lesley: .hhh An' ↑ Mark a:sked her f-b<u>a</u>ck ↓ for th'm this
>   evening 'n she s<u>ai</u>d .hh O<u>h</u> I thought Lesley had gi<u>ven</u> me the:se

In this case, the reported speech is direct; that is, it is presented as a reproduction or quotation of the (exact) words initially uttered by another speaker in another context. Indirect reported speech (or indirect quotation) is speech by another person that is summarized or paraphrased by the current speaker. In the example, the reported speech would have been indirect if Lesley had said something like, "she said that she thought I had given them to her." Tannen (1989) has suggested that the term *reported speech* be replaced by *constructed dialogue,* because not only is it likely that the speech was never uttered by anyone else in that form, but also the utterance is in any case transformed because it is part of the reporting context (the context in which it is currently uttered) rather than the reported context (the context in which it is alleged to have been uttered originally). She argues that "the words have ceased to be those of the speaker to whom they are attributed, having been appropriated by the speaker who is repeating them" (p. 101). Some analysts do use the term *constructed dialogue,* but *reported speech* is still the term that is usually used. It is not likely to raise problems for discourse analysis, in which reports of any sort are treated as part of the current discourse, not as reflections of utterances made by someone else. Discourse is always viewed as constructed on and for the current occasion; our concern would be with the function of attributing utterances to another speaker (Buttny, 1998).

Reported speech is an important concept in linguistics and literary work. It is also seen as a useful device in everyday discourse, for example, to make stories vivid and dramatic or to create involvement (see Tannen, 1989). Holt (1996) used a CA approach to analyze some of the ways in which speech is marked as direct reported speech (e.g., through the shift in intonation and use of the pronoun in the excerpt above) and its function in providing evidence. We add here that reported speech can also be marked by the use of finger movements that symbolize quotation marks. We also think that the term *like* can function as a marker of reported speech (as in, "She goes, like, I'm not going to do it that way") and that it may serve as a hedge on responsibility for getting the words exactly (i.e., as a device somewhere in between direct and indirect reported speech), but we have not yet studied this usage systematically. Reported speech has also been given attention in the context of footing, as a way of assigning responsibility for utterances to another person. It also figures in DASP as a way to make claims stronger and more factual, to work up different versions of stake and interest. (See Hutchby & Wooffitt, 1998, for an analysis of its use in interviews.)

Facework

As we noted in Chapter 3, we have some reservations about the way in which concepts of politeness and face have been used in discourse-analytic work (including our own previous work). Nonetheless, the various approaches to facework draw our attention to a wide variety of discursive devices and can be a rich source of ideas. In addition to the Brown and Levinson (1987) work that we discussed previously, readers may wish to consult MacMartin et al. (in press), Tracy (1990), and Wood and Kroger (1994).

Narrative

Narrative analysis refers to a large number and wide variety of approaches, within and across many disciplines and subdisciplines, for example, psychology (social, clinical, developmental, cognitive), communication, sociology, anthropology, and literary studies. They range from those in which the term *narrative* is used interchangeably with *account*; to those in which discourse is viewed as narrative because it has at least some features of conventional narrative structure; to those in which discourse (or its production and comprehension) is analyzed using narrative principles, that is, principles derived from those used to analyze narrative literary forms.

Approaches to narrative analysis can be broadly divided into social-constructionist approaches, in which the emphasis is on the role of the narrative in making sense of experience and constructing the self; literary approaches, in which the emphasis is on the narrative features of literary texts; and information-processing or cognitive approaches, in which the emphasis is on story structures and their relation to the comprehension, retention, and production of discourse and social action more generally. Social-constructionist approaches (e.g., Brockmeier & Harré, 1997; Sarbin, 1986) are likely to be most directly useful for discourse analysis, although they can vary considerably, for example, in the extent to which they view language as a route to internal or external events and their attention to the details of discourse. Narrative concepts play a role in DASP, and CA includes attention to various features of storytelling (see Appendix B). (See also Antaki, 1994, Chapter 6, and Edwards, 1997, Chapter 10, for discussions of narrative.)

Metaphor

We have discussed in Chapter 3 some of the ways in which discourse-analytic researchers have drawn on metaphors as an aid to analysis. We emphasize here that the metaphors used by speakers do not have to be particularly creative or striking or exotic to be worthy of analysis. One of the difficulties, however, is that metaphors are so pervasive, so mundane in all forms of discourse (Lakoff & Johnson, 1980), including academic discourse, that we frequently fail to notice them unless they are unusual (and this may be one of the reasons that they are able to function as they do). More generally, we can see accounts themselves as stories or as storied. Narrative approaches to discourse analysis not only rest on a central metaphor (with all of its auxiliaries, e.g., beginnings and endings, character, plot, etc.) but may also consider a wide variety of other sorts of metaphors within stories (e.g., of emotion; cf. Antaki, 1994, Chapter 6). And all of these metaphors can be analyzed for what they make available in relation to attributions of agency and responsibility, health, personality, and so on. (See Edwards, 1997, for general discussion of metaphor and discourse.)

Social Science Work

Almost any social science theory, concept, or study can be a source of ideas for discourse analysis, because such work concerns what people do, and, by and large, they do what they do in and through discourse (e.g., make comparisons and attributions; do gender and power). The discourse analyst can draw on particular substantive theories (e.g., just world), general theory and metatheory (e.g., psychoanalysis), and particular bodies of research (e.g., accounts, victimization, sociology of science) that can be found in anthropology, communication, literary studies, social psychology, sociology, and so on. But we emphasize that the way in which the discourse analyst employs concepts from these sources is usually quite different from the way that they are used in conventional work. For example, in social psychology, attributions are treated as cognitions, whereas in discourse analysis, they are viewed as discursive accomplishments (Edwards & Potter, 1992; see DASP in Appendix B). Similarly, notions such as social comparison and counterfactual thinking can be treated as discursive activities rather than as cognitive processes (see Chapter 9 for a social comparison example). The same sort of argument can be made with respect to notions from other disciplines, for example, sociology. That is, rather than viewing features of social structure, for example, social roles, as prior to and determinant of the particulars of social interaction, we see them as constructed in and through the discourse (see discussion of context).

Categories

Because we are interested in participants' categories, we need to be alert to those that might not appear in social science accounts but that do appear in everyday or colloquial discourse (e.g., "hotrodders," "good girls"; see Potter & Wetherell, 1987, pp. 128-132). There is a good deal of overlap; both everyday actors and social scientists employ categories of persons based on common physical or social categories (e.g., sex, race, age), personality types, and so on. We noted earlier that the business of categorization is problematic; we briefly reiterate and extend that point here. For example, whether a particular stretch of discourse constitutes description, interpretation, or explanation is disputable. This applies as much to the discourse of researchers as it does to that of participants, and we should question claims about discourse (or other) work as unproblematically descriptive, interpretive, and so on. Our terms and phrases (e.g., intensifiers, social comparison) have no inherent status as discursive devices, analytical concepts, and so forth. The issue is not whether we categorize our own terms correctly or incorrectly, but how we use them.

Collected Dossiers

In some instances, we can draw specifically on interpretations of discourse (in terms of devices, patterns, functions, etc.) that seem to be well-established in the literature. For example, conversation-analytic work on turn taking, adjacency pairs, preference structure, and so on is now extensive enough so that we do not need to reinvent the wheel when we consider how participants take turns, for example. We can build our analysis on those findings. Thus, Antaki (1994) interprets an utterance that implicates a negative self-image as "angling for her friends to rush in with a disagreement" because "we know (independently from the *collected dossiers*) [italics added] that there are strong norms for hearers to disagree with self-deprecation" (p. 73). Potter (1997) considers the use of "I dunno" by the late Princess Diana in a BBC television interview (noting that he picked out this fragment for several reasons: a broad concern with fact construction; an interest in the way seemingly trivial detail can be seen to determine the sort of action that is being performed; and to compare a discourse-analytic treatment with a cognitive-psychological approach to talk). He argues that "the best way into some materials like this may be to consider *other* materials or *other* sorts of findings" (p. 152). For his analysis, he draws on previous work showing that making a reference to the stake of the speaker is a principal way of discounting the significance of a person's action. He also considers the appearance of "I don't know" in materials from a relationship counseling session (see description of the study by Edwards, 1998, in Chapter 9), showing that it works as a kind of stake inoculation; that is, it works to prevent the undermining of a participant's description (of his wife's skirt length) as evidence that he is jealous. Potter then analyzes the appearances of "I dunno" in the interviews in terms of this sort of stake inoculation.

The use of previous findings can be very helpful, and it is likely to become increasingly so as discourse-analytic research accumulates. We stress that it is insufficient simply to invoke those findings as a justification for interpreting the discourse at hand in a particular way. That interpretation must still be justified or grounded (as we will discuss later) in the current discourse. As Schegloff (1992) took pains to note when he drew on two prior accounts of

storytelling to analyze a specific fragment of talk, he was using "analytic resources from 'the literature'" for a "detailed *analysis* of the empirical data as
embodying the phenomenon at issue, and not a broad subsumption of the data
under some analytic category or rubric" (p. 224).

So, what we have is a large, amorphous and fluid set of resources that can be
given shape by the analyst in relation to the purpose of a project and to the discourse itself. But ultimately, there is only talk—that of participants and of researchers—and the issue is the kinds of talk that we are going to put together. In
the end (in the "last analysis"), all we have is the discourse—not syntactic
units, rules, identities, preference structures, interpretive repertoires, and so
on—and our criterion for what can be used should be anything that helps us to
understand the discourse in a way that can be adequately warranted. At the
same time, it is helpful to remember Sacks's (1984) advice to treat what you
have "in an unmotivated way" (p. 27) rather than starting from ready-made issues or categories (see also Edwards, 1997, p. 89).

The resources that we have identified require familiarity with both the conventional and discourse-analytic literature. We offer next some suggestions
for the novice analyst that might be of more immediate use.

Strategies

Substitution

A useful strategy is to consider which utterance could reasonably be substituted for the utterance at issue. For example, in considering the possible function of *like* in an utterance, we can ask whether the phrase *for example* would
make sense as a substitution. If it can, we can see that the term is functioning in
a particular way (e.g., to explicate an argument); if it cannot (and there are numerous instances where this is the case for *like*), then we need to consider some
other possible function. Similarly, Harré (1995) has suggested the inventing
and testing of a verbal equivalent as a tool for identifying the function of nonverbal performances. For example, a cough can be read as "'Wake up! I am
about to make an announcement,' or . . . 'Look out! There is somebody
around'" (p. 150). That is, the cough can be viewed as the equivalent of a verbal
preannouncement, warning, and so on.

Reframing

We mentioned previously the strategy of reversal, that is, a technique
whereby problems are treated as solutions, and so on. More generally, the work
of interpretation can often benefit from a careful reframing of the sorts of questions that are addressed to the text, particularly in terms of the activities of the
speakers. For example, rather than asking if a text is coherent, it is more helpful

to ask what sort of text the speaker produces, for example, if the speaker makes the account coherent and how this is done.

Another sort of reframing involves questioning the kinds of categories deployed by participants in terms of the nature of the categories themselves. Respect for participants' categories does not necessarily mean that we take the categories as transparent or treat them at face value as a basis for social-psychological theorizing (see Wagner, 1995). We no longer assume, for example, that sex and age should be viewed only as biological rather than social categories. But the same concerns should be raised about other, less obviously problematic categories, such as those pertaining to psychological processes. For example, we should consider whether to treat utterances and the categories to which they refer as metaphorical. That speakers use the language of perception (e.g., when asked in studies of anorexia to make judgments about the size of their bodies) does not mean that we should treat their utterances as (or at least only as) a reflection of their ability to perceive size accurately, but as situated accounts. Such accounts can also be seen to involve moral or social categories and can be examined in terms of the sorts of actions for which they might provide a justification (e.g., refusing to eat because one is "too large"). Goodwin and Goodwin (1997) have shown how perception can be treated as part of the situated practices involved in various professions (e.g., chemists). (See also Edwards, 1997, for general discussion.)

Similarly, utterances framed in the categories of cognitive processing do not call for interpretations in cognitive terms, but rather in discourse terms. Again, this involves a reframing in terms of the more general discursive psychology perspective and a concern for identifying the social functions that perceptual or cognitive categorization may serve in a particular social context (e.g., making a claim appear objective; cf. Edwards, 1991). We need to be alert for the ways in which the language of one domain can be appropriated for use in another (e.g., explication, social accountability) by both everyday members and analysts. This orientation is one of the most important features of discourse analysis.

Multiple Functions

We have discussed previously the emphasis in discourse analysis on multiple functions. In attending to these, the analyst should also consider the possible hierarchical and sequential organization of the talk. For example, utterances such as "your essay might have been better organized" or "you could have dried as well as washed the dishes" could be interpreted as either criticism, feedback, or both. Further, we might decide that the speaker is doing feedback in order to criticize, or criticizing in order to give feedback. Our decision should depend on how the utterance is treated by the participants. For example, people are likely to express thanks for feedback (even when it is achieved by criticism), but not for criticism (even when it is accomplished by what under some circumstances might qualify as feedback).

Content

Another guide to interpretation is content (more specifically, subject matter) at the locutionary versus illocutionary or perlocutionary level, that is, what the participants are talking *about*. In the previous example, comments on an essay are likely (although not necessarily) to be viewed by participants as feedback, whereas comments on the performance of domestic duties are more likely to be seen as criticism. We underscore that discourse analysts are interested in content as well as style. As we discussed earlier, we reject that distinction, because content can be viewed at multiple levels, which themselves incorporate style. For example, content may be viewed in terms of function (e.g., "he criticized me"). We should also be alert for parallels in content at different levels. For example, a speaker may interrupt someone—function—when talking about interruptions—subject matter. The parallels may or may not be noted by the speaker; this sort of reflexivity is involved in explicit performatives (e.g., "I am asking you to shut the door") or, more subtly, in their denial (e.g., "I am not questioning your motives" as a way of questioning motives). Thus, content in some senses *is* style, and style *is* a kind of content. The point is that discourse analysts are not interested primarily or only in content in the usual restricted sense. Even in those kinds of analysis in which there is a strong concern with content in the traditional sense, for example, in work on interpretive repertoires, the focus is on the kinds of functions such repertoires perform, on the actions that they enable or constrain.

Participants' Meaning

This strategy originated in CA (see Levinson, 1983). It focuses specifically on a participant's interpretation of a particular utterance or set of utterances, that is, the meaning that is given to the utterance. The utterance can be the participant's own or that of another participant (including an interviewer). This does not mean that we ask the participant what was meant (as we discuss later); rather, it refers to the idea that the meaning of an utterance is in the very next utterance (Heritage, 1984). For example, a person may state, "The dishes are dirty." Her spouse may reply that he "is sorry for not keeping up with his chores"; that is, he treats the previous utterance as a complaint, rather than as a description. Or as Potter and Wetherell (1987) point out, a speaker's utterance may be in the form of a question, but "if the recipient treats it as an accusation the analyst is also justified in interpreting it this way" (p. 170). The next utterance by the same speaker can also show how she or he is treating the prior utterance. For example, a speaker who initiates a repair (notices or marks a source of trouble, e.g., by breaking off after the first sound of a word; Schegloff, Jefferson, & Sacks, 1977) or carries out a repair is interpreting the previous utterance as an error or trouble source. Repairs are "overwhelmingly done in close proximity to the turn containing the trouble source" (Nofsinger, 1991, p. 126).

We said that the meaning of an utterance is in the very next utterance. More precisely, the latter is "the most *prominent* [italics added] place at which the character of an action A is demonstrably appreciated" (Heritage, 1984, p. 245). As Heritage and Atkinson (1984) point out, "it should not be concluded that the way in which a speaker responds to a prior utterance can, in every case, be treated as criterial in determining how the utterance should be viewed analytically" (p. 11). Utterances that demonstrate a speaker's interpretation of a previous utterance do not necessarily follow closely that previous utterance. The same caution applies in the opposite direction, that is, when we look to a previous utterance for understanding a later utterance (a more obvious analytic strategy than the one we just discussed). For example, Antaki (1994) discusses a case in which a person about to leave a group of friends offers an utterance that appears to be admitting a failure ("I can't offer you any of Malcolm's sherry") and providing an explanation ("he hasn't got much")—an utterance that appears to make no sense at all. However, as Antaki points out, this utterance refers to the way in which "shortage of sherry" was a topic that was used to bring the person into the group approximately 200 turns earlier. The utterance becomes understandable as a closing of the encounter in a way that parallels its opening.

We have talked about looking at how a speaker treats an utterance, but the evidence that a speaker treats an utterance in a particular way is not always completely straightforward. In some cases, the evidence is relatively direct because of the semantics of the treatment. For example, "That's not quite right" can be seen fairly readily as an interpretation of a previous utterance as an error. In contrast, breaking off after the first sound of a word is less clearly a response to trouble in a previous utterance; it could also be a response to an unexpected noise or perhaps to trouble of a different sort (e.g., something caught in the throat). In some cases, a speaker may name explicitly the way she is treating the utterance, as in, "How dare you accuse me?" More often, we identify how a speaker is treating a prior utterance by making a judgment that what the speaker is doing in the current utterance (e.g., offering an excuse) must mean that the speaker interprets the prior utterance in a particular way (e.g., as an accusation). This evidence is more indirect, both in that it rests on our reading of the current utterance as an excuse (which may be a matter of semantics—"I couldn't help it"—or scaffolding—it is followed by an utterance that is arguably an acceptance of the excuse) and on the assumption that an excuse by definition is occasioned by an accusation. This assumption may not be problematic, but it does not yield "incontrovertible" evidence that the prior utterance is interpreted as an accusation; for example, an excuse may be offered in response to a simple "Hello" in anticipation of (and to forestall) an accusation.

The complexity of sorting out semantic and sequential evidence can be seen if we look at the use of terms such as *sorry*. For some people, the use is so ubiquitous that we might question its interpretation as an apology and its status as evidence that a prior utterance is seen as an accusation (or that a subsequent utterance is seen as an excuse). It is possible that some speakers take almost any utterance or potential utterance by another person as an accusation, correction, or reprimand of some sort; for them, the utterance is an accusation and so forth, although it may not be interpreted that way by most of us. Sorting out the possibilities might require attention to a sequence of subsequent turns by both the speaker and other participants, along with a comparison of the various sequences in which the term is deployed.

Similarity and Difference

This strategy (adapted from Potter & Wetherell, 1987) reflects the discourse-analytic principle of variability. As analysis proceeds, the analyst often comes across accounts or versions that seem either similar to previous accounts or different and potentially inconsistent or contradictory. Again, the analyst looks to the participant for guidance. Wetherell and Potter's (1988) work on identifying interpretive repertoires suggests three relevant features of the discourse. We consider these in relation to the work of Gilbert and Mulkay (1984) on the interpretive repertoires of scientists, to which we referred briefly in Chapter 3. In the empiricist repertoire, experimental data are given logical and chronological priority, the author's personal and social commitments are not mentioned, and laboratory work is conventional and follows from impersonal rules. The basic principle is that actions and beliefs are a neutral medium through which empirical phenomena make themselves felt. In the contingent repertoire, action and belief are depicted as dependent on speculative insight, prior commitment, personal characteristics, and social ties, and the connection between action, belief, and the phenomena under study is less clear-cut than in the empiricist repertoire. The basic principle is that scientists' professional actions and beliefs are importantly influenced by factors outside the realm of physical phenomena. The three relevant features are as follows. First, the appearance of the accounts or versions in different places would suggest that they are different (and potentially inconsistent). In the case of scientists' repertoires, Gilbert and Mulkay found that the empiricist repertoire was predominant in formal research papers, whereas the contingent repertoire appeared in informal interviews. The empiricist repertoire also appeared in the interviews, but usually in different passages of talk. Second, when the accounts do appear together, their use for different functions suggests that they are different. Thus, the scientists in the Gilbert and Mulkay work used the empiricist repertoire to account for their own "true" beliefs and the contingent repertoire to account for the errors of other scientists. Third, ostensible inconsistencies are notice-able to the participant as well as to the analyst. The scientists' use of a device (the "the truth will out" device; i.e., in time, the evidence will be clear) shows that they recognize the inconsistency between two versions or repertoires of scientific practice.

New Problems

As Potter and Wetherell (1987) point out, the use of linguistic resources to solve a particular problem will often create new problems. The appearance of new problems (and new solutions) can be used to aid interpretations of the original usage. Potter's (1984) analysis of scientists' use of the rule that theo-ries should be testable provides an example. In his examination of transcrip-tions from a psychology conference on theory, Potter argued that the function of accounts in which scientists describe their own theories as testable is to jus-tify one's own work. If Potter's explanation is a reasonable one, this should cre-ate a problem for the one scientist who was found to depict his own theory as relatively untestable (assuming that we are all keen to justify our work); evi-dence that it does pose a problem is provided by the scientist's characterization of his theory as equivalent to those classical theories that are also not testable. This move solves the scientist's problem (and confirms Potter's interpretation) in that it serves to justify his own work. However, it creates a new problem—how can the scientist then criticize any other theory that avoids refutation? He solves this problem by reverting to an explanation of the other work in terms of the questionable motives of those espousing that theory.

In some cases, the new problem is generated specifically by the way in which a speaker creates contradictions in solving a prior problem. For exam-ple, when scientists use empiricist and contingent repertoires, respectively, to describe research and to account for error, the contradictions between the two (especially if they are used together) may create a new problem, namely a chal-lenge to the dominant paradigm. Scientists may draw on the "the truth will out" device (i.e., that eventually, the empiricist repertoire will be shown to be supe-rior) to address this problem (Gilbert & Mulkay, 1984). That is, the device serves both to recognize inconsistency and to deal with the problem created by the inconsistency. However, the generation of new problems does not necessar-ily involve contradictions or inconsistencies; that is, it is more general than the criterion involving the treatment of contradictions. Further, the treatment of new problems also tends to unfold more sequentially than the treatment of con-tradictions.

Interpretation and Grounding

A discussion of interpretation leads inevitably to a discussion of grounding those interpretations, that is, justifying an interpretation of discourse by drawing on evidence in the discourse. We discuss grounding again in Chapter 10, but we mention the issue here because interpretation and grounding are not only related, but intertwined. First, the analyst must attend to the issue of grounding while carrying out interpretation, in order to assess whether the interpretations are likely to stand or if they should be revised. Second, grounding is not only part of the warranting of claims, but it can also suggest the interpretations on which claims are based. Strategies for grounding thus have a double role. Similarly, some of the strategies we have discussed above can be used not only to suggest but also to secure interpretations. (For example, Potter & Wetherell, 1987, refer to the last three strategies as analytic techniques for validation.) The strategies also anticipate later stages of analysis, for example, in relation to scaffolding and to ideas of similarity and difference that are involved in the identification of patterns.

However, not all of the strategies that can be used to generate interpretations simultaneously entail grounding, because they are not all concerned directly with the participant's orientation. By orientation, we mean an indication of what the participant finds meaningful. For example, if a participant summons another person who does not answer, and the participant repeats the summons, we could say that the first person orients to the incompleteness of the summons-answer pair (see Nofsinger, 1991, p. 54). Orientation need not involve awareness or deliberation (Potter & Wetherell, 1987). Rather, the analogy is to the plant turning its leaves toward the source of light. Orientation includes, but is broader than, the concept of "participant's meaning," in that it refers to a sequence or pattern of events and not just to the interpretation of a specific utterance. For example, the strategy of "similarities and differences" concerns whether a participant orients to two accounts as different or contradictory; the strategy of "new problems" concerns whether a participant orients to a prior utterance sequence as problematic. (Potter & Wetherell include only the first two of these under orientation, but we think that "new problems" also fits here.)

Orientation is also broader than the concept of participants' meaning in the sense that it involves not only how the participants see things, but also that they see things in a way that has implications for what follows in the interaction. That is, it is not only that participants notice something but that they do something with or about that noticing. For example, the scientists discussed above not only show their recognition that the two accounts (empiricist and contingent) are different, but also treat that difference as relevant for some further business, for example, to account for truth and error, to bolster the empiricist position.

We present one brief, further example (from Hutchby & Wooffitt, 1998, p. 68):

```
1    A:      flight information can help yo ⌈u:?
2    C:                                     ⌊yes could you
```

3   give me an ETA please on BA

4   three six five from bordecks?

5   (0.4)

6   A: three six five from bordoh? (.) yeah

This excerpt is from a call to the British Airways flight information service (transcribed to show the differences in the pronunciation of the word *Bordeaux*). As Hutchby and Wooffitt point out, the caller displays no recognition of having mispronounced the word *Bordeaux*; it is the agent who must repair the error. But explicitly repairing another person's utterance can be problematic; it draws attention to the error and might disrupt the smoothness of the exchange. But note that the agent does not simply correct the caller's mispronunciation. She first pauses after the production of the "trouble source" (Line 5). This gives the caller the opportunity to recognize and correct his error and "displays the agent's orientation to the preference [that is, the normative practice; see Appendix B] for self-repair over other-repair" (Hutchby & Wooffitt, p. 68). The agent also orients to the possibility that other- versus self-repair can be problematic in the way that the repair turn is constructed, that is, by repeating the details and using upward intonation. That is, she presents the information as a question to the caller for clarification.

In sum, what it means to ground an interpretation is to show that participants orient to the text in a way that supports that interpretation. As Schegloff (1992) has argued, we need to show not only that some particular features are relevant to the participants, but also that "they are *procedurally consequential* for the particular aspect of talk which is the focus of analysis" (p. 196). What this means is not just that participants notice or mark the feature in some way, but that it has consequences down the line. For example, in the study of responses to teases that we discussed in Chapter 3, participants not only showed that they recognized the tease but displayed an orientation to the tease as a problem, as can be seen in their subsequent serious response. We return to this issue in our discussion of context. But we want to note here that in using the term *consequences,* we are not talking about cause and effect in the usual Humean sense. Rather, the emphasis is simply on what follows in sequence. The utterances are connected by their appearance together and in some cases because they are connected by convention. For example, it is normative to follow a question with an answer—but the question does not "cause" the answer. We would say, rather, that a prior utterance sequentially implicates (Jefferson, 1978) or occasions a later one (see Nofsinger, 1991).

Before leaving the topic of grounding, we note two of the most common problems that arise in the novice's analysis of excerpts. They are in some ways mirrors of each other, in that one involves underanalysis and the other a kind of overanalysis. Both result in weak (and often uninteresting) claims. First, discourse analysis is not simply a matter of restating the discourse. Restating is not only repetitive, but it also tends to reify literal content. Nor is it a matter of paraphrasing the discourse. Paraphrasing is often employed in other qualitative approaches, for example, in the first stage of grounded theory; we see this as problematic because the paraphrase is then taken as the interpretation. The issue is not that the paraphrasing is simply description (and also repetitive); description is always interpretive (see DASP in Appendix B). Rather, it is that the interpretation so constructed is not warranted. Claims based on paraphrase are likely to be either unsupportable (not simply unsupported, i.e., made without evidence) or so obvious as to be uninteresting. It is not that discourse analysts never paraphrase (e.g., see the strategy "substitution" discussed previously). Rather, the rephrase is not taken as the interpretation, but as a way of helping the analyst to work out the interpretation, a way to go about identifying a possible function. The interpretation itself must be grounded in the discourse and must also be in discourse-relevant terms. For example, van Dijk (1997a) emphasizes the necessity of examining text or talk in terms of some theoretically based framework. As we have discussed, this does not mean that the analyst begins with or applies some particular set of theoretical concepts, but rather that the findings are framed in the context of relevant devices or concepts. Nor does it mean that all of the relevant devices or concepts have already been identified. As we suggested earlier, even the beginning analyst may note that a particular sort of utterance may work in a particular way that has not previously been articulated, and the analyst may thus come up with new devices.

The second problem occurs when an analyst hedges a claim because it is assumed that providing evidence would require going beyond the discourse. In many instances, there is sufficient evidence in the discourse itself. The problem arises when the analyst treats concepts that are discursive (in the discourse-analytic perspective) as abstract and hidden—and very often cognitive. For example, an analyst might suggest that the utterance "I meant to call you" can be interpreted in terms of the speaker's (good) intention and that it functions to construct the identity of the speaker in a positive way. The analyst then backs away from this claim because "I do not really have any evidence for such an intention and may be making an unjustified inference." But from the discursive-psychology perspective, one does not need evidence for this interpretation; the utterance itself, the expression of the intention, is what it means to have a good intention. It is evidence because it is viewed as constitutive of what it means to have an intention, rather than as simply correlated with, caused by, or reflective of an intention. Similarly, Sherrard (1991) states, "The assertion that nominalization obscures agency . . . implies intentional verbal encoding for these purposes and corresponding decoding by participants. These implications may be correct, but independent evidence is lacking" (p. 175). But for nominalization to obscure agency, no corresponding intention is required. This is what nominalization does grammatically—and what the speaker does with the nominalization is a matter to be identified in the discourse. This argument also applies to all sorts of other concepts conventionally viewed as "internal," for example, attitudes and attributions. "It was his fault" does not reflect an attribution: It *makes* an attribution. More generally, one can guard against the possibility of both over- and underinterpretation by remembering the general principles of discursive analysis.

Finally, we note that there is inevitably an issue of shared knowledge in the business of interpretation. As Jackson (1986) points out, this does not mean that an analyst can simply assume that others will recognize a particular feature in the same way, although they may well do so; the interpretation may require demonstration (evidence and arguments). For example, if Schegloff's intuition that "Are you busy?" is leading up to something were not shared, his analysis of presequences would have been challenged. At some point, however, we do need to fall back on our shared knowledge, including our knowledge of language and how to use it, of *language games* (Wittgenstein, 1953). Such knowledge is required simply to understand an analyst's claim, as well as to see that it is grounded in the text. We can never explicate everything; the problem is to decide whether the language of explication is itself shared or requires further explication. (For example, what does it mean to be "leading up to something"?) Even in the most empirical discourse-analytic approaches, such as CA, which stresses the primacy of data, the notion of fundamental features, such as a turn, rests on a shared understanding of what constitutes a turn, on a shared way of glossing or interpreting movements (alternating utterances) as the action of a turn. Both participants and analysts must rely to some extent on the taken-for-granted; this is one reason why analysis must involve a kind of scaffolding.

In sum, interpretation always involves keeping an eye out for grounding. For example, attention to a previous or subsequent utterance as a guideline for interpretation can simultaneously identify the evidence in the discourse for that interpretation. Nonetheless, there are limits to the necessity for grounding. Further, analysts should not be so concerned with grounding in the initial stages that they become overly constrained or cautious and unduly constrict the creative activity involved in interpretation.

Analysis II

Patterns and Context

We consider first the identification of patterns. We next present an example of working up an analysis. The chapter concludes with a discussion of context and of quantification.

PATTERNS

The identification of patterns as one proceeds across the segments of discourse is an important part of analytic activity. Patterns involve form or structure, the disposition or arrangement of parts or elements. Patterns can be synchronic (e.g., a particular usage by a particular participant) or diachronic (e.g., the turn-taking structure of a conversation). They involve essentially the recognition of relationships between features of discourse: within or across participants, within or across sections, within or across occasions, and so on. For example, in the study of conference transcripts described previously, Potter (1984) identified a regular pattern of accounting in which scientists described their own theories as testable but argued that other scientists tried to avoid testability. Patterns are sometimes difficult to recognize; novice analysts in particular are likely to think that they have only identified a collection of devices (e.g., of fact construction) or the elements of an interpretive repertoire. But the use of these devices is always occasioned and will always co-occur with something else about the circumstances or context of use, all of which provide ideas about possible functions of the devices. The identification of patterns also requires alertness, because patterns can be seen to occur at different levels (very fine details or relatively large chunks, e.g., one part of an interview vs. another) and to vary in extensiveness (a few vs. many instances) and complexity. Patterns are interesting in their own right; they also serve a critical role in the development and warranting of interpretations of structure and function. As analysis proceeds, the claims that are developed about the patterns and about the function and structure of the discourse are checked and refined against the segments that have been examined and against the remaining segments. This process will usually require the revision of claims and the reanalysis of segments. A critical part of the process is the search for exceptions.

Looking for Exceptions: Negative Case Analysis

The process of analysis can be seen as the continuous examination of new data (i.e., further data in the text at hand) to find cases or instances of discourse that will confirm developing claims, but especially to identify negative cases. Negative cases are exceptions that must be accounted for by showing how they can fit the claim, by adjusting or modifying the hypotheses, or by showing that they are outside the scope of the claim, that is, they involve a different pattern or claim. Like many of the other strategies discussed previously, the search for negative cases is relevant to interpretation and to the development of claims, as well as to the supporting of those claims. With respect to the latter, it builds a kind of testability into discourse analysis, although in a different way from that involved in conventional hypothesis-testing research, so that we prefer to speak of claims checking rather than hypothesis testing. The discourse mentioned in Chapter 7 (Potter, 1984) of the scientist who presents his own theory as not testable is an example of a negative case; it is an exception to the pattern of all of the other accounts and appears to contradict the claim that scientists (at least those in that study) describe their own work in self-justificatory ways. But as we noted, the claim is sustained by a closer examination of the scientist's reworking of the notion of testability such that a lack of testability is a positive characteristic, at least of grand theories like his own. Thus the case is an exception to the pattern, but not to the claim made about that pattern with respect to the function of the discourse.

A classic example of negative case analysis is the work of Schegloff (1968) on opening sequences in telephone calls. Schegloff identified a pattern concerning the distribution of turns between callers and answerers. All but one of the conversations in his collection of 500 cases could be described by a rule that "answerer speaks first." In the one case that did not fit, the caller spoke first. This could have been simply dismissed as a deviant case that proved the rule, as error variance. Or it could have been analyzed as a deviant case to see if it had particular features that explained why it differed. However, Schegloff adopted a different strategy, namely to go back to all of the cases and see if the original pattern could be reformulated to account for all of his cases. His solution was to treat the openings not in terms of the rule that the answerer speaks first, but as a form of a summons-answer sequence. The first move in a call is not the response of the recipient, but the summons, that is, the ringing of the telephone. However, in the one case in which the recipient of the call did not speak right away after the receiver was lifted, it was necessary for the caller to speak first, that is, to repeat the summons, following which the recipient spoke. The revised pattern, that is, summons (the ring; possibly repeated by the caller's "Hello") and answer (the recipient's response to the summons, e.g., "Hello" or name of an organization), accounts for all of the calls. As Hutchby and Wooffitt (1998) point out, this "formal description" is a more adequate one than the original and explicates the organizational basis common to all of the cases. As they also note, not all patterns can be so elegantly and simply described. But the work serves as an excellent model for dealing with exceptions.

Schegloff's (1968) analysis may strike some readers as having yielded only banal, commonsensical results. (Doesn't everyone, well, nearly everyone, answer the phone with hello, name, or number? So what if one person out of 500 didn't?) The history of science is littered with examples of solutions to profound questions that, once announced, are then seen as commonplace. The Second Law of Thermodynamics evokes those kinds of reactions from laypeople to this day. In the present case, Schegloff's solution must be seen as a triumph of trained ingenuity that solved the problem of one exception in a 500-item series by redefining the telephone conversation, by saying that the first item in the telephone conversation is *not* the hello of the answerer but the ring of the telephone, the summons. It changes the syntax of telephone conversations and raises a host of further questions that go beyond the structure of telephone conversations. How do you protect your privacy and gain freedom from imposition when every Tom, Dick, and Sally can summon you to engage in a conversation, in a social encounter (in this case, within your own four walls, in the evening during supper, perhaps to solicit funds for charity, to sell you something, to ask your political opinions). How is it that answering machines have become so popular? Do other forms of conversation have this pattern? And so on.

Accounting for exceptions in negative case analysis is not precisely equivalent to ruling out competing hypotheses or counterarguments (which is arguably a feature of all scientific work), because negative case analysis involves a search through the data for exceptions to one's hypothesis, rather than an assessment of alternative hypotheses concerning the data at hand. That is, we are dealing with counterinstances versus counterarguments. The two strategies are, however, closely intertwined and are carried out simultaneously in that a search for negative cases inevitably involves the consideration of alternative hypotheses. Note also that the consideration of negative cases is not equivalent to a consideration of "contradictions" in the data (e.g., where a participant makes two statements that seem to contradict each other, as we discussed above), because the contradictions are between instances of discourse, whereas negative cases involve contradictions between some instance of data and the claim that is being made. (Contradictions in the discourse may well support the claim being made, e.g., claims that a participant is ambivalent.)

This is important to recognize because there is otherwise potential for confusion between the concerns of the participant and the concerns of the analyst.

The combination of negative case analysis and a consideration of alternative claims is neither new nor unique to discourse analysis. It is essentially what is involved in analytic induction, "a method of both discovery and testing" (Jackson, 1986, p. 129). Some researchers using this method place relatively more emphasis on structural features of discourse than on (social) functions, or they are concerned to make a relatively more general claim about discourse. For example, conversation analysts can be said to use this method, and they tend to be more concerned with the identification of conversational phenomena (Hopper, Koch, & Mandelbaum, 1986) than with the social functions of these phenomena within a particular discourse. Further, Jackson argues, "The widespread view that analytic induction is a case study method is simply wrong" (p. 138). But this does not mean that the method cannot be used in work on some particular discourse (in which the generality of the claim refers to that discourse rather than to discourse in general).

In any case, we recommend that beginning analysts read some of the work on analytic induction, because it gives some additional ideas on how to work up support for claims. It is helpful in its emphasis on aberrant cases, in the way it plays on variability, and in the idea of "methodology as a way of generating arguments about empirical claims, rather than as a set of procedural guarantors of truth" (Jackson, 1986, p. 133). (In this view, procedures such as random sampling are seen as argumentative resources rather than guarantees of correct description.) Discussions of analytic induction also show that the method does not involve argument by example; rather, it involves making an argument *from* (or through the use of) example, or, more important, from counterexample (Jacobs, 1986). The concern about arguing by example arises in part because examples cannot be used to make claims about regularities. But this is not what is done in discourse analysis.

Work on analytic induction is helpful for its specification of different sorts of examples, particularly negative cases; discourse analysts have tended not to distinguish among different sorts of exceptions. For example, Jacobs suggests that the basic evidence for a pattern is paradigm cases or prototypes, that is, clear-cut cases that are obvious to any reader. (As he notes, *prototypical* means prototypical in appearance vs. typical in occurrence). However, this sort of confirmatory evidence is insufficient. Minimally, there should also be a set of clear examples with high internal diversity. In addition, the analyst should include cases that are less obvious or that are fringe cases, and the analyst should show why they are fringe cases (e.g., in terms of features of the pattern that are missing). Finally, there should be cases of clear deviation; again, if a claim is adequate, it ought to account for such deviations, mistakes, or failures.

Patterns of Laughter

Analysts may be interested in patterns primarily because they are useful in the development and warranting of claims. However, the identification of patterns can also be the primary aim in discourse-analytic research. This is often the case in CA work, for example, the Antaki and Wetherell (1999) study of showing concessions that we described in Chapter 3. We present here another example of such work in order to show how the identification of patterns and the use of exceptions can be framed as a series of steps. Our presentation does not necessarily replicate the way in which the work was done; the point is to show one of the many possibilities that are available for carrying out analysis systematically, as we discussed previously.

Jefferson (1984) analyzed conversations in which people talk about their troubles and found recurring instances in which the person telling the trouble produced an utterance and then laughed, whereas the listener did not laugh (see, e.g., p. 346).

> S: I've I've stopped crying uhheh-heh-heh-heh-heh,
> G: Wuh were you cry::ing?

She compared this pattern to those patterns in which both participants laugh (a well-established phenomenon that also occurs in her data) and also to patterns in which the second person does not laugh, but where the previous utterance involves something other than a trouble that is not laughable (e.g., a bad joke). She argued that the speaker who laughs in the course of troubles telling is doing "a recognizable sort of job" (p. 351)—namely, showing "troubles-resistance." In turn, the listener who declines to laugh at the trouble is demonstrating "troubles-receptiveness."

This hypothesis is assessed through the examination of apparent exceptions. First, there are some instances in which both the troubles teller and the listener laugh. In all of these cases, it can be shown that the troubles teller has introduced some sort of buffer topic or time-out. That is, in the course of talking about the trouble, the teller may make a joke or bring in an amusing anecdote. But it is notable that it is always the troubles teller, not the recipient, who introduces such material and further, that troubles recipients do not bring in relevant material of their own (e.g., a similar story), even though this is usually the case in conversation. In other words, although there is an exception here to the pattern of laugh/not-laugh, it can be accounted for in terms of the sort of material involved. That is, laughter by the listener that is occasioned by buffer topics can be seen here as showing troubles-receptiveness, an interpretation supported by the listener's concomitant failure to introduce or follow up such topics.

The second exception to the basic pattern of laugh/not-laugh involves the recipient's laughing, but not the teller; that is, it reverses the basic pattern. This occurs in only one case, a case that is quite complex. Jefferson identifies a number of instances in which the person telling the troubles shows herself to be troubles-receptive, rather than troubles-resistant. Jefferson (1984) argues that although it is usually the responsibility of the teller to show resistance (and of the listener to show receptiveness), the teller's failure to do so will then be addressed by the listener. That is, a balance is maintained between receptiveness and resistance; this is usually achieved through the laugh/not-laugh pattern, but it is also preserved in the single exception to that pattern. Jefferson's analysis is much more detailed and complex than we have been able to show here. We hope nonetheless that it shows the way in which the analyst can work up an interpretation that accounts for both basic patterns and exceptions.

We raise here one additional point with respect to patterns. They often involve the identification of a sequence of actions at a relatively abstract level, particularly in work in which pattern identification is the major goal. Thus, for example, Antaki and Wetherell (1999; see Chapter 3) identified a pattern of proposition, concessions, and reprise (which they described as "glosses" of the actual utterances). In other work, we see patterns such as story preface, request to hear story, and story; or trouble source, next-turn repair initiator, and repair (see Hutchby & Wooffitt, 1998, for these and other examples; see also Appendix B on CA). Readers may wonder whether there is a standard collective term for such patterns, but there does not appear to be one. Rather, there are a variety of different terms that have been used or that might be appropriate, including *pattern* or *structure, canonical format* and *schematic representation* (both used by Hutchby & Wooffitt), *template, prototype, exemplar, model,* and *paradigm.* Although there may be concerns that such terms may encourage reification (C. Antaki, personal communication, February 25, 1999), there may be some advantage to having a more specialized term for abstract patterns because it can underline their regularity and generality. And it should not be problematic if we remember that regardless of how well a particular pattern has been established in previous work, we still need to show its operation specifically in the discourse at hand.

WORKING THROUGH AN ANALYSIS: AN EXAMPLE

Most of the analyses that we present in this book come from published reports. Reading about these reports, or even reading the reports themselves, can give a good idea of what an analysis looks like in the end. But it cannot convey very easily the process of doing the analysis. So we want here to give an example that illustrates this in a little more detail, although our account will of necessity omit a good deal—and make the process appear to be a good deal more linear than it was. We have selected an example of work in which we have both been involved (Kroger & Wood, 1998; Wood & Rennie, 1994), because it allows us to say more about those aspects of doing analysis that tend not to appear in published reports. The research is different from the Jefferson work in several ways. It involved interviews rather than everyday conversations; it was carried out largely within the DASP rather than the CA tradition; and it was concerned not primarily with the identification of patterns, but with what was being done in the accounts and the discursive strategies used to accomplish this. It illustrates yet another way of working through the various components of analysis, as well as some ways in which analysis can draw upon the various notions that we discussed in Chapter 7.

The research involved open-ended interviews with eight women who had been raped by dates or acquaintances. The original aim was to examine the ways in which the women negotiated their identities, on the assumption that we would see something rather different from the picture given by conventional research, in which issues of blame, responsibility, and so on tend to be treated in static, dichotomous terms. However, as we mentioned in Chapter 6, we found as we listened to the tapes and read the transcripts that the struggle to name what had happened was a major theme of the interviews. We therefore selected for analysis all of the segments that involved this theme as well as those related to identity.

Excerpt 1 [Wood & Rennie, 1994, p. 130]

> And you know, I saw the ad [for the study] two weeks ago, and I read it, and I'm going, "Well, let's go and see this person [interviewer]. Let's find out whether it was an actual rape." (Ann, Lines 500-506)

This excerpt nicely expresses uncertainty about whether or not the event that occurred was rape. Examination of the other interviews showed that Ann (a pseudonym) was not the only woman to do so; all of the other women except one not only reported questioning at various times after the event whether or not they had been raped, but continued to question this during the interview. So we looked more closely at all of the passages in which they did so, examining the specific ways in which they attempted to come up with an answer. We give one example here.

Excerpt 2 [p. 130]

> Something that I'm still, I'm calling this date rape, as you said it's rape. I see rape as more violent, but maybe. (Ann, Lines 1292-1294)

We see here Ann's attempt to combine the two possibilities for describing the event ("date rape"); she goes on to say it is rape, but she specifically marks this as the interviewer's formulation and then backtracks by differentiating date rape

from rape. However, this distinction is weakened by its framing as her perception (vs. the stronger phrasing that could have been used, "Rape is more violent") and by the contrastive conjunction *but* that follows it (although the
alternative is both hedged by *maybe* and unspecified).

The two versions offered here of the same event appear to be inconsistent.
As we discussed previously, one way of strengthening the claim of inconsistency is to show that the ostensible inconsistencies are noticeable to the participant as well as to the analyst. We see such evidence in Excerpt 1, in which Ann
refers to finding out "whether it was an actual rape" (implicitly contrasting the
two versions). Further, her linkage of "you know" to this utterance assumes
that the interviewer also recognizes the inconsistency. The reference to the inconsistencies is consequential; that is, it is worked up as a motive for participating in the study, namely, to address the inconsistencies. Her recognition of
the inconsistencies is also marked by their framing in reported speech ("and
I'm going"). Her use of the discourse marker *Well* to initiate the reported
speech along with the plural pronoun (*Let's*) can be seen to point to the possibility that sorting the matter out may not be easy, that it will require joint effort
(an interpretation for which we provide further support momentarily).

Through looking at these and numerous other excerpts in similar ways, we
gradually worked up the claim that the women see two different ways to construct their sexual experience (rape or date), but that neither of them fits the
women's own experience. We say more about the details of these formulations
below in our discussion of intertextuality. Our focus here is on the claim that
naming their experience as one or the other is seen as difficult.

Excerpt 3 [p. 133]

It's just something that happened. (Kim, Lines 254-255)

We see here the use of "Dummy it" (Penelope, 1990), that is, the use of a pronoun whose referent is unspecified, not named.

Excerpt 4 [p. 130]

It's hard to separate the rape from the date situation (Kelly, Line 352)

The claim of difficulty here (along with other statements by Kelly) rests on the
assumption that rape and a date can and should be separated. Further evidence of
sorting out what happened could also be seen in the accounts of two women who
discussed speaking with the man involved sometime after the event. One frames
her motive for doing so as an attempt to answer the question, "Am I imagining
things?"

After working up our provisional claim about the problem of naming the experience, we moved on to consider the segments that we had selected as relevant to identity.

Excerpt 5 [p. 138]

I'm so separated from it [the rape] now, I'm happy now. I mean before I was still so close to that feeling. (Lyn, Lines 963-965)

Excerpt 6 [p. 138]

You have to get past the self-blame before you can actually look at yourself as a victim. (Kelly, Lines 602-603)

Excerpt 7 [p. 138]

I'm a lot further along than some of them [other women in a support group]. (Mary, Lines 816-817)

What struck us about these excerpts was the use of distance and temporal metaphors; we thought that one of their functions was to negotiate a victim-nonvictim identity. In Excerpt 5, the contrast between separation (in the present) and closeness (in the past) serves to compare past and present selves; Lyn was a victim, but now she is not. In Excerpts 6 and 7, the metaphors are incorporated within a further metaphor, that of the journey. For Kelly (Excerpt 6), the journey involved three stages: moving from a nonvictim to a victim and then again to a nonvictim identity. In Excerpt 7, we also see social comparison used to achieve both identities (Mary is different from some, but not all, of the other women in the group). (Social comparison was a strategy used by many of the women both to compare victim and nonvictim identities and to compare experiences of the event as rape or date.)

We looked therefore for further evidence of the negotiation of identities and for the specific ways in which this could be done.

Excerpt 8 [p. 138]

I can't believe that it happened to me. (Lyn, Line 961)

Phrases such as "it happened to me," as we see here, and "it's just something that happened" (Excerpt 3) were common in the interviews. Grammatically, this structure serves to construct the woman as a victim or, more generally, a patient. But there also multiple instances of grammatical features that constructed the women as nonvictims, as agents.

Excerpt 9 [p. 132]

> The whole thing I was thinking the whole time was it's my fault because I
> shouldn't have been, my parents always told me you don't go out with a boy
> alone and don't go and do this or do that. (Barb, Lines 70-74)

The explicit acceptance of blame here is appropriate only for a person positioned as a nonvictim, as an agent, a positioning supported by the use of a modal
(*shouldn't*; see Pragmatics, Appendix B) and other expressions that encode obligation. This (self-)positioning is reinforced by the use of extreme case formulations ("the whole thing," "always"; Pomerantz, 1986; see CA, Appendix B) and
through the device of listing. The stress here is on a kind of moral failing, but
there are other failings associated with agency and blame.

Excerpt 10 [p. 136]

> Sometimes I would think that I was kind of stupid doing what I did, like not
> trying to get away more, or stuff like that. (Leslie, Lines 290-292)

Excerpt 11 [p. 136; in response to the question of whether she blamed herself]

> If I hadn't crawled out my window, if I hadn't been so friendly to him, if I had
> worked harder in getting away, you know, in a sense, yeah I did. (Leslie, Lines
> 612-615)

We see in Excerpt 11 a more indirect construction of failing than in Excerpt 10
("kind of stupid"), one that is worked up in the form of a counterfactual
argument.

   This presentation works up the process of analysis in a somewhat clearer order than actually occurred. For example, we were sometimes struck by some
grammatical feature, and only then did we consider function. The presentation
does not convey adequately the way in which the analyst picks out some aspect,
tracks it within a case, then across cases and back again. But it should give
some sense of what happens as the analyst begins to pull ideas together. One of
the things that happened in this analysis was that we began to see the ways in
which the working up of two different identities paralleled the construction of
the two different versions of the event, versions that implicate the woman as
victim or nonvictim. And it was this sort of patterning that allowed us to generate a coherent set of claims around what the women were doing with their accounts and the various discourse devices and strategies that they deployed.

   The generation and presentation of claims was not as straightforward as it
appears here. For example, we were faced with the question of how to organize
the analysis: Should we organize it around specific devices (e.g., grammatical), strategies (e.g., social comparison), or functions (e.g., negotiating the

rapist's identity)? Should the analyses be presented case by case or across cases (neither of which would capture the process of going back and forth between the two that characterized the work of analysis). As we considered different possibilities, we found ways to modify our claims, to work them up in more detail, in combination with further listening and reading. And we found that, as we discussed previously, the process was very much like trying to organize material for a review paper. In the end, we decided to present the analysis across cases in terms of the basic functions—event formulation and identity construction—because it allowed us to highlight the various patterns in the most general way (Wood & Rennie, 1994). At that point, we were satisfied that we could warrant the claims we had made. But this is not the same as saying that the analysis was complete. In the course of discussing the work in a subsequent paper (Kroger & Wood, 1998), we looked at the data again and worked up some additional claims (as we will discuss later).

We have tried to convey some sense of how one goes about the process of analysis and to emphasize the way in which analysis begins with and keeps going back to the discourse, drawing on various concepts if and when they appear to be useful in working up our understandings. There are other accounts of the process that readers may want to look at, for example, Hutchby and Wooffitt (1998) and Potter (1997). But again, the best way to appreciate what is involved is to get one's feet wet with data of one's own (the Nike strategy—Just do it!). There are, however, a few remaining issues.

CONTEXT

It has become commonplace to emphasize that social action does not occur in a vacuum and that we thus need to consider the context in which it occurs in order to analyze and understand it. This seemingly unproblematic statement masks the lively discussion and debate that is ongoing in discourse analysis around the notion of context and what it means to consider it. The issues are so complex that we cannot begin to do them justice here; there are some excellent and extensive treatments available in several collections (e.g., Duranti & Goodwin, 1992; Tracy, 1998; Watson & Seiler, 1992) and in specific articles (e.g., Schegloff, 1997; see also references later in this work). Rather, we point briefly to some of the issues and focus on some suggestions for dealing with issues of context as a practical matter in analysis, although we run the risk of oversimplifying both the literature and our own position.

Context is often taken to refer in a general way to information that is outside the text that is being analyzed, that is, information about settings, circumstances, social roles, demographic variables (age, sex, race, etc.), and so on. This sort of information is sometimes referred to as extrinsic context (e.g., Schegloff, 1992), in contrast to intrinsic context, that is, the parts of a text that are outside the particular segment is analyzed at any particular moment.

We shall assume for our purposes here that the use of the latter sort of context is not only desirable, but necessary. We follow the CA position that talk is "doubly contextual in being both *context-shaped* and *context-renewing*" (Heritage, 1984, p. 242). Utterances rely on prior utterances for their production and interpretation and themselves contribute to the context for subsequent utterances. This contextualization of utterances is a procedure that is relied upon by participants themselves and is hearable-visible in the discourse that we are analyzing.

The more difficult problem concerns the use of extrinsic context (or broad context; see Tracy, 1998). Extrinsic context includes not only the information we mentioned above, but also comments made by people about a prior episode in which they participated and about their talk on that occasion. The use of this latter sort of information is perhaps obviously problematic for the sort of discourse analysis that we have been discussing in this book, in that comments on the second occasion can only be considered in their own right as yet another discourse and not as a route to the prior discourse. But what about the setting, the characteristics of participants, and so on? Can we draw on these to analyze our data? Should we distinguish between different sorts of such contextual information (e.g., about demographic variables vs. the setting; cf. Duranti & Goodwin, 1992; Tracy, 1998)? The strategy that we want to recommend here is a simple one. It follows the arguments of Schegloff (1997) and others (e.g., Antaki, 1994; Potter, 1998a) that context is only to be used in formal analysis if it is relevant to participants. And by context we mean all sorts of external contexts (e.g., class, ethnicity, sex-gender, race, age; general properties such as power; institutional orders, such as the legal order; and settings, such as ecological or cultural settings; cf. Schegloff, 1992, p. 195).

Why make this move? As Schegloff (1997) points out, the problem is not that it would not be true to say, for example, that a person is a woman or an American or a professor and so on. The problem is that all of these categorizations (and many more) are true. How do we select among them? Further, how do we select those that are relevant to the participants? For example, if we know that participants in an interaction differ substantially in age, we may be tempted to interpret features of action in intergenerational terms (and perhaps even call the interaction "intergenerational"). But as N. Coupland (personal communication, May 14, 1994) has argued, age may not be relevant to the participants; they may orient instead (or in addition) to role or race or gender and so on. How do we know that a particular feature is relevant (and not simply confounded with some other feature, e.g., in the way that age may be confounded with status; Antaki, 1994, p. 192)? If a particular contextual feature is important to the participants, we should be able to see this in some way or another in their discourse, to show that they orient to it, that it is, as we discussed earlier, procedurally consequential (Schegloff, 1997). Further, this requires us to specify precisely what it is about that feature that is important. It cannot simply be glossed as age or race or gender, because all of these can be described or worked up in many different ways (including their categorization variously as personal or situational or social, which is why we do not distinguish between different sorts of external context on an a priori basis). As Schegloff (1992) points out, there is a tendency to treat context as understood; it is "not so much subjected to analysis . . . as it is 'invoked'" (p. 193).

We note further that the problem is not only or necessarily a problem of using analysts' versus participants' categories. The distinction is by no means a clear one (Potter, 1998a). Categories such as race, gender, medical exam, and so on are participants' as well as analysts' categories (Antaki, 1994). The issue is rather, which category or categories are relevant now, are used in the current discourse, in what sense, and how. (See, e.g., Edwards's, 1998, point about being Irish, which we consider in Chapter 9.)

Another reason for adopting this strategy is a broader theoretical argument:

> Structures, systems, cultures, and so on are "occasioned" phenomena, which exist only in the practices of participants. They exist nowhere else. Particular participants at particular moments, in particular strips of discourse, constitute what they refer to as "the system". . . . Having constituted "the system," participants then orient themselves to it as if it had an objective existence prior to and independent of their discourse. (Watson, 1992, p. xx)

That is, we need to ground context in the discourse not simply as a way of demonstrating that a particular feature is important to the speakers, but because this is the only place that context can be found (if not in the discourse at hand, then in some other discourse or discourses). Regardless of one's position on this broader claim, the requirement to ground context in the discourse has a practical virtue. As Edwards (1997) has discussed in relation to the issue of identifying speakers' intentions, it gives us "a principled way to *stop* doing it (i.e., identifying) . . . *for any one instance of talk* we could go on forever, attributing to participants all kinds of reasons for saying things" (p. 95).

It is crucial to emphasize that the recommendation is not to ignore context, to leave out what is important, but to be very careful about how it is brought into analysis. One possibility is to broaden the scope of the analysis (Antaki, 1994) by extending the boundaries of the interaction under analysis. For example, we may find that there is no orientation to age in the interviews that constitute the text of our analysis. However, discourse that occurred prior or subsequent to those interviews (e.g., preinterview talk) might support an analysis in terms of age and could so be considered if it were available. In this case, it arguably becomes part of the internal context (further demonstrating the problematics of certain analytical distinctions, such as the internal-external; see Antaki, p. 191; Schegloff, 1992, p. 197).

It is also important to point out that "this approach does not imply that analysis is being done without ethnographic knowledge, as if everything relevant is to be *discovered* in the talk" (Potter, 1998a, p. 31). As we discussed earlier, analysis cannot proceed without a great deal of shared knowledge, not the least of which is (and is supplied by) the language itself. And as we noted above with respect to analyst and participant categories, this knowledge is also shared at least partially by participants and analysts. Shared understanding makes materials "coherent and analysable" for both participants and analysts (Edwards, 1998, p. 23; see also Hutchby & Wooffitt, 1998, pp. 112-113). Sometimes, ethnographic research is necessary. For example, in analyzing conversations between teenagers, we have needed help in understanding references to "2 Pac" (as in "yeah so 2 Pac's not dead eh?"), although we had no problem in appreciating the discussion of Elvis and whether he is dead. Similarly, in looking at data from a wedding in England, it was helpful to be told that Waitrose is an upscale store (which we might have assumed, perhaps inappropriately, from the utterance that followed: "pass them [some of the groom's things] over to you Julie [bride] if that's OK . . . in a Waitrose bag. Alex [the groom], I know you are very posh and all that"). But as Schegloff (1992) notes, "the relevance of whatever has been learned through fieldwork (or in any other manner) must be warranted as relevant to the participants by reference to details of the conduct of the interaction" (p. 223). That is, we not only need to know the meaning or sense of some item for the participants, we also need to show that and how it is meaningful to them.

In a similar vein, we shall probably want to use information about the circumstances and setting in which an interaction occurred in order to set the scene for the text that is to be analyzed. This is not done to justify any claims about the text (e.g., that it involves "therapist talk"), but to make it comprehensible for the reader by pointing to some possible contexts in which the text would make sense. This move should not foreclose possibilities for analysis as long as we are clear about the provisional status of the information as context specification, for example, by distinguishing between our version of context (i.e., the circumstances under which the discourse was collected, e.g., in the therapist's office) and the participants' version (the circumstances identified by the participants as relevant; see Edwards, 1998, pp. 19-20).

Researchers may overestimate the difficulty of grounding context in the discourse; there are numerous examples of how to do this. Heritage (1997) looks at some of them in his discussion of conversation analysis and institutional talk (see also Appendix B on CA). Hutchby (1999) discusses the way in which power can be considered a feature of and resource in interaction, for example, by looking at the asymmetrical distribution of argumentational resources. There are a number of examples of the way in which social identities can be examined by looking at discourse identities, that is, participant identities (e.g., the teller and recipient of a story) that are "integral parts of conversational activities" (Nofsinger, 1991, p. 163). For example, Greatbach and Dingwall (1998) show the way in which participants invoke discourse identities that are consistent with the social (specifically institutional) identity of divorce mediator. Chapter 9 presents some other examples of how analysts have dealt with identity as a participants' concern. (See also Wood & Rennie, 1994, and the previous discussion of this.)

Gender is often seen as an aspect of context relevant in all social interactions (Tracy, 1998, p. 10). And gender will almost invariably be indexed or marked in some way if only because this is built into most languages (e.g., via pronouns, naming practices, and so on). But we need to consider specifically whether the marking of gender is procedurally consequential, whether there is a "consequential tie" for the participants between (some aspect of) gender and a "particular facet of their conduct" (Schegloff, 1992, p. 196). Hopper and LeBaron (1998) show how this can be done in terms of a three-part sequence by which "gender creeps into talk." We present a very brief and simplified summary of their argument.

Excerpt 1 [Film: Strangers in good company; two bird-watchers talking about a singer bird; p. 62]

Cissy:	He was- (0.2) he was so pla::in, .hh wasn't he
	(1.8)
→	I'm saying he, it might be a she . . .

Gender is indexed in the first line; this sort of indexing often passes unnoticed in conversation. Here, however, we see in the second line an explicit noticing ("I'm saying he").

Excerpt 1 [continued, p. 65]

Cissy:	I'm saying he, it might be a she, huh huh huh=
Mary:	=If it sings it's a he.
Cissy:	Oh, oh is it really?
Mary:	There are very few <u>female</u> birds that sing, which is one of those .hhh sa:d things.
Cissy:	Oh, I didn't know that?

Cissy's noticing is taken up here by Mary, who asserts the relevance of gender, following which gender becomes a central focus of the encounter. "To summarize: A gendered activity may emerge as the extending of themes raised by a previous gendered noticing" (Hopper & LeBaron, p. 66). That is, gender creeps into talk "through an action series of three phases: peripheral use, noticing, and extension" (p. 69).

There are many different ways in which participants bring in context (and many ways to show how they do so). For example, we see in the Hopper and LeBaron (1998) work that the issue is not simply whether gender is in or out. Rather, Hopper and LeBaron show that the salience of gender gradually

increases on a turn-by-turn basis. More generally, one advantage of the emphasis on grounding context in discourse is that it allows (and requires) us to be
more precise about the particular element of context that is consequential (Potter, 1998a) and to improve our understanding of context by attending to distinctions within contextual features that are often framed globally. For
example, we can see that in constructing an identity as a victim, the women in
the Wood and Rennie (1994) study were orienting to power. Powerlessness is
part of what it means to be a victim (which we can also see elsewhere in the
women's discourse). Power here involves the notion of power *over*. But the
women in the study also constructed identities as agents; power in connection
with agency stresses the notion of power *to*.

There are nonetheless concerns among some discourse analysts about the
sort of technical or formal analysis (Schegloff, 1997) we have been discussing,
even among those sympathetic to arguments about the need to demonstrate
procedural consequentiality. For example, Coupland, Holmes, and Coupland
(1999) have questioned whether such demonstration should be a "universal obligation for discourse analysts/pragmaticists who want to incorporate aspects
of 'social context' into their interpretations" (p. 1238) and have suggested that
it is an overly restrictive criterion. Concerns have arisen in part because of
Schegloff's (1997) claim that such a criterion is needed to offset the possibility
that analysts, particularly those who adopt critical and political stances, will
simply impose their view of context and conduct upon participants, and, further, that "serious critical discourse analysis presupposes serious formal analysis, and is addressed to its product" (p. 184). Wetherell (1998) has argued that
a complete or scholarly analysis (in contrast to a technical one) must go beyond
the limits set by this requirement and include the "argumentative threads
which are hearably *not* [italics added] part of these participants' orientations
and everyday sense-making" (p. 404). She proposes a more synthetic analysis
that would also include critical, particularly poststructuralist, concerns (e.g.,
around issues of ideology, power, sexism) and that could be evaluated not only
according to the criterion of grounding or demonstration, but also in terms of
other criteria, such as coherence and plausibility. Schegloff's (1998) response
to this argument is (in part) that we should not underestimate the reach of CA.

We cannot engage all of the elements of the debate here. Again, we attempt
to offer some suggestions for practice, including the use of intertextual analysis as a way to incorporate external context in the sense of larger societal discourses and texts (see our discussion of this issue later in the work). We are
sympathetic to Schegloff's concern that analyses that are not grounded in participants' concerns can constitute an unwarranted imposition, a form of academic hegemony; moreover, such analyses are unlikely to bring about social
change (as can be seen in numerous examples of failed interventions, social
programs, etc.). At the same time, we agree with Wetherell that analysis should
aim to do more than identify what is of concern to participants. In particular,
we think that it is crucial to identify what is not hearable—not because it is

nonetheless implicated in some way in the discourse (which seems to be the thrust of her argument), but because it is *not* implicated. For example, Wood and Rennie (1994) made the point that one of the notable features of the discourse of women in their study of rape was that this discourse made almost no use of concepts of gender oppression, of coercive sexuality, and so on. So although we might attempt to understand their experience in these terms, *they* did not—which is precisely the point. As critical analysts and feminists, we would aim to make these perspectives available to them, rather than impose these perspectives on their experience. Should the identification of what is not (hearably, visibly) there be considered a part of formal analysis? This is a possibility, but we might then be constrained to identify all of the myriad possibilities that are not there. We could instead draw on a notion of orders of analysis.

Orders of analysis are not the same as levels of analysis. By the latter, we mean the way in which smaller units are part of larger units; for example, "lexical choice is a part of turn design; turn design is a part of sequence organization; sequence is a part of overall structural organization" (Heritage, 1997, p. 179). As we have discussed earlier, analysis involves a recursive process of working across these multiple levels, both within and across cases, a kind of scaffolding that is both sequential and hierarchical. Analysis is not unlike mowing a lawn where this involves starting at the center and proceeding in ever-widening circles while overlapping with the previous pass. The move to outer layers or higher levels of analysis can be seen as a way of extending context by bringing more into the text. All of this is first-order analysis; that is, all of the interpretations are grounded in the text (the mower is always in contact with the lawn). Second-order analysis would focus on the analysis of the text— on the interpretations, claims, and so forth, rather than on the text itself. (Stand back and look at your mowing job or, in Schegloff's terms, at the product of your formal analysis.) The aim here would be to identify the ways in which your analysis could be seen in relation to issues of ideology, culture, and so on, and in particular, with respect to what is not there from your perspective as an analyst and a critic.

Another way to bring in notions about culture, ideology, and other features of context would be to address them in a discussion section (a possibility mentioned by Schegloff, 1997, p. 186, and one that we have also considered in relation to the use of face as an analytic concept; MacMartin et al., in press). This could be done in lieu of or in addition to a second-order analysis. We would probably opt for the latter. The second-order analysis would stick more closely to the formal analysis and would also be constrained to identify alternatives, particularly those hinted at (although not clearly specified) by the rhetorical organization of the discourse. The discussion could range more broadly, including the consideration of "why" questions for those so inclined. We agree that it is important to develop strategies for considering alternatives, for going beyond what is immediately available (see also Tracy, 1995). One of the strengths of critical discourse and poststructuralist approaches is that they draw attention to some of the possibilities. There are different views on how these should be treated, on how we may include these sorts of analytic concerns in our work, but their inclusion is consistent with the idea that discourse analysis is not simply a method or empirical account.

Intertextual Analysis

Intertextuality is a term with multiple meanings (Potter, 1996). Potter suggests that it can be understood as a set of relationships of quotations between texts (with each text consisting at least in part of quotations from other texts) or as a relationship between different genres or forms of discourse and representation or as the use of the central metaphors in one area of discourse in another (pp. 78, 95). In the sense of relations among quotations, all texts are intertextual, but analysis is not intertextual unless it takes account explicitly of such quotations. For example, for Fairclough (1992a), "intertextual analysis shows how texts selectively draw upon *orders of discourse*—the particular configurations of conventionalized practices (genres, discourses, narratives, etc.) which are available to text producers and interpreters in particular social circumstances" (p. 194). Like linguistic systems (*la langue*), orders of discourse are social and historical resources—abstractions that are realized in particular texts, although any "particular text may draw upon a plurality of genres, discourses or narratives" (Fairclough, 1992a, p. 195). Intertextual analysis "presupposes accounts of individual genres and types of discourse" (Fairclough, 1992a, p. 195).

We shall try to put these notions a bit more simply. We have said that we must demonstrate the way that context is a concern for participants, that it is grounded in their talk. We can draw upon the idea that we discussed above, namely that context (orders of discourse) exists only in the practices of participants (broadly speaking, in their discourse), rather than treating the notion of context as some abstract, general "out thereness." But this does not preclude the possibility that some particular context is relevant in other texts besides the one at hand. Intertextual analysis can enhance our analysis of context by allowing us to consider how it is worked up in those specific other texts.

Fairclough (1992a) gives a number of examples of intertextual analysis within the CDA perspective. We consider here one example from our own work. In the analysis of interviews with women who were raped by someone who was not a stranger, Wood and Rennie (1994) argued that the women's accounts could be viewed in terms of two interpretive repertoires. The Hollywood (or "standard" rape) repertoire includes sexual intercourse without consent; certain kinds of identities (a villain and a victim, who are strangers); brutality; violence, and a set of motives (power and escape). The consensual sex (or date) repertoire includes sexual intercourse, but with consent; different identities (e.g., friends, lovers); and shared motives (sexual satisfaction, love). (See Kroger & Wood, 1998, for further elements.) The relevant repertoires can be seen as orders of discourse concerned with sexuality and gender that the women both drew on and reproduced. This looks like intertextual analysis—except that the argument was not explicitly or specifically intertextual. That is, although Wood and Rennie presented evidence for their claims that the women were working up their formulations of events in terms of these elements, they did not show specifically that the women were drawing on repertoires, because they presented no evidence for the operation of such repertoires outside the text that they analyzed. (This is also the case for much of the other work that has been done on repertoires.) Kroger and Wood (1998) reconsidered the Wood and Rennie work with a specific focus on intertextuality. They drew on research by Coates et al. (1994) on Canadian court decisions (described in Chapter 3) that demonstrated the way in which those decisions incorporate (what were identified as) interpretive repertoires for stranger rape and consensual sex, the repertoires described (independently) by Wood and Rennie.

The Kroger and Wood (1998) intertextual analysis would be even stronger if it had also been able to draw on work focusing directly on these repertoires and orders of discourse, particularly work that shows the distribution and operation of such repertoires in North American culture (see Fairclough's, 1992a, comment above on presupposed accounts). Nonetheless, we think that it demonstrates the way in which analysis that draws on context as articulated in specific other texts (including talk and written texts) is not only more broadly social than analysis that considers only the functions of discourse within a specific interaction: It can also contribute more generally to identifying the way in which certain features of context are realized in multiple texts. As Fairclough (1992a) argues, intertextual analysis "crucially mediates the connection between language and social context" (p. 195). Intertextual analysis does not defeat the requirement that we show that (and how) participants themselves orient to context. But this requirement does not necessarily mean that participants must orient to orders of discourse as intertextual or must identify intertextuality in any specific or explicit way (although they may do so, for example, by using reported discourse or drawing upon social science literature in the course of working up an argument). Rather, the analyst must show that the participant's orientation can be understood intertextually and that intertextual analysis contributes an enhanced understanding of the participant's orientation and discourse.

Summary

Context is a problematic notion. As a noun, context refers to what is "with" the "text," what occurs before and after a specified word or passage or the situational background or environment relevant to some happening. Context is thus always shifting, depending on what one specifies as text or as relevant. So we are better off to think of context not as an object, but as a process or activity, and to ask not what goes with the text, but what is put with the text (as captured in the origin of the word in the Latin *contexere,* to weave together). And as we do with other actions, we can ask what is being done with statements about context. Schegloff (1992) suggests (only partly facetiously) that "context" may be used simply as a polemical device, as a way of saying "what I noticed about your topic that you didn't write about" (pp. 214-215). Statements about context can also be used in relation to analysis, understanding, discussion, the generation of hypotheses, and so on—and they should be evaluated in terms of the claims that are made. But doing context is also (and must be, for certain sorts of claims) a matter for participants, who construct, make relevant, and orient to context. For example, footing can be said to involve the provision of information (e.g., about authorship, circumstances) to be used in the interpretation and assessment of a particular utterance. In other words, context is a problem for both participants and analysts (Potter, 1998a).

We have taken a very broad and undifferentiated approach to context in order to stress the importance of participants' orientations—what they include, their distinctions. This approach reflects the one that we have taken to the issue of analysts' categories more generally; that is, we need to see if they are relevant to participants and how participants can be said to be doing social comparison, intention, facework, gender, race, and so on. (Recall the O. J. Simpson trial, in which attorneys were said to be "playing the race card," that is, invoking specific formulations of what it means to be an African American, specific versions of the history of race relations, and so on.) All of these categories exist as they are worked up in texts—the everyday talk of participants, the "dossiers" of analysts—and they can be reformulated as discursive activities, activities that are carried out by participants and analysts alike.

QUANTIFICATION

Discourse analysis is primarily an analysis that is carried out by using words, that is, discursively, rather than by using numbers or quantitative techniques (which are often treated interchangeably, although they are not equivalent, in that one can quantify without using numbers and use numbers without quantifying, i.e., nominally). The issue is not the use of numbers or of quantification per se. Rather, the problem is with scientistic assumptions that quantification is the only sort of analytic activity that is meaningful, that only those aspects that can be quantified are worth considering, and that statistical tests are a route to some sort of transcendent truth. Such tests still appear to be worshipped, despite frequent reminders of the limits of significance testing (e.g., Cohen, 1994). It needs to be reiterated that qualitative analysis can be highly useful, if not essential, in many cases and that quantitative approaches may well be unscientific, if used inappropriately.

Discourse analysts are concerned with what people are doing or not doing, how they are doing it, and how it is connected to other things they are doing, rather than with how often they are doing it, how much they are doing it, and so on. The latter sorts of questions could be addressed quantitatively—and would need to be if researchers were concerned to assess the strength of relationships between features or variables, the distribution of certain features of conversation across various participants or occasions, the statistical significance of those relationships or of differences of some sort between people, and so on. But these are not the primary concerns of discourse analysts.

More important, there are good reasons *not* to quantify. The major problem is that quantification can ride roughshod over meaning, that we may only be counting the countable. The use of numbers to designate categories or quantities is at best premature if those categories are unclear (Tracy & Carjuzáa, 1993) or if quantification is conceptually inappropriate; for example, judgments of guilt in criminal trials are not a matter of degree, although they may be in civil trials in which judges or jurors are asked to apportion responsibility. The fundamental issue is that quantification requires coding (in the sense of interpretation and categorization), but coding cannot be done acceptably until discourse has been analyzed, given that meaning shifts with context and that context itself is constantly shifting. (See Schegloff, 1993, for a much more detailed discussion of this issue and of other issues related to quantification.) Without careful analysis, there is a great danger of unjustified interpretation and selectivity; it is not possible to avoid the imposition of oversimplified analyst's categories and the omission of essential features. It is a moot point whether the coding of unanalyzed discourse data is an improvement over the use of questionnaires and scales in which attributions and selection of meaning are almost wholly neglectful of the participant's views (Potter & Wetherell, 1987).

Quantification is also problematic with respect to the preservation of meaning if it represents averages. For example, an average score for a group is misleading not only because it does not apply to everyone, but because it may not apply to anyone. This seems particularly ironic if the researchers are psychologists, concerned as they ostensibly are with individuals, not with statistical abstractions. We are reminded of the old joke about economists; they put one foot in the fridge and one in the oven and conclude that it is room temperature. The same is true for averages across units other than persons. For example, Schegloff (1993) has pointed out the dangers of adding up the number of times people laugh in an hour and then concluding, for example, that they laugh once per minute. Clearly, people do not laugh once per minute; if they did, it would mean that they are not sensitive to the proper occasions for laughter. And Harré (1978) has alerted us to the problems of the meaning of distribution involved in probability statements. For example, the statement that there is an 80% probability of laughing during a conversation of particular type and duration could mean either that every person in a group of 10 has an 80% chance of laughing, or that 8 people will laugh and 2 will not. We need to be vigilant about preserving the individual discourse features and their relationships to each other and to their occasions of use, and about avoiding the inappropriate use of aggregates, averages, and distributions.

These arguments do not mean that discourse analysts do not use numbers or quantification. Rather, it means that "quantification is no substitute for analysis" (Schegloff, 1993, p. 114) and that its role is limited to functions that are not strictly part of analysis, although it may be important for preanalytic work. Thus, discourse analysts avoid quantification in the form of significance testing of analytical claims, but they may use quantification in description or in the coding for selection that is prior to analysis. Numerical expressions may be used to describe the number and frequency of particular features of discourse. For example, Harwood and Giles (1992) examined the presentation of the elderly in six episodes of a popular television series. They reported that there were approximately 28 to 55 age markers per show, which meant an "average of between one and two age markers per minute!" (p. 419). Discourse may also be appropriately described using nonnumerical quantitative expressions, for example, *overwhelmingly, ordinarily,* or *occasionally.* Schegloff (1993) has argued that this sort of informal quantification (or what we could call *ethnoquantification*) is not weaker than statistical or formal techniques, but that it involves a different sort of account. Informal quantification reports an

> *experience* or *grasp* of frequency, not a count; an account of an investigator's sense of frequency over the range of a research experience, not in a specifically bounded body of data; a characterization of distribution fully though tacitly informed by the analytic import of what is being characterized. (p. 119)

We are reminded of the Woody Allen film in which two different assessments of the frequency of sexual intercourse ("all the time," "hardly ever") are provided by two different characters in relation to the same count (three times per week).

Both numerical and nonnumerical expressions may be used to describe patterns. For example, Harwood and Giles (1992) reported that age markers were present in almost half of the humorous utterances in the television episodes that they examined, and that almost 90% of the more than 200 age markers coded occurred within a humorous context. They also expressed the latter pattern nonnumerically: "Non-humorous age-marking is relatively rare . . . whereas humorous age marking appears to occur as a matter of course" (p. 426). In their study of intellectual discussion, Tracy and Carjuzáa (1993) reported that "faculty members talk more than graduate students" (p. 192). None of these authors reported statistical tests in support of their descriptions. Such tests could have been done, but they would be unnecessary, because the claims are not really the point. (They can be adequately supported by what is sometimes called the "eyeball test," i.e., ethnostatistics.) Rather, the point of the descriptions is to establish significance not statistically, but in the sense of importance (Schegloff, 1993). The frequency of age-related humor suggests that the television show studied by Harwood and Giles (1992) may be an important source of images of aging and the elderly and deserves more detailed analyses. It also justifies the interpretation of the show by Harwood and Giles in intergroup terms—"or at least potentially so (for younger viewers)" (p. 420). For Tracy and Carjuzáa, significance (importance) resides in the implications of talk by faculty members to which the difference in talk between faculty and students draws attention. Finally, the sorts of descriptions we have been considering here are important because they give the reader a sense or feeling for the data, for how it looks overall.

Quantification may be helpful for selecting data. For example, a researcher may wish to quantify (numerically or nonnumerically) various features of discourse in order to select for analysis a particular feature that occurs frequently or rarely. Quantification may also be helpful in the detection of patterns for analysis (using either conventional or ethnostatistical procedures). The co-occurrence of particular features of discourse can suggest that there may be particular functions of those features. Instances of co-occurrence can then be analyzed to identify any such functions, with instances in which the features do not co-occur considered as in negative case analysis. It is difficult to find examples of studies that employ this strategy (but see Freed & Greenwood, 1996). Studies in which researchers identify patterns of co-occurrence through statistical analyses are plentiful; however, the patterns are usually presented as the outcome rather than the starting point of analysis. For example, in a study directed in part to Schegloff's arguments about the problems of quantification, Wilson and Zeitlyn (1995) attempted to identify the relationship between the use of person-referring expressions and features of the social and conversational context. Among other matters, they assessed the distribution of different types of kin referents according to the status of the referent (e.g., self vs. addressee). It would seem reasonable to make claims about this distribution because the categories involved are not contentious. There is no disagreement about what counts as a kin term (e.g., *father*) or about whether that term refers to the speaker (father) or the addressee (son), at least in this study. Similarly, the identification of a first-person pronoun in English is a straightforward matter. Coding is not inevitably problematic, particularly where the categories involve features of talk (vs. of persons) and are treated as nominal rather than ordinal (with tests of patterns therefore involving chi-square or log-linear procedures).

However, there are probably relatively few "transparent" categories; for example, the categorization of vocal sounds as "talking" (as in the Tracy & Carjuzáa, 1993, study) may not be completely straightforward. The classification of "humor" (as in the Harwood & Giles, 1992, study) is another example. Even grammatical categories can be problematic: A grammatical question is not necessarily an interactional question (Heritage & Roth, 1995). Use of these sorts of categories would require analysis before they could be used as part of a claim about distribution. This is not to suggest that researchers are thoughtless about their use of categories, but that the attention that is given or the analyses that are done are insufficient. For example, Wilson and Zeitlyn (1995) considered the relationship of person-referring expressions to types of speech acts. Although they make a careful argument for their coding of the latter, the nontransparency of that coding is apparent in both their reliance on interrater reliabilities and the failure of the latter to equal 100%. In a study that was also directed toward Schegloff's concerns about quantification, Heritage and Roth examined a number of bases for coding, including the category "questioning," in order to assess quantitatively claims about the extent to which news interviews are marked by a pattern of interviewer questions and interviewee responses. Their consideration of grammatical, pragmatic, and turn organization criteria is quite thorough, but as they admit, the coding scheme that they develop is still unable to capture all relevant instances.

The sorts of coding difficulties that we have been discussing would not be an issue if the codings were not used in the making of distributional claims—but they are. For example, Wilson and Zeitlyn (1995) claim that the proportion of expressions referring to the addressee is greater for topic-changing than for non–topic-changing utterances, despite their acknowledgment of the limitations in coding topic. Similarly, Heritage and Roth (1995) claim that their coding procedure enabled them to demonstrate significant convergence between questioning and turn organization. However, Heritage and Roth are not particularly enamored of this possibility, although they point out that quantitative assessment may be necessary for some sorts of applied work. They suggest that such assessments can offer a picture of "order in the aggregate." They cannot "compete with the sensitivity and specificity of single-case analyses of which they are properly aggregates" (p. 53) but can be complementary to such analyses.

The strategy that we propose here treats the quantitative assessment of relationships neither as complementary to analysis nor as evidence for claims about relationships, but as a preanalytic activity. It avoids the problems of using unanalyzed or underanalyzed categories in the identification of patterns, because no claims are made about those patterns. The patterns are merely a starting point for the selection of material for analysis. In the course of that analysis, we can both check those patterns and, more important, assess their functions. If it turns out that the patterns do not hold up, there is no threat to the claims that are the focus of interest. The use of contentious codes is thus not problematic, although it is desirable to use those that are as uncontentious as possible because they can provide a finer basis for selection. Nor is the use of ethnostatistics problematic, again because no claims are made about the patterns so identified.

In sum, discourse analysis can make use of statistical tests of the conventional sort perhaps to select material for analysis. But statistical tests cannot be used for analysis. The coding that they involve is for selection rather than for interpretation and categorization, which involve and are part of analysis. We are not suggesting that statistical analyses can never be used to support discourse claims; rather, the sorts of claims that can be so supported (because they do not involve inappropriate coding) are not likely to be very interesting on their own. For example, the claim that faculty members talk more than graduate students would not be worth the research effort required for its substantiation (Tracy & Carjuzáa, 1993). In contrast, the major claims of interest to discourse analysts in most cases cannot be assessed using conventional statistical procedures; where they can be (e.g., because the appropriate analyses have been carried out), they would be redundant, because the questions at issue have already been answered, and answered more thoroughly. Such procedures are not a higher form of analyses, but a less refined one. They may nonetheless be useful for certain practical purposes. We think that this position is compatible with the injunction to use quantification and statistics when they are useful and appropriate (an injunction honored more in the breach than in the observance) and to avoid the fallacy of misplaced precision (Fischer, cited in Lowry, 1974). Lowry argues that this fallacy can take several forms: "Some numbers are used inappropriately, some are simply nonsense, others imply measurement of something that might not be quantitatively measurable, while still others obscure the fact that nonquantitative measurements or assessments may be more significant" (pp. 49-50). We would emphasize that this fallacy involves *misplaced* precision; precision itself is an important goal and certainly so for discourse analysis.

COMPUTER-ASSISTED ANALYSIS

In line with the arguments of the previous section, we would emphasize that computer programs can be useful, but that we have not yet found any that are suitable for carrying out discourse analyses. Pfaffenberger (1988) presents a useful discussion of various issues involved in the use of microcomputer programs in qualitative research of various sorts (particularly ethnographic and grounded theory styles, but excluding discourse analysis). He distinguishes between the sorts of programs that involve the use of computers for the storage and retrieval of textual data and those that involve data analysis. The latter include programs for automatic data analysis (e.g., word frequency and content category analysis) as well as knowledge-based strategies, particularly expert systems. We find that none of these are really useful for discourse analysis. The automatic programs are focused on (inappropriate) quantification, and the expert systems that have been developed to date cannot begin to replicate the interpretive activities of the discourse analyst (in part because of their inabilities to deal adequately with context).

Other researchers (e.g., Huberman & Miles, 1994) use a broader notion of analysis than does Pfaffenberger (1988) and thus would classify most of the sorts of programs he includes in his first category (storage and retrieval) as programs for analysis. As Huberman and Miles point out, all such programs have built-in assumptions about theory; our concern is that the programs that are currently available are based on theories that do not fit readily with a discursive perspective. For example, Ethnograph (Seidel & Clark, 1984) and NUD•IST (Richards & Richards, 1990) involve hierarchical relationships and assumptions about these that are compatible with grounded theory but not with discourse analysis.

From our perspective, all of the search and retrieval programs involve analysis in some sense, if only because they employ codes that almost always require at least minimal analysis. We have discussed above the problems that this entails, namely that the analysis required is not carried out properly or thoroughly, thus creating difficulties of premature coding when the codes are used in analysis. We think that these difficulties are exacerbated by the availability of programs that can use those codes. We are thus quite wary about the use of computer programs (beyond the word processing required for the creation of transcripts) and suggest that at best we talk about the possibility of computer-assisted preanalysis in order not to delude ourselves into thinking that there is a substitute for the painstaking process of doing discourse analysis "by hand." However, we do see a place for various sorts of software programs. For example, they are probably essential for the sheer management and organization of material, especially for research that involves large and heterogeneous data sets. They can be helpful for searching for and retrieving instances of usages, topics, or linkages for analysis. To detect patterns, researchers may wish to use programs that can carry out or be linked to programs for statistical analysis. For many small projects, the simple search capacities of word processing programs may be sufficient. But there is only a peripheral role for computers in discourse analysis.

Identities in Talk: Research Examples

In Chapter 3, we discussed discourse-analytic research on a variety of topics in order to convey some sense of the range and possibilities of such work. Here, we present research examples to demonstrate different ways of looking at the same topic. We selected the topic of identity, because it is a concern that has received a good deal of attention in discourse analysis in a number of traditions. It has also been a central topic in conventional social scientific work. So we can also see here the contrast between discourse-analytic and conventional approaches by showing some of the ways in which we can understand identities in talk.

INTELLECTUAL AND INSTITUTIONAL IDENTITY

Tracy and Carjuzáa (1993) examined the enactment of identity in intellectual discussion; we consider here some of their examples of introductory comments by speakers at a weekly colloquium series.

Excerpt 1 [p. 177]

> The book, uh, was, uh, based on research I was involved in while still a graduate student and then a post-doctoral . . . where we had a major grant. . . . What I want to talk about today is something completely different . . . I have a grant from. . .

What is the speaker doing? He mentions grants and having had a book published, but not all of this information is relevant to the topic of the talk he is giving ("something completely different"), and in any case, the information was already provided by the person who introduced him. As Tracy and Carjuzáa argue, in referring to his past novice status and his new focus, the speaker constructs himself as an experienced academic. Further, he is highly competent (a book, grants) and very much engaged in his current project.

Here are two other speakers.

Excerpt 2 [p. 177]

> What you're going to hear about today is a paper in process.

Excerpt 3 [referring to a flyer describing the colloquium series; p. 178]

> flyers . . . are really nice, but, uh, I must say it kinda ups the ante a little bit on these colloquia.

In contrast to the first speaker, these speakers downplay their responsibility for the work they are about to describe. As Tracy and Carjuzáa note, phrases such as "paper in progress," "pilot study," "tangent," and so on (e.g., "sketch a framework") are commonly used by presenters and serve to suggest that the person has not been working on the ideas for very long and therefore they are not very polished, are subject to revision, and so on (p. 178). Similarly, the suggestion that one is giving an informal talk rather than a formal lecture (a contrast invoked elsewhere by the speaker in Excerpt 3) serves to license a lower level of presentation and to minimize the risk of failure.

The analyses discussed above focus on the ways in which colloquium participants construct intellectual identity. But participants have other concerns, for example, the construction of institutional identity, that is, one's rank as assistant professor, full professor, graduate student, and so on. Tracy and Carjuzáa (1993) considered two sorts of discourse. First, audience members were interviewed about how they saw their role at colloquia. For example, a tenured faculty member describes himself as a listener and offers an account for his failure to comment throughout the semester on topics on which he might be presumed to have an opinion. He thus constructs a position that faculty should not be silent (otherwise, why offer an account?). A graduate student comments: "The questions I ask are in the main exploratory, explanation . . . I think that's probably unique among graduate students" (p. 182).

Second, Tracy and Carjuzáa (1993) examined the way in which participants in interaction with a speaker orient to rank in relation to the kinds of questions they ask.

Excerpt 4 [p. 182]

> I have, I have, uh, a question about your, the paper . . . Uh, since I've not done comparative analysis, it's sort of asked more for my own knowledge, um, and it's not a loaded question.

Excerpt 5 [p. 183]

> I'm not as familiar with this individual as you are. Let me ask a question that I don't have an answer for.

In this context, giving an account for doing what one is doing (asking for information) when no one has asked for such an account suggests that this is an unusual sort of activity for the speaker, that the speaker usually provides information, and is therefore at a reasonably high level of institutional status. As Tracy and Carjuzáa point out, the statement that "it's not a loaded question" could also be seen to establish rank, in that it is much more likely that a senior rather than a junior person would be in a position to ask such questions. Both members of the audience note that they are seeking information—knowledge, an answer—in a way that suggests that they usually do have the knowledge, the answers. Tracy and Carjuzáa argue that the formulation of the speaker in Excerpt 5 in particular suggests that he often does ask questions to which he has the answer, a rhetorical device typically associated with teachers rather than with students.

As we discussed in Chapter 7, discourse analysts, particularly conversation analysts, often use the term *orienting* in discussing the actions of speakers, a term that can be problematic for beginning analysts. To say that speakers are relating or orienting to rank (or to any other feature) is to argue that rank is relevant to the speaker, or is an issue for the speaker. But such action is not necessarily done in any explicit or obvious fashion. For example, speakers do not say, "I'm a full professor, I don't usually ask questions for information." However, we can ask if the discourse could be paraphrased this way, which would suggest orienting to rank as a possible interpretation. But paraphrasing is not analysis, so we need to do more. One way to support such a reading is to ask what the references to knowledge and answers are doing in the utterances. They are not needed to ask a question, so they must therefore be doing something else, such as implying that this is not a usual activity of the speaker and that he is thereby orienting to rank. In Gricean terms (see section on Pragmatics in Appendix B), the inclusion of prefacing remarks about one's knowledge, the work one has done, and so on violates the maxim of relevance.

Discourse virtually always has multiple functions, even at the level of a single utterance. In addition, the functions are often interdependent. In the present case, as Tracy and Carjuzáa (1993) point out, it is not only that participants construct both sorts of identity, but that the doing of one serves or has implications for the other. For example, we can see how the speakers employ references to rank in their construction of competence (in Excerpt 1 above).

Our discussion does not do justice to the analytical possibilities of the discourse reported by Tracy and Carjuzáa (1993; see complete paper). We mention here only one further point. By constructing various versions of competence and commitment with respect to the work to be discussed, the speakers also constrain subsequent interaction in different ways. That is, these constructions have consequences for the trajectory of the interaction. They make available different sorts of possibilities for subsequent contributions by audience members, for example, encouraging or foreclosing the asking of difficult questions. Further, they provide different attributions (or "attribution out(s)" as Tracy & Carjuzáa put it, p. 177) for the speaker's failure to address questions adequately; one is not necessarily incompetent because one has not considered all the possibilities for carrying out work that is only just beginning. These claims could be checked by examining the sorts of questions asked by the audience and the speakers' responses. We note here the use of a concept, attribution, that appears frequently in conventional social psychology. However, as we discussed in Chapter 7, in discourse analysis, an attribution is a discursive act rather than a cognitive entity.

AGE IDENTITIES

We consider next some conversational discourse from a study by Coupland et al. (1991), in which the focus was on the ways in which contrasting age identities are coconstructed by an older woman talking to a woman of her own age and to a woman who is younger than she is. The conversations come from a corpus of videotaped interactions between women who have been asked to get to know one another.

Excerpt 1 [pp. 195-196]

1	May:	so er (.) we've got our Christmas party next Friday
2	Nora:	oh yes
3	May:	so I'm hoping I don't have two parties t overlapping one another

.

11	Nora:	once a week well I don't go out at <u>all</u> in the ⌈nights
12	May:	⌊my (.) er my
13		friend calls for me ((breathes)) we go to the Columbo
14	Nora:	oh yes
15	May:	we've got a little room and we do a lot of charity work for the
16		Home Towers [a local hospice]

.

26	Nora:	occasionally one or two of the family will come take <u>me</u>
27		somewhere and
28	May:	yeah
29	Nora:	bring me back home again like you know
30	May:	oh I go up <u>every</u> weekend to my family

Both of the women in this conversation are over 75 years old; in these and other excerpts, they present quite different pictures of their social activities and their life circumstances and thereby construct contrasting age identities. In these relatively few lines, May reports not only a number, but also a variety of different sorts of engagements; she is clearly an active and involved social participant (notwithstanding her dependence on others in some cases for transportation, etc., an inference that is available in other segments of the discourse). Further, each of these reports makes available further dimensions of May's identity: She has friends and contact with family members, she helps others, and so on.

It is clear that in this sort of analysis, at least, discourse analysts do rely heavily on "content," but, as we have discussed earlier, content is not a simple matter, nor can it be separated from style. May's claim to friends, family, invitations, and so on is not direct and, in some instances at least, not particularly obvious; she does not say explicitly, for example, "I am active, I have friends, and so on." Rather, these features of her identity are constructed through her reporting of activities, reports that require certain assumptions if they are to make sense. In addition, as Coupland et al. (1991) point out, May constructs her identity in relation to Nora. It is not only the content of her contributions, but their extent, in contrast to Nora's brief and passive utterances, that contribute to her identity construction. And when Nora does make a more extensive contribution ("occasionally one or two of the family"), May ups the ante, so to speak, by stressing that her own family visits are "every" weekend, rather than occasionally.

The various ways in which discourse analysts deal with issues of content can also be illustrated in the Coupland et al. (1991) analysis of the conversation between May and Jenny, a 38-year-old woman. May describes her weekly lunches with three generations of her family. Jenny interjects with, "So you're not lonely are you?" (p. 199). May subsequently reports her practice of giving sweets and pocket money to her great-grandchildren. Jenny responds with, "Gosh you manage to do that as well do you!" (p. 200). Although Jenny's comments describe a positive state of affairs, they both reflect and perpetuate the assumption that loneliness and financial hardship are relevant to someone who is old. There are other inquiries from Jenny that might seem positive (e.g., "do they er arrange anything for you to go away on a holiday?" p. 198; "and you're allowed to go there [to a holiday camp] is it yes?" p. 199); as Coupland et al. point out, these utterances also foreground the dependence of someone in May's position.

It is not always easy to generate and warrant these sorts of interpretations; how might the analyst go about this? The analytical work of Coupland et al. (1991) is facilitated by their familiarity with the literature on discourse and aging, as well as by the availability of a larger corpus of discourse than we have presented here. What else can be done, particularly by novice analysts? As we have discussed previously, one strategy is to consider the alternatives to what was said, a strategy that is also used by Coupland et al. For example, in the case

of the holiday, Jenny does not ask May whether she likes the camp, if she has
decided to go there this year, and so on; her questions are framed in such a way
as to constitute May as a patient rather than as an agent. And Jenny's question
about loneliness might more suitably have been replaced by comments or questions about May's family (or indeed, by a comment on her own family; overall,
this interaction reads more like an interview than like an everyday conversation.) What is *not* said becomes part of the analysis. A final feature of Jenny's
questions that deserves attention by the analyst is their syntax; the questions
are phrased in such a way as to call for responses that deny difficulties (loneliness, etc.). But at the same time, they all focus on limitations rather than opportunities or advantages.

In some conventional perspectives, concerns around identity construction
tend to focus upon the activities of one or another speaker. In relation to the
analyses we have just discussed, the analyst might be tempted to stop at the
ways in which May constructs her identity (the conversation with Nora) or has
her identity constructed for her by Jenny. But for a more complete analysis, the
analyst must always be concerned to identify the ways in which identity construction and other discursive accomplishments are interactional achieve-
ments. For example, after Jenny's comment on May's report of giving pocket
money, May responds, "That's sixty pence comes out of me every week!"
(Coupland et al., 1991, p. 200). May thereby aligns with Jenny's reformulation
of May's positive action "as a struggle for economic survival" and thus contributes to the construction of her own identity as an older person with problems
(p. 200). This example also illustrates how a response by one person (May)
serves to warrant our interpretation of a previous utterance (Jenny's) as implicating negative rather than positive aspects of May's situation, an interpretation that may seem overdone if we look only at the surface content.

Coconstruction is also demonstrated in another segment of the discourse
between May and Jenny, in which May begins with a positive evaluation of the
cost of the lunch available at the Day Centre.

Excerpt 2 [p. 201]

```
6   May:     and of course you couldn't cook a dinner
7   Jenny:   no not for one (.)   ⌈you can't be bothered you see
8   May:                          ⌊for sixty pence
9   Jenny:   no no (.) no

10  May:     but erm (.) you know it's erm (.) as I say I I
11           when I'm home I er (.) er butcher comes round and
12           I order something and I goes to cook it oh I don't
13           want it I gives it to the dog
14  Jenny:   do you (.) mm
15  May:     I don't want it
```

Jenny's interpretation of May's evaluation as reflecting a lack of interest in cooking for herself reiterates stereotypical concerns about the old person's lack of interest in cooking for one. More remarkable about this excerpt is the way in which May not only shifts her original assessment and picks up Jenny's formulation, but also claims to have originated Jenny's view ("as I say") and then extends it from not wanting to cook to not wanting to eat. As Coupland et al. (1991) point out, this construction (tea-and-toast syndrome in the gerontological literature) with its implications for depression and health is an interactional accomplishment. It does not belong only to Jenny or only to May; we might say that Jenny initiates and May completes it, but this would fail to recognize that Jenny's comment picks up on that made by May in a prior turn.

This sequence again alerts us to the necessity of working with both prior and subsequent stretches of discourse, both for interpretive and warranting purposes. We can point to May's reply to Jenny as justification for a claim about what Jenny is doing. It also reminds us more generally to keep an eye out for the ways in which people claim responsibility for their utterances (an important feature of the DASP approach; see Appendix B). There are many ways of doing such claims besides "as I say" or "I say," for example, "I think" or "it seems to me." We should also assess other functions of such phrases, for example, serving as hedges on the claim—making it weaker, distinguishing the speaker's position taken from that of another person, and so on. (Our interpretations along these lines will depend not only on the discourse context, but also on stress and intonation, e.g., "as *I* say" vs. "as I sa::y".)

We hope that even though they have seen only fragments of the discourse between May and Jenny and, especially, between May and Nora, readers will have been struck by the contrast in the identities constructed for May in the two conversations: the passive and dependent May struggling with loneliness and impoverishment is in effect a different person from the active, lively, and humorous May. Findings such as these are important both theoretically and practically. They demonstrate the advantages of the discourse focus on what people are doing with what they say, rather than upon what they "are" in some permanent sense (which is taken to be reflected in what they say), and of the discourse emphasis on variability as both a substantive theme and an analytic tool.

PRONOUNS AND SELVES

One feature of discourse that lends itself to the construction of multiple identities is linguistic: the personal pronoun. There has been a good deal of work on the social psychology of personal pronouns within both social psychology (e.g., Brown & Gilman, 1960; Kroger, 1982; Kroger & Wood, 1992) and linguistics (e.g., Mühlhäusler & Harré, 1990). A major focus of such work is on the way in which the exchange of particular pronoun forms (e.g., *tu* and *vous*) both reflects and constructs relations of status and solidarity. However, the empirical basis of claims about the functions of pronoun usage (and address exchange more generally) tends to consist of the analysis of decontextualized fragments of discourse. More recently, however, there has been work on pronoun usage in longer segments of discourse in particular situations.

One of the studies in this vein is that of Sabat and Harré (1992). They argued that "selfhood is publicly manifested in various discursive practices such as telling autobiographical stories" (p. 445). They distinguish two senses of the term *self*: personal identity (Self[1]) and public persona (Self[2]). Self[1] has no content; it is a structural feature. It is not simply manifested as discourse but constituted in discourse. First-person discursive practices express (vs. reflect) Self[1] through indexing our sayings as ours. Sabat and Harré applied these ideas in their analysis of clinical material (interviews and conversations) involving three patients with Alzheimer's disease.

Excerpt 1 [p. 450]

J. B.:   I don't want to cause problems for my wife, family.

Excerpt 2 [p. 450]

J. B.:   I know who I am.

Excerpt 3 [p. 451]

J. B.:   She says I don't think you should be working anymore.

Excerpt 1 shows the use of first-order or simple indexicals (*I, my*). The speaker indexes reports of experience as his. Excerpt 2 shows the use of embedded or iterated indexicals: the experience *who I am* that is indexed as the speaker's is embedded in a further indexical utterance, *I know*. The speaker treats himself grammatically as both object and subject. Excerpt 3 entails the use of even higher-order indexicals; not only is the reference to self ("you") from the viewpoint of another person ("she"—the social worker), but the utterance is indexed as that of the other person ("I").

We comment briefly on the ways in which other linguistic devices figure in self-construction. Sabat and Harré (1992) maintain that, in contrast to the singularity of Self[1,] there are multiple Selves[2.] Further, these selves have content in the form of a repertoire of personae manifested "in clusters of behaviour displayed in the appropriate social context" (p. 446) and are maintained in interaction with others through multiple discursive practices. We have discussed a number of these practices above. One sort of specifically linguistic device that is implicated in the construction of Self[2] is verb tense. For example, one person with Alzheimer's disease in the Sabat and Harré study was introduced by, "This is Henry. Henry was a lawyer" (to which Henry objects with, "I AM a lawyer"; p. 443). Because Selves[2] also have content, we can analyze the semantic features of discourse for the sorts of identity claims that are made or disputed, for example, "lawyer" and, in Excerpt 1, husband and father (via "wife," "family").

Sabat and Harré were concerned to demonstrate that despite the effects of the disorder, persons with Alzheimer's disease do not suffer a loss of self, at least in the sense of Self[1] However, Selves[2] can be lost because of the way in which persons with Alzheimer's disease are positioned by others. The work does contribute to our understanding of a serious problem. As a study of identity, it is limited because of its specific focus on linguistic features and its relative lack of finely detailed attention to other ways in which identities are worked up and undermined in talk (e.g., via attributions about competence). Nonetheless, it can be drawn on more generally by the discourse analyst to consider the various functions of personal pronouns: to display self, to take or assign responsibility, and so on. For example, Jane's reference (see Buchanan & Middleton, 1993, and see Chapter 3) to "*their* memories" when she could have said simply "memories" serves (in context) to support the implication that such memories may not be of interest to others. And we have discussed how May takes over Jenny's view by introducing her phrasing of it with "as I say" (see the previous discussion of Coupland et al., 1991). Such work alerts us to the way in which seemingly trivial shifts in discourse (e.g., saying "the" vs. "my") are worthy of attention; we draw particular attention to those that involve grammar (article vs. possessive pronoun) in addition to semantics (Bob's vs. John's), because they are less likely to be noticed by the beginning analyst.

AUTHENTICITY

The notion of social comparison has been a mainstay of social psychology since Festinger (1954) introduced it 45 years ago. Widdicombe and Wooffitt (1990) have put the concept to use in the context of DASP. In their initial reading of interviews with 26 young people who identified themselves as punks, rockers, gothics, or hippies, they noted that speakers' comparisons often stressed the theme of genuineness or authenticity versus shallowness; they then focused their attention on three specific sorts of comparisons and the conversational devices through which speakers claimed authenticity.

The first comparison is between the groups and an external standard, specifically, commitment to the group.

Excerpt 1 [2Punks; R = Respondent; Widdicombe & Wooffitt, 1990, p. 262 (line structure modified)]

1 R: There doesn't seem to be a lot of thought in gothics. They just
           seem to be like

2   the front—it's a pose 'innit and it's just like a fashion going
           through.

3   Like they'll probably be something else in another couple of
           months.

4   There's nothing behind it. Like skinheads—at least they've got
           something behind it.

5   Although I'm not into it. The same with rastas, fucking whatever,
           hippies—

6   and like they're genuine they've got genuine feelings behind what
           they're doing.

7   But I can't see what gothics have got.

The idea that genuine members should have an investment in their group is worked up in three ways. First, reference is made to the shallowness of the sub-culture that is complained about. In Excerpt 1, Line 1, we see the implication that gothics join the group without thinking much about it; further, this idea is presented as a considered judgment of the speaker ("There doesn't *seem* to be"). Second, there is the claim that membership in the subculture is short-lived ("just like a fashion going through," Line 2). Third, there is a reference to groups that do meet the standard ("skinheads . . . rastas, fucking whatever, hippies"; Lines 4-5), a reference that includes all other groups and thereby serves to emphasize the failure of gothics to meet the standard.

The second comparison is between the past and the present of the subcul-ture.

Excerpt 2 [2Punks; I = Interviewer, R = Respondent; Widdicombe & Wooffitt, 1990, p. 265]

1 I: What's, what's punk all about?

2 R: Well, it was about—it was just a meaning, a—it was a meaning at
          first.

3   I don't think it is—so much now.

4 I: What do you mean, "meaning"?

5 R: Well, against—the system, and against—well, basically—the
          system—

6   the police and all this sort of thing. I think basically—some of it,
          it still is a bit now.

7   But I think it started off more like that.

In this excerpt (as in others), the speaker points to a feature of the past that makes it preferable to the present (in this case, the meaning). But there is also an effort to show that this quality has not altogether disappeared (Lines 3 and 6). In describing the subculture in this way, the members can not only point to the origins of the group as genuine (vs. a matter of fashion), they can also show their own genuine commitment by identifying themselves with that past.

The third comparison distinguishes between younger (more recent) and older (long-standing) members.

Excerpt 3 [1Punk; Widdicombe & Wooffitt, 1990, p. 267]

1	R:	The punks, now, right, they just like a racket, you know, and they just
2		like getting into trouble. If you get into trouble now or if you're in gaol,
3		you're great, you're a hero. But when I was a punk at first, right, it used to be
4		good, because we just used to have a laugh and not get into trouble and that.

Excerpt 4 [1Punk; p. 267]

1	R:	you know who's been a punk for a long time and old punks are the best punks.

Excerpt 5 [2Gothics; p. 267]

1	R2:	It's going downhill really. And a lot of really naff people are latching on to it
2		because they like the style.

In these excerpts, the comparison favors the old members. The comparison is accomplished via temporal markers (*Now, at first, old,* which indicate time vs. age per se), tense (present vs. past), and durative verbs (*going downhill*). The evaluative aspects are achieved via positive and negative words and phrases (getting into "trouble"; note also the use of *just,* which serves to mark this negative characteristic of new punks as their only attribute). Such comparisons serve to enhance the speaker's own identity, through the emphasis on the positive aspects of the subgroup (old vs. new) to which the speaker belongs in comparison to those of others in the group.

This rather general analysis can be strengthened by establishing more precisely how denigration of the new members is accomplished. Widdicombe and Wooffitt (1990) show in other excerpts how the speakers use three resources: labeling the new members in specific derogatory ways (e.g., "mini-goths," p. 268), emphasizing the shallowness of new members ("latching on," "trendy," "dabbling in the outskirts," p. 269), and ascribing prototypical features (e.g., punk music now is a "racket," p. 270). By identifying the specific content (in the form of adjectives, category labels, metaphors, etc.) through which speakers construct the denigrated qualities of new members, the analysts strengthen their reading of the discourse as doing comparison and negative evaluation. Furthermore, the specificity of the evaluation of new members as inferior provides a more precise assessment of one function of the discourse, namely to enhance the identity of old members not so much in a generally positive way, but by emphasizing the authenticity usually accorded to the founders of a movement. As Widdicombe and Wooffitt point out, however, precisely the same resources that are used in descriptions to work up the inferiority of new members can also be used to do the opposite, that is, to show that the new members are more genuine than the old members. Such is the flexibility of language.

In sum, the Widdicombe and Wooffitt (1990) study provides another demonstration of the importance of social comparison and suggests its particular relevance for work on identity. We stress that social comparison is viewed here as a discursive rather than a cognitive matter, and we emphasize the necessity of identifying precisely the discursive devices that are involved in making comparisons. In a similar vein, we note that an important finding of the Widdicombe and Wooffitt study concerns the way in which motivation (in this case for joining a group) can serve as a linguistic resource (not a cognitive construct). Motivation was worked up by the participants in the study as an important feature of "being" a member of a particular group, rather than simply "doing" the activities associated with membership.

The Widdicombe and Wooffitt (1990) study contrasts with those of Tracy and Carjuzáa (1993) and of Coupland et al. (1991) in that it is concerned with a specific aspect of identity (i.e., its authenticity) rather than with the sort of identity that is constructed (e.g., faculty member, old person). Nonetheless, it shares with them several features, most notably a lack of specific attention to sequential organization and a focus on the achievement of identity or some feature thereof. We turn now to a study in which the relative emphasis is on identity as a tool rather than an achievement (Antaki & Widdicombe, 1998).

THE RELEVANT THING ABOUT HER

Edwards (1998) analyzed data from the first two sessions in a series involving a couple taking part in relationship counseling.

Excerpt 1 [pp. 20-21]

```
177 Counsellor:    ↑Oka↓y so, (0.5) for me list↓enin:g, (.) you've
178                 got (0.5) rich an:d, (.) complicated lives, I
179                 nee:d to get some histo⌈ry to put-        ⌉
    .
191                 Right. And you::'ve >been married< how many years:,
192 Connie:         Just °twelve years now.°=
```

```
193 Jimmy:        =Thirteen years ⌈in September.⌉
194 Connie:                      ⌊thirteen years⌋ in September.=
195 Counsellor:   =°Okay.° .hhh And you have how many children.
196 Connie:       Three children.
197               (0.7)
198 Counsellor:   And they are::
199               (0.7)
200 Connie:       ⌈One iss⌉
201 Jimmy:        ⌊twelve ⌋
202               (0.3)
203 Jimmy:        ⌈Eight⌉
204 Connie:       ⌊just ⌋eleven, (0.3) one is (0.2) just seven, (.)
205               and the other eight.
206 Counsellor:   El-eleven:, ei⌈ght, (.) and seven.⌉
207 Connie:                    ⌊eight and seven.  ⌋Yeh.=
208 Counsellor:   =Fine.
```

Edwards examines the various sorts of identity work done in this session. We shall come to the details in a moment. But we want to mention first Edwards's comments on the way in which the transcript itself sets up identity categories. That is, the counselor appears merely in role, whereas the couple are identified by name (albeit pseudonyms). This implicates their personal identities, but not that of the counselor, as relevant to the analysis. Edwards argues that these identifications reflect the material under analysis. We agree that this practice is not necessarily problematic; presumably we will see in the data the ways in which such identities are made relevant by the participants. But we think that Edwards's point is an important one and that it should make us careful in how we identify the participants in an interaction. There is no reason why we should not call the participants by the names that they use for each other. But names often also identify a person by gender (as here). As we discussed in Chapter 8, we need to be careful not to bring into analysis these sorts of categories unless we can show that the participants themselves orient to them (see Tracy, 1998, pp. 25-26).

We see first how the counselor establishes the interaction as a counseling session (continuing some prior talk not shown above) and provides for various kinds of identity categories for the couple (marital status, parenthood, etc.). Edwards (1998) points out that these look like routine details, but that the participants do go on to make something out of them. For example, Connie corrects Jimmy's report of the children's ages (Lines 201-205), and the counselor takes up this version as the appropriate one (Lines 206-208). "These start to identify her (for them and for us) as the one who owns best knowledge of the children" (p. 23). Edwards also addresses the ways in which marital status and other demographic details are used as resources in that and subsequent excerpts. We shall not present these here, but instead, we pick up the main part of the analysis in which Edwards focuses on uses of the category terms *girls* and *women*.

Edwards (1998) begins with the notion that these are separate if somewhat fuzzy categories, with a variety of different associations, for example, age and marital status. What is important, however, is how they are applied to the same individuals, how they manage "discursive, rhetorical business, in signalling, in some bit of talk about someone . . . the relevant thing about her" (p. 24).

Excerpt 2 [Connie has been talking about how Jimmy left her and how she later found him living with someone else; she attributes his walking out to his relationship with this woman; p. 25]

80 Connie:	=To explore: what happened ex<u>actly</u> y'know, because
81	I <u>c</u>an't ac<u>cept</u> (1.0) I <u>can't</u> ac<u>cept</u> (1.0) y'know: (.)
82	wh<u>a</u>t he's <u>telling</u> me, (0.5) y'know? = =I just belie:ve
83 →	that this girl was here all alo:ng, (0.2) and that's why.

Edwards suggests that the use of "this girl" rather than "this woman" "downgrades her status, if not her threat, as an unattached, unmarried, available, possibly young, female" (p. 25). He notes that one cannot rest an analysis on a single word; these categories are functional because they can invoke different possibilities without acting as an explicit claim that could be easily countered.

Excerpt 3 [p. 26]

98 Jimmy:	(. . .) U::m (0.8) it's >n<u>ot</u> right< to sa:y that (0.5)
99	>I didn't <u>leav</u>e Connie for another woman.<
100	(0.6)
101	but (0.4) I was liv-sleepin' away for (0.5) 'bout
102	three- three weeks (.) ↓four weeks three weeks (0.4)
103	whatever, (0.6) when I moved <u>in</u>: (.) w<u>ith</u> a wo- girl,
104	which I <u>did</u> have (1.0) uh: a bit of a fling with (.)
105	when Connie went on h<u>o</u>liday last year.

In this excerpt, which follows shortly after Excerpt 2, we see again the terms *girl* and *woman*. Here, Jimmy denies that he left Connie "for another woman" (a recognizable idiom for this activity), a claim consistent with his own version of long-term marital strife. But in Line 103, he repairs his (beginning) use of *woman* to *girl,* switching from the denied and general category to the particular person with whom he admits having moved in. He thus aligns with Connie's use of the term *girl,* at the same time downgrading his relationship with her and countering Connie's claim that there was something more serious going on "all along" (Excerpt 2, Line 83).

Edwards (1998) then considers the way in which Connie uses both of the terms when talking about herself and her friends. She has been complaining that Jimmy is unreasonably jealous about her nights out with her friends, whereas Jimmy has countered that he knows what she is like (in other excerpts not analyzed here).

Excerpt 4 [from Session 2; p. 27]

```
1375 Connie:      >What I would like to be able to do is, < when my friend
1376              rings me up, (0.5) every six weeks, or: when they're
1377 →           having a ↑girls' night out, >to be able to say,< (.)
1378              "yeh I'd love to go." (0.7) Without (0.2) THAT meaning,
1379              (.) going out with my frie:nds (.) doesn't have anything
1380              to do: (0.2) with not wanting to sit in with you.
```

The identities invoked here work together with other categories, such as activities and places. Connie talks about wanting to go out with her "friends" (not any old people) for a "girls' night out," the purpose of which is to have a "chat" about some problem that a friend has (not shown in Excerpt 4), and which is not even instigated by Connie (Line 1376; the friend calls her). It is all quite harmless. In a later excerpt (not shown here), Jimmy takes up Connie's description ("when you're out with the girls," p. 29), but he neglects to mention that this event comes about in response to a call from a friend wanting to talk about her problems. He goes on to agree with the counselor that he is worried that she "might end up in bed with someone else" (p. 29).

Edwards (1998) suggests that the category "girls" "is nicely appropriate for . . . sexual developments—nicely, that is, for Jimmy's version of things" (p. 29). And what we see later is that Connie (having been asked to tell her side of things) again talks about "going out with the girls" but then reformulates their identities as married women.

Excerpt 5 [p. 29]

```
1846 Connie:     . . . when I go out with the gir:ls, it's a:ll married
1847             women talking about our ki:ds or somebody rin:gs (.)
1848             .hh they have a pro:blem, y'know (.) "d'you fancy go-"
1849             (.) that's uh- (.) the gir:ls night out
```

We see again here how the relevant identities are worked up by combining such descriptions with a number of category-relevant activities (e.g., talking about their children) and places (quiet pubs—not shown here). As Edwards notes, "the category 'married women' does not get used here merely because that is *what they are*. . . . Its use attends to local, rhetorically potent business in their talk" (p. 31).

In sum, Edwards (1998) shows how various identity categories, together with other descriptions, are used as a resource by Connie and Jimmy to work up their individual versions of what is going on in their marriage—the nature of their problems, who is to blame, and so on. More generally, we see the ways in which people in interaction invoke categories, how they make them relevant by what they use them to do. As we discussed in Chapter 8, these categories are and must be the business of participants. As Edwards notes in this study, there are some obvious categories that could be relevant—for example, that the couple is Irish, the counselor English—but they do not turn out to be important for the participants. This does not mean that there is no mention of these; for example, Jimmy and Connie do talk about England and Ireland as places in their discussion of various events, but they "make nothing at all of *being Irish*" (p. 32), at least in these sessions. Edwards concludes with a helpful discussion of how this sort of approach contrasts with that taken in social-psychological theories such as self-categorization. For example, there is little interest in the latter in the categories that people use nor in how they are used. Rather, the concern is how people place themselves into categories (as analysts know them) according to situations. The older approach differs greatly from the discourse-analytic approach, in which not only identity categories but also situations are a matter for participants themselves to work up, treat as relevant or not, and so on.

SUMMARY

We have distinguished between the analysis of identity as an achievement and as a tool, but as the studies here show, achievement and use are intertwined activities for participants. They are also reflexively constitutive; that is, the discursive construction of identity enables certain sorts of activities, and those activities contribute to the construction of identity. For example, the identity of counselor that is achieved (in part) through the sorts of questions that are asked also warrants the asking of those questions. The issue is whether the analyst wants to put one or the other activity in the foreground; this will depend in part on the analyst's specific interests, but also on the way in which participants orient to these activities (e.g., the attention they give to working up or contesting a particular identity). In any case, we want to be sensitive to the particulars of how identities are achieved, collaboratively constructed, and deployed in specific circumstances (i.e., interviews, everyday or institutional interactions, written texts of various sorts).

We have discussed various pieces of work throughout the book, sometimes including additional or alternative interpretations to those offered by the author or authors. Our purpose was to help readers to develop a sense for how to carry out analyses on the ground, as it were, and for the various ways of approaching analysis depending on one's substantive and analytical interests—and on the data. But we have also been concerned to show that there is no simple, clear-cut path to follow in doing analysis, no single criterion for selecting an approach. The discourse-analytic perspective is a constructionist, even a kaleidoscopic one. This flexibility is one of the hallmarks of discourse analysis; the flexibility has many advantages, but it can also be a source of insecurity. So we have tried to demonstrate the way in which the main features of the perspective are played out in analysis: variability (e.g., in identities, in the way that devices are used); discourse as action (its functions and effects); and the focus on discourse in its own right, rather than as a route to internal events. In relation to this last feature, we emphasize again the way in which discourse analysis does not entail a wholesale rejection of previous work, but rather, it often involves the reworking of old concepts in new ways, for example, the treatment of attributions and comparisons as discursive activities rather than as cognitive structures or processes. Such concepts, along with others that are often considered to be central, such as "intention" and "motivation," are constituted rather than reflected in discourse. They are not cognitive, but linguistic or pragmatic concepts (Widdicombe & Wooffitt, 1990).

We have commented on some of the ways in which researchers have attempted to warrant their analyses, to provide support for their claims. The next chapter focuses specifically on this issue.

PART IV

EVALUATION AND REPORTING

Warranting in Discourse Analysis

CONVENTIONAL CRITERIA

Warranting consists of providing justification and grounds for one's claims. This is a requirement for all scientific endeavors. In psychology, warranting has come to mean reliability and validity, as defined in standard texts on method (e.g., Rosenthal & Rosnow, 1991), and these have assumed operational forms that are deeply embedded in the positivist theory of science. Such notions can no longer be taken for granted. But the critical scrutiny of such historically weighted concepts as reliability and validity requires special care. We want to retain what is useful while suggesting necessary innovations. We see our discussion of warranting as providing information to those interested in the alternative conceptions of reliability and validity that have emerged in discourse-analytic work. It is not intended to offer alternative ways of meeting conventional criteria for reliability and validity.

Instead, discourse analysts use a different set of criteria, criteria that reflect an alternative metatheoretical and epistemological perspective. The concepts of reliability and validity as usually employed are intelligible at best only in the treatment of matters as matters of res naturam. But it is not that straightforward for work in res artem, where there are multiple meanings and versions, none of which are "true" in the sense of correspondence to a single, material reality. That is an ambiguity we cannot escape. As Tracy (1995) put it:

> reliability and validity, as traditionally conceived . . . presume there is an objective world to be known . . . that differences are a result of measurement error

(lack of reliability) and that when differences exist, there is one accurate representation of what is (validity). (p. 209)

Clearly, we need to look at alternatives.

We deal first with some preliminary matters. As we discussed in Chapters 5
and 8, there is at most a limited role for quantification in the warranting of
claims, and we shall not consider it further here. Similarly, we have addressed
questions about generalizability in Chapter 5, in the context of sampling. As
we discussed in that chapter, there are differences between conventional research and discourse analysis, both in the nature of claims and in the ways they
are warranted. Discourse analysts emphasize that what counts as the same or
different (e.g., circumstances, actions, etc.) itself involves a claim and can often be problematic and that the notion of relevant samples and populations requires careful consideration. Nonetheless, discourse analysts are as concerned
with generality as are other researchers.

Reliability

Reliability (repeatability of findings across samples, raters, measures, parts
of measures, over time, etc.) is considered to be the minimal requirement for
warranting in conventional approaches. If a finding is not stable, there is no
point in asking whether it is valid, that is, whether it reflects a true score or relationship (where *true* refers to the state of the world).

There are two issues to be considered in relation to reliability: the notion itself and its meaning in relation to validity. First, there is the idea even in conventional research that there are different sorts of repetition: for example,
operational versus conceptual replication (or the repetition of movements vs.
meanings). Our interest is in the repetition of concepts or meanings. But the es-
tablishment of such repetition relies upon the examination of measurements or
movements (e.g., the moving of a lever on a "shock" machine in the Milgram,
1974, experiment is taken to index the concept of obedience). Conventional
approaches assume that the relation between operations and concepts is
unproblematic; for discourse analysts, such relations are multiple, contentious, and socially constructed. Conventional approaches also assume that reliability can be assessed independently of context. That is, although the value of
variables might vary across contexts, their nature does not; they are still the
same variables. This is a reasonable assumption in relation to res naturam. For
example, the volume of a gas might vary from one environment to another, but
the concept of volume does not change. This is not the case for the social world,
in which meaning is inseparable from context. Different movements (including the utterance of words) can have the same meaning in different contexts;
the same movements can have different meanings in different contexts. This

makes it much more difficult to assess whether or not there is repetition or reliability on the level of concepts.

More fundamental is the issue of what counts as a repetition (and what counts as context). From a discursive perspective, repetition is like other categories in that it is not a fixed and obvious event, but something that is negotiated within a particular context. Judgments about reliability thus always involve some sort of inference or theoretical interpretation, not simply in terms of how much agreement there must be (if using quantitative criteria), but in terms of which aspects or features of an event are important. (See, e.g., Tannen, 1989, on the argument that a seemingly new utterance is a repetition because it has been uttered before at some time, by some speaker, whereas at the same time, the utterance of words that have been uttered before is not a repetition because it occurs in a new context.)

But let us assume that we can agree that the same result was obtained in two different studies, or that two different raters have categorized discourse in the same way. Can this be used as evidence for the independent existence of the phenomenon? Discourse analysts would make no such assumption. The repetition of a result speaks as much to the similarity of the total set of assumptions and procedures by which it was produced as it does to the existence of a phenomenon outside that set. And the consensus involved in "interrater reliability" is as much a reflection of the socially constructed nature of the sorts of judgments that are made as it is grounds for the truth of those judgments. That is, people's use of consensus to argue for the "out thereness" of some event does not mean that consensus can be taken unproblematically as support for the claim that the event exists independently of the speakers (see Edwards & Potter, 1992).

Conventional researchers sometimes ask the questions, What if two analysts disagree? How do we decide which one is correct? We have already noted our response to the second question, namely that it is the wrong question because there is no single correct response. Both interpretations are equally correct—or incorrect. In response to the first question, we need to ask: What does it mean to construct the two versions as a disagreement? In what sense are they incompatible? Exploration of the versions may show that they involve different sets or levels of analytical concepts, different views of context, different scope, and so on. Interpretations themselves are always contextualized and provisional. There is always the possibility of a new interpretation, in part because the context is always changing to include the previous interpretation as well as other developments. The focus should therefore be on closer examination of the two versions; if they are both adequate (supported by the text), one can go on to ask whether one is more useful than the other, more appropriate for one purpose than another, and so on.

None of this means that discourse analysts avoid repetition. On the contrary, discourse analysis involves repeated readings of the text, the redoing of analyses both in the analysis and write-up stages, repeated questioning of the analyst's own stance, and so on. It just means that we do not make repetition a criterion of warrantability. Rather, repetition is part of the careful attention to detail and the concern for refinement that are major features of discourse-analytic work.

Validity

The conventional notion of validity in psychological research assumes that the goal of research is to produce findings that match as closely as possible the real state of the world, that is, the world as it exists independently of our notions about it. In contrast, the discursive perspective emphasizes the way in which the world is constructed discursively, both in the sense of discourse about the world and in the sense that discourse is part of the world. Because discourse is socially constructed, it has shifting and multiple meanings. The analyst's account or interpretation of that discourse is thus only one version of its meaning—and cannot be said to be true or false. Truth and realism are themselves social, that is, discursive constructions. There is thus no basis for selecting one account over another on the grounds that one is a truer or more valid version of the world, a better account of "how things really are."

This is a simplified version of "epistemological relativism," which is usually contrasted with conventional or realist positions. (For more detailed discussions, see, e.g., Potter, 1996.) Adopting this position is not to deny "reality" (i.e., the existence of physical objects), but to remove correspondence to reality as the primary criterion for evaluating discursive research (while perhaps also holding a position of material realism). For some discourse analysts, this involves a focus on the discursive means by which reality is itself constructed.

Further, adopting this position does not mean that there are no criteria for selecting among versions, that any version is as good (or bad) as any other. Nor does it mean that relativists must remain politically neutral (if this were possible). There are two sets of such criteria: scientific and moral. The scientific criteria for selecting among versions are, like the criteria in conventional work, socially constructed, disputable, negotiated, and arguably arbitrary (e.g., like $p < .05$). We might say that they involve a kind of social realism. We discuss those in detail below. The moral, value-relevant, or political criteria reflect the fundamental notion that discourse is action. Thus, we need to consider what we, as analysts, are doing in our discourse (e.g., how we are constructing versions of persons) and what we are doing through our discourse (e.g., what the consequences of such constructions might be). From this perspective, it is not possible for any scientist—natural or social—to claim that his or her work is value-neutral. But the implications are even stronger for the social scientist, because people care what is said about them and are directly affected by it, whereas rocks do not care and do not feel the effects (Hacking, 1992).

WARRANTABILITY IN DISCOURSE ANALYSIS:
SCIENTIFIC CRITERIA

The basic premise for the discourse analyst is that the "social" world does not exist independently of our constructions of it, so it does not make sense to ask if our analyses are valid in the sense that they are true, that is, that they correspond to an independent world. But discourse analysts do not reject altogether the notion of validity. Rather, we attend to other meanings of the term *validity* that are more closely related to its origin in the Latin *valere,* to be strong. Thus, we are concerned to show that our analyses are "sound; well grounded on principles or evidence; able to withstand criticism or objection," "effective, effectual, cogent" (Webster's, 1976, p. 2017) or that they are "based on evidence that can be supported; acceptable; convincing," "properly derived from accepted premises by the rules of logic" (Funk & Wagnall, 1974, p. 1479). Given the usual understanding of the term *validity* in relation to truth and in its focus on empirical indices, it would be both confusing and misleading for discourse analysts to talk about validity, although they may be driven to do so for rhetorical purposes. Rather, we propose criteria for warranting that transcend reliability and reformulate validity.

We propose that an analysis is warrantable to the extent that it is both trustworthy and sound. Dictionary definitions and everyday use provide some clues. For example, Webster's defines *trustworthy* as "worthy of trust or confidence; dependable; reliable" (1976, p. 1964). *Sound* has multiple meanings, for example, "whole; unimpaired," "free from imperfection," "founded on truth; strong; valid; reliable; sensible," "thorough; complete" (Webster's, p. 1733). Such definitions are of limited use, partly because the meanings given are often circular. For example, *trustworthy* is given as a meaning for *reliable* (but *repeatability* is not; Webster's, p. 1526). In a general way, we mean that trustworthy[1] claims are those that can be depended upon not only as a useful way of understanding the discourse at hand, but also as a possible basis for understanding other discourse, for further work, and so on (because they are derived from accountable procedures, are systematic, etc.), whereas sound claims are solid, credible, and convincing (because they are logical, based on evidence, etc.).

The following analogy may be helpful in giving the flavor of what we have in mind. Imagine that you are concerned about retirement and want to be assured that your investment portfolio preserves your assets and will be a good basis on which to plan your future. You need to trust that the person who does your investing (e.g., your spouse, banker) does not spend the money on other items, does not take foolish or unnecessary risks, and keeps track of the investment decisions and outcomes. But you also want to know that both the overall portfolio and its individual components are sound investments, which they will be if they are not overly volatile or have expense ratios that are too high, if they are based on both internal (national) and external (international) sources, and if they are neither too concentrated nor too scattered. The requirements or criteria for trustworthiness and the requirements for soundness could be distinguished in terms of process versus product (or what is done vs. what is accomplished, or perhaps illocutionary vs. perlocutionary force). This distinction captures the idea that warrantability consists of more than simply following a set of procedures.

Rather than defining these terms more specifically, we show how they are constituted through the criteria that follow and the ways in which these are achieved. The set of criteria that we propose draws upon a variety of suggestions that have been made about warrantability in discourse analysis (e.g., Potter & Wetherell, 1987; Tracy, 1995). Our concern is to draw these together in an integrated way, such that specific criteria can be seen in the broader context of the relationship between method and theory. That is, there is a theoretical foundation for the warranting of claims, a set of theoretical and metatheoretical statements that concern the nature of data, of claims, of coding and analytic procedures, and of the relationships among these. The precise manner in which criteria are met will depend in part on the specific nature of the claims that are made (e.g., their specificity or generality, whether they concern the existence or interpretation of a specific utterance or of a pattern, etc.; see Jackson, 1986, who discusses various sorts of claims in the context of a perspective on methodology as a way of generating arguments rather than as a set of procedures treated as rules to be followed).

The way in which criteria are addressed depends also on their nature; that is, some are empirical, some conceptual, and some logical. Some criteria are relevant to both trustworthiness and soundness. The criteria are also concerned with different levels: Some are internal and some external to the data, the analysis, and the overall work.

There are a number of reflexive elements involved in warranting that reflect the linkage between theory, method, and warrantability. A report of research is subject to the same considerations as any other report. There is overlap between the ways in which participants (or authors, etc.) themselves warrant the claims that they make in their discourse. And, as in other reports, some activities of warranting are done by the analyst, some by the reader, and some by both. Warrantability is a coconstruction, and, like analysis, it rests on shared knowledge, although this does not diminish the responsibility of the analyst to do warranting as thoroughly as possible. However, compared with conventional researchers, discourse analysts give much greater prominence to reader evaluation (Potter, 1998b), an emphasis that both results from and is encouraged by the greater transparency of discourse-analytic work. Finally, we note that a judgment about the warrantability of any specific piece of work, that is, its trustworthiness and soundness, is (and can only be) an overall, qualitative judgment that is not tied solely to any single criterion.

CRITERIA OF TRUSTWORTHINESS

Orderliness and Documentation

Orderliness applies to all scholarly work, and its meaning is relatively straightforward. In the present case, it refers to the clarity and orderliness of the way in which the research in all its aspects was conducted and recorded and is reported.

Documentation is also shared in many ways with conventional forms of research. It involves a clear description of all facets of the research, including how the data were collected and how the researcher went about doing the analysis. In discourse analysis, the documentation of procedures and the display of the arguments contribute to the reader's trust that the analysis was carefully done, but the soundness of the analysis rests on different criteria. Nonetheless, the documentation of procedures is important as a minimum requirement, not so that the research can be replicated, but to provide a context for understanding claims. Documentation of data and data excerpts is particularly important because "readers of discourse analytic studies need to be able, to an important extent, to perform their own evaluations of the analytic conclusions" (Potter & Wetherell, 1994, p. 63). There is an increasing call for researchers to make available the transcripts of text that were used in their analyses, even for journal articles (in which the transcripts may appear as an appendix). In sum, documentation points to the accountability of the researcher, who is answerable for the way in which the research was carried out.

Audits

The notion of accountability can also be linked metaphorically to other domains to suggest criteria and methods of warranting; this has been done by some researchers in their discussions of qualitative or naturalistic research. For example, Guba (1981) describes an approach that involves the metaphor of a fiscal audit. An auditor of a company's books examines the methods of accounting that have been used and certifies that the entries and calculations are correct. In relation to the first task, Guba suggests that researchers should establish an "audit trail" that will permit an external auditor

> to examine the processes whereby data were collected and analysed and interpretations were made. The audit trail takes the form of documentation (the actual interview notes taken, for example) and a running account of the process (as in the form of an investigator's daily journal). (p. 87)

He proposes that researchers should arrange for a "dependability" audit to be done. These suggestions are similar to those that we have made, except that we include documentation and the account of process in the research report, and leave the dependability audit to the reader (and editors and reviewers).

Guba (1981) refers to the second task as a "confirmability" audit, that is, one that certifies that "data exist in support of every interpretation and that *the interpretations have been made in ways consistent with the available data*" (p. 88). In contrast to the first task, which largely addresses process (the activities of the researcher), this task involves an assessment of the quality of the "product," that is, the set of claims that are made. We deal with this aspect in the Criteria of Soundness section. (See also Huberman & Miles, 1994, for discussion of auditing within more conventional qualitative approaches.)

CRITERIA OF SOUNDNESS

Orderliness

As with trustworthiness, this criterion also applies to all scholarly work, not just discourse analysis; however, discourse-analytic reports are more detailed and explicit about showing that the criterion is met. Both the analysis and the reporting of the analysis should be orderly. However, because discourse analysis is so highly recursive, orderliness will be much more complex than in more conventional forms of research.

Demonstration (Showing vs. Telling)

Demonstration is arguably the key requirement for warrantability; it reflects the core of the analytical work. Demonstration is the central feature in the report of that work, specifically in the analysis section, which is why that section is so critical for establishing warrantability. It is crucial to show the argument through presenting the steps involved in the analysis of excerpts rather than simply telling the reader about the argument and pointing to an excerpt as an illustration. Demonstration is essential to ensure analysis of discourse rather than mere description. It makes two contributions to warrantability: In providing an opportunity to check the analysis (effectively redoing and refining it), it serves both to ensure the soundness of claims and to display their soundness. This does not involve reproducing the whole analysis, but it does mean demonstrating the sequences of analysis that capture the logic of the argument, including revisions and exclusions of hypotheses.

Demonstration means showing how the interpretations of individual excerpts (the subclaims) as well as the overall claims (about patterns and their interpretations) are grounded in the text. The criteria for grounding involve considerations that we have previously discussed in the chapters on analysis. The difference between grounding in analysis and grounding in warranting is that the emphasis during analysis is on doing interpretation and generating claims, whereas the emphasis here is on supporting those interpretations and claims. Potter and Wetherell (1994) argue that in discourse analysis, warranting is separate from analysis in the sense that how the analyst arrives at an interpretation may be different from how the interpretation is justified, whereas these processes are the same in conventional work, in which warranting consists largely of following procedures correctly. The criteria are ordered roughly from specific to general (i.e., from interpretations of particular utterances to claims about patterns); the latter can be said to build upon the former, in that meeting the more general criteria both requires and confirms that the preceding criteria have been met.

Orientation

The first set of criteria for grounding concerns the participant's orientation. There are a number of ways to show that this is consistent with the analyst's interpretation. They essentially involve aspects of discourse that we have already discussed in Chapter 7. In the first instance, for example, the analyst can draw on grammar, content, and meaning:

1. The use of grammatical features that encode social or psychological orientations (e.g., modals of obligation, agentless constructions) can support a treatment of utterances in terms of such features.

2. The incorporation by a participant of (lexical) content relevant to a particular category, relationship, and so on (e.g., age, parenthood) supports the interpretation of that category as one that is relevant to the participant.

3. The recognition or treatment by a participant of a particular utterance in a particular way (e.g., as an insult or a tease) supports the giving of that particular meaning or the treatment of the utterance that way by the analyst. However, as we discussed in Chapter 7, we need to do more than show that participants orient to a particular feature in particular ways, that it has a particular meaning or is relevant for them. We also need to show that it is procedurally consequential, for example, in terms of similarities and differences or new problems.

4. If the participant treats two utterances (or sets of utterances) as similar, different, or contradictory, the analyst is also justified in treating them in these ways.

5. If a participant treats her or his own previous utterance as creating a problem (by offering a subsequent utterance directed toward the problem), the analyst can treat the previous utterance as one that creates that problem.

Note that our reading of the criterion of new problems as proposed by Potter and Wetherell (1987) is at odds with some interpretations that we have seen. The criterion is sometimes read as equivalent to fruitfulness (see Tracy, 1995). However, fruitfulness concerns the analyst's claims and their relationship to future research activities, whereas the Potter and Wetherell criterion of new problems refers to participants' ways of dealing with these in the text at hand.

Claim Checking: Patterns

Analyses and claims are not just about the individual bits of discourse and their interpretation. They are also about patterns and must be supported by accounting for exceptions to the patterns (e.g., by revising the claim or limiting its scope) and by discounting potential alternatives or counterclaims. A pattern is explained by showing "how particular structures may satisfy functions that variations cannot and . . . how those structures get built up from their component moves"; excerpts are used to "justify a technical description of [the pattern]" (Jacobs, 1986, p. 153). The requirement to rule out competing hypotheses or claims is, of course, not limited to discourse analysis. Further, both discourse analysts and conventional researchers recognize that one cannot rule out all other possibilities. However, discourse analysts are likely to argue that there can be multiple alternative claims that are equally good at accounting for the data. Thus, the goal is to produce a set of claims that accounts for all of the data while acknowledging the possibility of making an argument for more than one set of claims.

The criteria of orientation and claim checking also apply to intertextual analysis. As we have discussed in Chapter 8, intertextual analysis includes and extends intratextual analysis and can therefore serve to strengthen that analysis. Intertextual analysis can also be used to address criteria other than demonstration; we consider these possibilities below.

Summary

The making of claims rests upon inference by the analyst: What must X mean to the participant if she or he does X in these circumstances? An inference is supported both logically and empirically; it relies both on the shared knowledge of a common language and of how the language is used and on the logic of semantics and usage. It may draw on previous work (e.g., empirical studies of adjacency pairs), but the primary empirical evidence is the set of utterances at hand. It is important to look for more evidence to confirm an inference, particularly in cases involving indirect evidence. One can strengthen one's claims by showing how they are supported across sequences of discourse as well as in isolated instances (as in, e.g., the study by Antaki & Wetherell, 1999, discussed in Chapter 3). And although in most instances the analyst will be unable to present all of the relevant excerpts for a particular claim, most or all of the *different* sorts of excerpts or evidence must be included and considered thoroughly.

There is one other critical issue involved in analytic work. We have suggested above that there are many similarities between the activities of analysts and the activities of participants. Participants and analysts are both involved in looking for new data and making inferences, although participants tend to be less reflexive, less explicit, and less systematic than analysts. But we need to keep straight whether we are talking about what participants are doing or about our own activities. Otherwise, we risk the sort of confusion we have described in relation to the criterion of new problems, as well as some others that we identify below.

Coherence

Coherence is a criterion that refers to the set of analytic claims that are made about the text. Its application requires that there be an identifiable set of claims, a requirement that may seem obvious, but that is not always met (Jackson, 1986). Further, the claims must be clearly formulated in order to be seen as coherent. Coherence requires that claims be grounded, but coherence is not the same as grounding. Grounding is concerned with the relationship between the analysis and the text (both individual items and the text as a whole). In contrast, coherence concerns the nature of the analysis, or, more precisely, the entire set of claims that are made. Grounding can be seen as a textual criterion (about the text), whereas coherence is an analytic criterion (about the analysis)—and in contrast to demonstration, coherence is primarily a matter for the discussion section of the report, as are the remaining criteria. The link between demonstration and coherence is analytic induction, that is, accounting for exceptions and ruling out alternative claims. Analytic induction works both indirectly and directly in relation to coherence. To the extent that alternatives are discounted via grounding in the text, the minimal requirement for coherence is met. But the exclusion of alternatives is also a requirement for coherence—and there are other ways to do so. For example, we would not rule out the possibility of using data from outside the text (including hypothetical instances) to strengthen the case.

A coherent claim, then, is one that has accounted for exceptions and alternatives. Potter and Wetherell (1987) argue that this requirement (what they refer to as confirmation by exception, i.e., confirmation via having searched and accounted for exceptions) is a particularly relevant aspect of coherence. More generally, this feature is one of the main contributors to the rigor of discourse-analytic work. The necessity to account for all cases is a much more stringent criterion than the "$p < .05$" criterion of conventional research. We might say that there is no "error" variance in discourse analysis, only variability that needs to be accounted for.

Coherence is not simply about accounting for loose ends. A coherent set of claims will account for both the broad, general pattern and the details of individual sequences (Potter & Wetherell, 1987). As Tracy (1995) puts it, it is insufficient to have individual instances of analysis "that are persuasive but collectively go in different directions" (p. 210); rather, they must cohere together in a well-developed argument. A coherent analysis will show the reader how the discourse is put together and "how discursive structure produces effects and functions" (Potter & Wetherell, 1987, p. 170).

We include under coherence the requirement that a set of claims should also be characterized by a clear and adequate explanatory scope. Intertextual analysis can serve to strengthen the coherence of claims by locating them within a larger social context and making their scope explicit. The adequacy of scope can also be assessed by comparing the set of claims to the goals of the research (Tracy's, 1995, criterion of "how well a specific study accomplishes what it espouses to be about," p. 210).

We raise a cautionary note about coherence. We think that this criterion is sometimes misinterpreted. For example, Sherrard (1991) states, "Coherence means the success of the analysis in revealing the coherence of the discourse" (p. 172). In our view, coherence refers not to the discourse, but to the analysis, the set of claims about the discourse. Sherrard's reading of Potter and Wetherell is understandable; Potter and Wetherell are themselves not clear on this point. For example, they talk about "giving coherence *to* [italics added] a body of discourse" (1987, p. 170), suggesting that coherence both involves an activity of the analyst and refers to a feature of discourse. We see this confusion as another instance of conflation of the activities of participants with the activities of analysts. It also illustrates why we need to distinguish grounding and coherence as criteria of warrantability: Grounding is about participants' orientations, whereas coherence is about analysts' claims. This does not mean that the coherence of participants' discourse is not an issue or that it cannot be analyzed. But claims that participants' discourse is coherent and the identification of the ways in which participants make their discourse coherent need to be grounded in their discourse.

Plausibility

Plausibility as we use the term refers to whether or not a set of claims is acceptable (or more strongly, praiseworthy—deserving applause). *Plausibility* can also be used to mean "seemingly true"; that meaning could also apply here if we emphasize the hedge on truth. Tracy (1995) suggests that "a first criterion for interpretive analyses is that analyses be plausible and persuasive" (p. 209); good interpretations should bring clarity, should direct attention to what is usually unnoticed, and should yield a sense of insight. We see Tracy's specific requirements as related more to what we have discussed as grounding than to plausibility. Although plausibility is in part achieved by grounding, what we have in mind here is the way in which a set of claims makes sense in relation to other knowledge—both implicit and explicit. That is, although a set of claims should help us to see in new ways, it should also seem reasonable in terms of what readers as social beings already know about social life and in terms of what readers as analysts know about the sorts of claims that have been made in the literature. Intertextual analysis concerns linkages to discourses available in the culture and to texts available in the literature. It can thus contribute to plausibility on both of these counts.

Where claims are likely to be challenged on the grounds of implausibility, it is incumbent on the analyst to address the issue explicitly. This requirement is not unique to discourse analysis. Analysts who make any sort of claim that seems out of line with existing work must take pains to show that such work does not render their claim less worthy—for example, by pointing out features of the other work that are different (e.g., different sorts of texts, discourse producers, or occasions) or by challenging that work. Discourse analysts also have the option of arguing for the plausibility of both claims and of comparing their virtues on other grounds. (Again, this is not different from conventional work, in which one account may be preferred over another on grounds of, e.g., parsimony.)

Plausibility is an interanalytic criterion; it involves a comparison between analyses or sets of claims. It asks how other work that has been done bears on the merits of this set of claims. In grounding, the analyst may draw on other work that has, for example, identified particular devices, patterns, and so on. However, that work is used simply as a starting point, and the device, pattern, and so on must be grounded in the text. Potter and Wetherell (1994, p. 62) discuss this activity in their section Cross-Referring Discourse Studies. In contrast, plausibility involves the comparison of a claim to other work. The difference is that in the case of grounding, one looks for a warrant in the text; in the case of plausibility, one looks to other work for a warrant.

Fruitfulness

Potter and Wetherell (1987) identify fruitfulness as "the scope of analytic schemes to make sense of new kinds of discourse and to generate novel explanations" (p. 171). As they note, this criterion is not unique to discourse analysis but refers to all scientific explanations and theories. They suggest that it is in many ways the most powerful criterion—a reasonable argument to the extent that this criterion incorporates and goes beyond the previous criteria we have identified. In contrast to plausibility, the direction here is from the present work to other work; that is, we consider the implications of the present work for other work, rather than considering the present work from the perspective of previous work. Fruitfulness can be considered an extra-analytic criterion. Tracy (1995) suggests that fruitfulness means that a good study should be "intellectually implicative for the scholarly community. It should suggest productive ways to reframe old issues, create links between previously unrelated issues and raise new questions that are interesting and merit attention" (p. 210).

There are numerous ways in which research can be fruitful. For example, Potter and Wetherell (1987) point to the work on sequences of conversation that suggests solutions to the fundamental problem of accounting for indirect speech acts (Levinson, 1983), and they discuss the ways in which the concept of repertoires elucidates aspects of scientific discourse. Wood and Rennie's

(1994) work points to some previously unidentified issues in the formulation of rape, such as the role of the rapist. Because intertextual analysis embodies linkages to other texts, it may be especially helpful in pointing to such implications.

Summary

We have proposed a set of criteria for assessing the soundness of a particular piece of research; we have not addressed the issue of evaluating a program or body of research. This would involve the present sorts of criteria as well as specific considerations around the scope and interconnectedness of research. Apart from orderliness, which concerns the research as a whole (data collection, analysis, report), the criteria are hierarchical, in that each can only be addressed after the previous criteria have been met. We have drawn on previous suggestions but have attempted to go beyond these to provide a more integrated and extensive account that is grounded in the metatheory of discourse analysis.

There is one procedure, often mentioned in connection with the evaluation of research, that we have not yet considered: triangulation, that is, the use of multiple methods, sources of data, and so on (see Huberman & Miles, 1994). The idea is that using information from different sources or angles can allow us to identify the correct version or position. There are a number of problems with this argument. First, as Potter and Wetherell (1987) point out, the use of multiple sources tends to increase rather than reduce variability; that is, triangulation is not really possible. K. Danziger (personal communication, February 25, 1987) argues that the combination of different methods on the grounds that combining them will cancel out their different weaknesses is just as likely to result in the compounding of those weaknesses. Triangulation is inconsistent with the principles of discourse analysis in that it assumes that different versions (from different methods, etc.) can be taken as a route to something behind them, and further, that there is one correct version; it fails to recognize sufficiently that observations are affected not only by theory but also by conventional methodological imperatives. Triangulation is itself a qualitative, discursive activity, not a set of mechanical calculations.

This does not mean that there is no merit to the idea.

> Triangulation reflects an attempt to secure an in-depth understanding. . . . Objective reality can never be captured. Triangulation is not a tool or a strategy of validation, but an alternative to validation. The combination of multiple methods, empirical materials, perspectives and observers in a single study is best understood as a strategy that adds rigour, breadth and depth to any investigation. (Denzin & Lincoln, 1994, p. 2)

The adoption of this view is a way to address the sorts of concerns raised by Fairclough (e.g., 1992a) as well as issues of generality. Triangulation is itself not a criterion of warrantability; rather, it can contribute to the likelihood that work will be seen as warranted.

We add one final and reflexive note. We have stressed that discourse analysis cannot simply be reduced to a set of procedures or methodological rules. As Billig (1988) has argued, all good scholarship includes "individual quirkiness" (p. 200), a commitment to making judgments about the importance of material, and a willingness to make judgments that may vary from those of other scholars. It takes experience and interpretation seriously. It emphasizes the breadth and depth of knowledge and an ability to connect seemingly unrelated phenomena that can only be achieved by the widest possible reading. We underline that our discussion of criteria of warranting does not mean that warranting can simply be reduced to these criteria. It also requires scholarly judgment.

WARRANTABILITY: MORAL CRITERIA

We have argued above that it is insufficient to evaluate research claims on scientific criteria alone. As discourse, research accounts have effects beyond the mere communication of a set of "findings." It is incumbent on researchers to assess work in terms of its moral implications and to articulate the criteria on which they do so; the failure to take a stance is itself the taking of a stance. The case for making one's stance explicit may seem more compelling for research that addresses acknowledged social problems (see our discussion in Chapter 1), but we need to recognize that all research has implications for whether or not some matter is identified as a social problem and how that problem is framed (Spector & Kitsuse, 1973).

The limited attention we give here to moral criteria reflects the relative lack of discussion they have received, not a lack of importance. Tracy (1995) is one of the few researchers to offer specific proposals. Working within the framework of action-implicative discourse analysis (see Glossary), she suggests three criteria that connect moral and scientific considerations. The first criterion is "helpful problem framing"; the problems of practice should be formulated at an appropriate level of abstraction and should suggest ideas about how to act. The second criterion is that the explication of discursive techniques should both capture how practitioners cope with problems and suggest how such problems might be transformed. The third criterion is that the research should offer formulations of "situated ideals" that would both incorporate participants' solutions and suggest normative principles. Tracy suggests that individual studies need not address all criteria but should meet at least one of these. There are relatively few studies that meet these criteria—and even fewer that address explicitly the ways in which they do so.

The moral and political aspects of research have not been entirely neglected. Critical discourse analysts do attend to this aspect of discourse analysis, for example, in discussions of the reflexive issues in studying power.

Fairclough's (1992a) arguments for textual (including intertextual) analysis include a political reason, namely that such analysis is an important resource for social science that has critical objectives. Feminist researchers have probably given the most attention to moral and political aspects of research, often in the context of concerns about the implications of epistemological relativism. For example, Gill (1995) argues that the problem with the relativist notion about the equivalence of versions is that it does not allow for political interventions. She proposes that social transformation should be an explicit goal of discourse-analytic work. Fairclough's proposals and the discussions by feminists and other critical social researchers can be helpful in addressing issues of moral accountability in research. There should be more consideration of these issues, although we would be wary of efforts to reduce concerns about the worth of research on moral grounds to any sort of simple checklist.

Our discussion of warrantability, as is inevitably the case, reflects our own ontological and epistemological commitments, so we think it appropriate that it conclude with a brief summary of those commitments. We are material realists in that we think it makes sense to talk about a physical world and in that we believe one can more or less "get it right" about the nature of that world. But this position is not particularly relevant for the work we do as social discourse analysts (although we do view transcription in this way; that is, we can ask whether a transcription accurately represents particular sounds, i.e., physical aspects of an interaction; see Tracy, 1995, p. 209). With respect to what we see as the social world, we are epistemological relativists, in that we think that versions of events cannot be evaluated in terms of truth because they involve actions and not occurrences, meaning and not movements. However, they can be evaluated on moral criteria and can be judged as better or worse; that is, we are not moral relativists.

NOTE

1. Other writers have discussed different versions of trustworthiness in relation to nonconventional forms of inquiry. For example, Guba (1981) identifies four "naturalistic" terms for aspects of trustworthiness that are labeled within the "rationalistic" or "scientific" paradigm as internal validity, external validity, reliability, and objectivity; Guba also proposes alternative methods for addressing those aspects in naturalistic work.

Writing the Report

Discourse analysis is an open-ended, recursive activity, and the analysis of discourse and the writing of the research report are both discursive activities. It is thus more difficult to separate them as clearly as one can when using more conventional research strategies. We shall see how this works in a moment. However, we shall start with the assumption that the researcher has finished the analysis, is relatively satisfied with the sorts of functions and patterns that have been identified and the claims that have been generated and assessed, and is ready to do the report. We first present an overview of what an ideal report might look like and then consider in more detail the section that is different from conventional reports and hence most likely to be problematic, namely the results or analysis section.

Our general recommendation is to follow conventional styles of reporting. We do this despite recognizing that those styles perpetuate a set of assumptions and values that are antithetical to the tenets of discourse analysis. American Psychological Association style is particularly problematic in this respect. But alternatives are few, underdeveloped, and difficult to bring off. More important, unconventional work often encounters resistance even when presented in conventional fashion, so it would be unrealistic to push for the acceptance of both new work and new forms. We reluctantly recommend walking the thin line between purity and practicality for the time being. This recommendation should not keep an inspired soul from inventing new styles.

OVERVIEW OF REPORT

The introduction can be modeled on conventional reports in form and content, although there are some features of the latter that may differ slightly. We can begin as usual with identification of the topic or problem to be addressed and reference to the pertinent literature. Depending upon the intended outlet

179

for the work, authors may or may not include an argument for and explication of the discursive perspective and discourse analysis, although they should identify the particular approach to discourse analysis that was taken (e.g., CA, DASP).

The methodology section is also relatively straightforward, although the relevant information is sometimes subsumed in the introduction or under other headings, for example, "The data (set)." This section should include the usual information about the nature of the data, how they were obtained, and, as appropriate, the rationale for the selection of the material (nature of the sample and sample size). It should also identify (usually by reference to an appendix) the transcription conventions that are used, with a comment on any variations of previous versions. The methodology section may also include an overview of the analysis.

The next section of conventional reports is usually called "Results." But this heading is less appropriate for discourse analysis, because the corresponding section in a discourse-analytic work does not simply present the output of some set of analytic procedures. Rather, it includes a good deal of "raw" data (discourse excerpts) and also presents the actual (re)doing of the analysis, or at least enough of the analysis for readers to see what was done and to see the basis for the claims that are made. "Analysis" is thus a more suitable heading for most kinds of discourse-analytic work. This section includes some elements that might conventionally be viewed as discussion in that it includes the rationale for specific claims, and, especially, because it is explicitly interpretive. (In contrast, much of the interpretive work of conventional analysis goes on before the data are collected, e.g., in decisions about observational procedures, questionnaire items, etc.)

The report usually concludes with a discussion section, which is conventional in the sense that it involves stepping back from the discourse and from the immediate analysis: Claims are elaborated and summarized, and their implications are considered. Authors may wish to argue here for the advantages of the work; it would certainly be appropriate to acknowledge its limitations. The discussion does not require a specific section on warranting (justifying claims and conclusions). Aspects of warrantability of the research that is being reported (e.g., generalizability, coherence, etc.; see Chapter 10) that have not been attended to in the analysis section should be addressed in the discussion, and the discussion should pull all of these points together.

Discussions conventionally include suggestions for future research, particularly work that could address the limitations of the reported research, for example, with respect to the sample of participants or discourse. In discourse-analytic work, the suggestions may also include proposals for further analysis of the discourse on which the report is based, for example, involving an examination of different sorts of themes. For example, in Wood and Rennie (1994), we excluded consideration of the ways in which women constructed their sexual identities because of the limited space available and because of the constraints on reporting extensive analyses of even relatively small data sets.

The report concludes as usual with a list of references. It may also include a number of endnotes, which tend to be used more frequently in this sort of work. Such notes are used in part to report technical details without disrupting the flow of the analysis (e.g., concerning features of the discourse itself, its transcription and presentation, although these are sometimes reported in an appendix). In part, the use of notes reflects the nature of discourse-analytic work, particularly its reflexivity, so the notes may include the acknowledgment of other versions, commentary on the analysis itself, and so on (see Madigan, Johnson, & Linton, 1995).

ANALYSIS

This is usually the most difficult section for analysts, especially novices, to write up in a formal report. It involves a great deal of detailed, painstaking, sometimes tedious work—tedious in part because it requires reanalysis or further analysis as one goes about presenting and discussing the discourse. But this section is critical because it serves as a check on the analysis and the claims the analyst wishes to make and because it provides evidence for the quality of the analysis. As Potter and Wetherell (1994) argue, "Often it is only when the discipline of presenting a study publicly necessitates filling in all of the steps that flaws and problems appear" (p. 64).

The first task is to organize under specific sections the analytic work that has been done; this can be done by topic, function, features of discourse, and so on—whatever makes the most sense given the particular project. In some work, it may be appropriate to organize the work on a case-by-case (by participant or document) basis, at least initially. Organization in itself involves a kind of analysis, in that the way in which one organizes material makes a theoretical or conceptual statement; this is always the case, but it may present particular challenges in discourse analysis because of the complexity of the material, the lack of standard procedures, and the inexperience of the analyst. And the researcher may need to try several different ways of organizing the material before she or he is satisfied.

There are nonetheless some general principles. First, it will invariably be necessary to use several sections and subsections (and possibly sections within the subsections). Subsections are required because of the hierarchical structure of discourse and analysis and because they enable a sharper, more detailed focus than one can achieve by starting with an attempt to say something general about discourse. The (sub)sections should address various (sub)topics or (sub)functions and should have corresponding headings (e.g., "Formulating rape"; "Avoidance"). The (sub)section can begin with a brief overall statement about what is going to be demonstrated in the form of a general (not detailed) identification of what the discourse is about, what is going on, its structure, or the devices employed. The statement should not simply repeat the discourse;

rather, it should give some indication of what the analyst has to say about it. So it should not include a quotation or paraphrase of the text (although quoted bits of text are sometimes included in the heading of a section, e.g., if they constitute a telling or dramatic demonstration of the function, etc. to be discussed). It is this sort of repetition that gives the sense that an analyst is not telling readers anything that they cannot see for themselves, that the analyst is simply describing the discourse. The statement is followed with a demonstration of the analysis (about which more in a moment). The (sub)sections conclude with a summary of the claims that are being made about the discourse.

There are no strict rules about how to organize and frame the analysis section, in part because of the multiple ways in which we can see discourse and the terms used to describe it. For example, we sometimes use the same term to refer to both a function and a device. This often reflects the connection between the device and the function accomplished; for example, *avoidance* can refer both to what is accomplished in a particular stretch of discourse and to the specific techniques by which speakers avoid mention of something (e.g., the use of passive voice without the identification of an agent). And sometimes the topic of interest will be a particular concept or device rather than a substantive topic. The critical point is that regardless of how the analysis is organized, the claim that is embodied in that organization and in the introduction to each (sub)section is backed up with a clear exposition of the steps that took the analyst to that statement and of the details of the claim. We need to watch that we do not simply fall back upon the presentation of examples, because the documenting of the original analysis will suffer, with two consequences for warranting: The analysis will be unchecked and the reader will be unable to see how it was done. Keeping the introduction brief and general helps to avoid this tendency.

Finally, there are organizational issues that arise when one is doing discourse analysis that involves working with two or more specific approaches (e.g., CA and CDA). These issues are also theoretical, in that they concern both whether and how one can combine different approaches within one analysis. As we noted in Chapter 2, there are some analysts who would argue that different approaches are simply incompatible, whereas others have suggested that the combination is not only possible, but desirable or even necessary (see Edley & Wetherell, 1997; Fairclough, 1992a). We take the latter position, although we recognize some of the difficulties it entails. In particular, there are questions concerning how to incorporate different levels and different sorts of concepts into the analysis and, especially, the write-up. For example, should one attempt to apply all levels to each excerpt as one goes along, or should one work with one level at a time? Where should the linking of the different levels take place, within the analysis or in the discussion section? The answers will likely require some experimenting; they will also vary depending upon the levels and specific approaches involved. There has not been a great deal of discussion of these issues—and certainly no agreement on how to proceed. We have offered some suggestions on this matter in Chapter 8. For the novice analyst, the best approach at the present time would be to read as many reports of multi-layered analyses as possible. Notions from the discursive perspective along with substantive theory and previous research may be helpful in providing a general orientation to the linking of analyses at different levels or within different approaches; however, they will not provide specific, detailed guidelines for doing so, and one has to be careful that the use of theory as it is sometimes understood does not jeopardize close attention to the text or impose unwarranted assumptions.

One solution to the problem of presenting analyses from different approaches or analyses that address different levels is to write them up as separate reports, for publication in different sorts of journals, as appropriate. For example, Antaki and Rapley (1996) analyzed interviews between psychologists and people with intellectual disabilities for the way in which the psychologists manage the paradox of official definitions and ordinary usages in assessments of quality of life. Houtkoop-Steenstra and Antaki (1997) analyzed the same data for the ways in which interviewers delivered questions that encouraged particular sorts of responses. The practice of writing multiple papers about one data set is the reverse of that in conventional research, in which one paper reports the analyses of several data sets (although this may also occur in discourse research, as we discussed in Chapter 10 in relation to triangulation). The difference reflects the nature of discourse-analytic work, in which the amount of discourse (data) is usually extensive and multifunctional and can be analyzed in multiple ways. We could say that one data set contains many studies, whereas in other research, one study covers several data sets. The Coupland work on conversations involving older women is also a good example of this sort of publication practice; the study we described in Chapter 9 and a number of others are all based on the same data set (cf. Coupland et al., 1991). Edward's work on counseling data is another example (see Edwards, 1997, 1998; the 1998 study is described in Chapter 9).

In sum, the organization of the analysis section (and of the report more generally) is a crucial issue. It is a way of making the analysis systematic and of demonstrating that this is so; it thus contributes to warrantability. Furthermore, because it involves theoretical as well as practical matters, it is inseparable from the sorts of claims that are being made, which also has implications for warrantability.

Demonstration

Demonstration basically involves the presentation of one or more discourse excerpts, followed by their detailed analysis. That is, the analyst explicitly names features of the discourse that were picked out; identifies their possible functions and effects; offers hypotheses about patterns; points to further features of the discourse that conform or not to these patterns; and provides a running commentary on how these features may work, the rationale for formulating hypotheses, and so on. Excerpts may themselves be introduced with a brief statement, or they may be presented immediately following the introduction to the (sub)section in which they appear. Introducing the excerpts is helpful if the analyst wants to make a number of points within a section (effectively creating subsections, but without headings). The introduction may identify the excerpt in relation to the point that is being made or the topic that is being addressed, or it may provide the context in which the excerpt appeared, so that the reader can see its relevance. Again, it is important to avoid simply repeating or paraphrasing (parts of) the discourse, either before or after the excerpt is presented. This is not always easy; you need to be sure that the reader has indeed noticed the "obvious;" you also need to identify it in order to talk about it. Knowledge of certain discourse devices is helpful here. For example, rather than saying something like, "In this excerpt, Mary refuses Bob's invitation," you can embed this point in the statement you want to make about Mary's refusal, for example, "Mary's refusal of Bob's invitation serves to construct her identity as a 'cold fish,' as can be seen in Bob's subsequent turn" (see Edwards & Potter, 1992, pp. 69, 71).

The requirement to include discourse excerpts provides constraints on the report. But their mere inclusion is insufficient; one cannot simply make some sort of claim and give an excerpt as support (see van Dijk, 1997a). Rather, the analyst must go through the excerpt in detail in order to show how a claim is grounded—a point that we have made repeatedly because it cannot be emphasized enough. The advice given to novice writers of literary work to "show not tell" if they want to make their writing engaging and convincing also applies here; in this case, it works by ensuring that there is sufficient evidence for the claims of the analyst. But there is an additional reason. In writing up the analysis in this way, in reproducing it, the analyst is inescapably required to redo the analysis. This reworking, which occurs in the context of a reorganization of the original analysis, provides another check on the soundness of the claims. It is somewhat like taking a visitor along a path that is for you well-traveled. You are able to point out all of the features that you have studied in the past, but in describing them to someone else you see them in a new light and notice variations that you may have missed on your previous trips. The various examples of analysis that we have included throughout the book (especially in Chapters 3, 8, and 9) should give some idea of what it means to work through an excerpt and a set of excerpts, although readers should consult the original studies to see how these look in the context of a full report.

We comment briefly on terminology. The term *excerpt* is not accidental; our choice depends partly on etymology. We avoid the term *example* because it implies that the analysis was completed previously (behind the scenes as it were) and is simply being reported on. This is true only in part; a good portion of the analysis is done in the here and now of the write-up. The term also suggests that analysis involves arguing by example, which is not the case (at least as this expression is usually understood; see "Warranting" section). Finally, *example* implies a representation of generality, but this is a claim that must be made and supported explicitly in the analysis. *Excerpt* is more precise than other possible terms in that it refers specifically to that which is picked out from a text (e.g., compare *extract,* which does not necessarily refer to texts and which may suggest an inappropriate concentration of that which is extracted). In emphasizing the process of selection, *excerpt* serves as a reminder of the analyst's active role in both analysis and write-up (vs. simply "finding" and reporting).

How does the analyst select the excerpts to be presented in the report? This question can provoke considerable uncertainty, particularly for novice analysts. To some critics, the process is casual, arbitrary, or overly selective. Potter and Wetherell (1987) talk about the inclusion of a representative set of extracts, but they do not specify precisely what is to be represented. It is possible to be systematic about selection by considering the requirements of the overall analytic strategy along with the particular claims involved. We recommend the inclusion of all the types of excerpts identified by Jacobs (1986; paradigm, fringe, and deviant; see Chapter 8) and if possible, of several instances of each type. There is no necessary relationship between the number of excerpts selected for the report and the number of such excerpts in the discourse. In any particular section of the analysis, there may be few excerpts of one type and large numbers of another; in the latter case, only some excerpts should be selected, with an emphasis on diversity. Where there is a choice to be made between two excerpts that seem essentially similar, the analyst might want to base selection on the criteria that we have discussed above. For example, if you already have an excerpt that is analyzed in relation to contradictions, you might wish to select a second excerpt that involves new problems in order to broaden the base of support for the claim. Finally, excerpts may be selected with an eye to the possibilities of intertextual analysis. As always, the selection of excerpts is provisional. As the analyst works up the report, interpretations and claims may be modified, and the final set of excerpts may be different from those that were selected at the end of the analysis stage.

Another issue concerns the extent to which one includes data other than those that are the focus of analysis. For example, when an analyst draws on some device or pattern that has been identified in previous work, it can be useful to include a display of the relevant data from that work in the course of defining the device. However, this should be done sparingly, or it can distract from the analysis at hand. Again, one possibility is to include this sort of information in an appendix. This is probably more feasible for work other than journal articles (e.g., grant proposals, monographs, dissertations).

Like the original analyses and the working up of the report, the final analysis section of the report is itself cyclical. Excerpts are analyzed, patterns identified, and tentative claims made. Variations are presented and analyzed to see if they conform to the pattern. As part of making claims, the analyst also must deal with exceptions to the pattern; this involves further discourse excerpts, further analysis, and possible modification of the claim. In other words, a section or even a subsection does not simply conclude with a claim or set of interpretations. Rather, claims are explicated along the way; further, there are likely to be multiple layers of patterns and interpretations.

A final caveat. The analysis and reporting phases of discourse-analytic work are similar in several ways. Both phases are cyclical and require analytic work. And both phases require discursive work in that, in contrast to conventional, quantitative approaches, doing the analysis itself involves writing. But the two phases are not the same. Reporting does not entail a simple repetition, representation, or reproduction of the analysis as it was previously done. As we have discussed, the prior analyses will involve numerous (re)cyclings through the data and the analyses, consideration of and working through different ways of organizing, and so on. In contrast, the final report involves the concise, selective presentation of well-considered analytic work, including instances of actual (re)analysis. We might say that analysis involves writing *out,* whereas the report involves writing *up.* Writing out is doing analysis; writing up is both presenting and doing analysis. But analysis in the former case essentially covers all of the discourse and preserves the identity of individual cases and of the original order; in the latter, the discourse is ordered and organized for specific purposes (e.g., it may or may not be presented on a case-by-case basis), and only selected excerpts, points, and claims are presented. And in the writing out, analysis begins with the discourse, whereas in the report, the discourse requires some sort of introduction.

We stress these differences between the two phases to avoid blurring their similarities and linkages. Blurring is particularly likely if the analyst is showing analytical work in progress to others, as in the case of novices or students for whom there is a need to produce some written work as evidence of analytical activities, for example, to show to a dissertation committee. Blurring can engender problems. Attempts at any sort of straightforward reproduction of the analysis in the report would make the report far too long for publication. On the other hand, the notion that one needs to do reanalysis in the report can foster a premature anticipation of reporting that is likely to make the analysis not only shorter, but much less thorough, precise, detailed, and grounded—in other words, less well thought out. And if in anticipation of writing up the work, the analyst approaches analysis with claims already formulated, the scope of the analysis and its grounding in the discourse will also be curtailed. In doing analysis, keep an open mind; in writing the report, put yourself in the shoes of the audience.

The analyst therefore needs to distinguish clearly between writing out the analysis and writing up the analysis in the report and to keep in mind what she or he is doing during each phase, despite the similarities between them. At the same time, we can never lose sight of the fundamental requirement for the report that in presenting analysis it also does analysis. The report in this sense is another analysis, the latest although not necessarily the last version; there is continuity as well as similarity across the two phases.

Postscript

When is discourse analysis appropriate? Not unexpectedly, we argue that it is a suitable approach for many questions in the social sciences. Even those questions that do not seem to be a matter of talk can benefit from being framed in this way. For example, one way of studying eating disorders has been to ask whether sufferers have distorted perceptions about their body size. But we can also examine accounts about one's body not as matters of perceptions, but as situated sayings, and we can consider how the language of perception can serve as a warrant for particular actions such as restricting food intake. We can also rethink questions that have been framed in previous work in terms of frequencies, degrees of relationship, and generalizations. Regardless of the topic, there are questions that would benefit from a discursive approach, although it requires some experience to frame these appropriately. There is another consideration. Researchers should ask themselves whether a discourse approach is compatible with their own skills and inclinations, because it does require a feel for and interest in language as well as the ability to feel comfortable with analytic procedures that are less mechanical and linear than those with which many people are familiar and that require fine attention to detail.

GETTING STARTED

We encourage beginning analysts to read broadly, to go beyond methodological discussions to a wide variety of research reports (see References). There are a number of associations that produce newsletters or other publications that provide examples of research, personal accounts, information about workshops and conferences, book notices and reviews, and suggestions for publication outlets.[1] Discourse analysts do not have to be linguists, although it is helpful to refamiliarize oneself with basic grammatical concepts.

The best preparation is simply to get started as soon as possible. Because discourse is everywhere, one is never at a loss for samples on which to practice. Reading the newspaper, listening to a conversation, and watching television all provide opportunities for asking what people are doing, not just what they are saying. When you are ready to start a specific project, start small and remember that there are many forms of suitable discourse, including written discourse. (In our experience, too many beginners simply assume that they should conduct interviews and do not consider other possibilities.)

There are a number of sources that can be helpful for working on analyses (see Chapter 7 and Appendix B). If possible, try to work with others (particularly those who have some experience), perhaps joining a group of like-minded researchers (or forming one of your own). If you are working with spoken discourse, begin by making transcripts together; the discussions this engenders are often enough to start you on your way with analysis. Collaboration is important not only for developing ideas and learning about the process of analysis. It also forces you to do the sort of grounding and warranting that you will eventually do for readers, but in this case with immediate feedback. Unfortunately, one of the drawbacks of using discourse analysis for many forms of student work is that student work is expected to be done independently. But this requirement should not preclude discussion of the analysis as you go about working it up (see also Chapter 11 on writing out vs. writing up analysis). Be prepared to take breaks at various points in the process of analysis (see Potter & Wetherell, 1987); this can be another advantage of working with others. And most of all, expect at least some of the time to expend a good deal of effort working on very small bits of discourse.

Writing Proposals

We have argued that discourse analysis does not (or should not) require more justification than any other approach. This position may not be realistic in the case of theses or dissertations or in the writing of proposals for such work, for grants, and so on. We have acknowledged that more information may be needed for discourse work when readers are not familiar with it, and this can provide us with an "out." That is, we can draw on the discursive strategy of doing justification (without characterizing it as such) via doing description— except that proposals and theses may require even more detail than would be expected in a report on the research. As in the report, you should include information about discourse-analytic assumptions, about the kind of approach you are taking, and about your plans for data collection (perhaps including brief discussions of why you may not be able to specify these completely until the work is under way and of possible modifications). You should also include a discussion of the warranting strategies that you will use.

In our experience, the most critical section of proposals is the one that does not appear in the report because it is superseded by completed analysis. It is the section in which you show how you will go about doing the analysis, not only so that readers will know this, but also so they will know that *you* know what you are going to do. This requires that you imagine what your data might look like and that you present various instances of this discourse along with their analysis. There are a variety of sources of such instances: pilot or preliminary work, previous research, literary and media discourse, public and private archives, your own personal research archive (assuming that as you go through your daily life you have been collecting interesting bits of discourse that might someday serve analytic purposes). You will probably use a mixture of these, along with various hypothetical or constructed instances.

Another strategy that might be appropriate for some work is to begin with a set of notions (e.g., interpretive repertoires) or a list of devices and then to consider for each a sample of relevant discourse that would exemplify or illustrate the device, as we have done in a number of places throughout the book (e.g., Chapter 7, Appendix B). For example, your research might address the various ways in which witnesses in a trial work up their testimony as factual. You should try to do more than simply illustrate devices; that is, you should show how the devices are played out in the discourse. But you probably also need to point out that this is not the way that analysis is actually done, that you will be starting with the discourse, not the devices, and that what you have done is only a limited version of analysis.

In sum, for proposals you actually have to *do* (some) analysis—as in the report itself. In discourse work, analysis is always with us, whereas in most conventional approaches, analysis is ahead of us at the proposal stage and behind us at the report stage.

GENERAL ISSUES

The requirement that one spell out in the proposal how one will go about doing analysis raises a more general question; how explicit can and should we be in articulating our "method" of discourse analysis? It is clear that there is not one perspective on discourse analysis, but many, and there is thus not *a* method of discourse analysis. Potter and Wetherell (1987) have argued that there is "no *method* to discourse analysis" (p. 175) in the traditional sense. Rather, discourse analysis includes a broad theoretical framework and suggestions for studying discourse. The stages they identify are "intended as a springboard rather than a template . . . discourse analysis is heavily dependent on craft skills and tacit knowledge" (p. 175). We think that their points are well-taken, but they are not exclusive to discourse analysis. Method of any sort always involves some sort of theoretical framework, at least implicitly, along with craft skills (or conventional psychology would not require so many hands-on methods courses) and tacit knowledge. Still, we can say a good deal about our activities; discourse analysis is teachable in some systematic way, although it encompasses elements of craft skills that have to be practiced under the guidance of a more experienced analyst. But that is not really different from the kind of hands-on training that people require to become successful particle physicists or molecular biologists. There is always an undefinable element in scientific research that cannot be exhaustively codified in textbooks on method.

Nonetheless, we do not see the "problem of translating a skill into a technique" (Hepburn, 1997, p. 33) as an excuse for eschewing any attempt to do so. (As with all discourse, we focus not on the truth of a statement—in this case, whether it is indeed (too) difficult or undesirable—but on what might be done rhetorically in the making of such an assertion—avoiding the troublesome task of explicating as clearly as possible what it is that we do.) The effort can benefit not only newcomers to discourse analysis, but all of us who have an interest in such work. However, we would argue for a bottom-up as well as a top-down approach. That is, in addition to attempting to articulate what we do in a general way, we must be careful to do so in relation to our specific projects. Explication of the analytic activities involved in an individual piece of research can both draw on and contribute to the development of the discourse-analytic perspective.

We would be remiss if we did not turn a critical lens on discourse analysis itself. We have mentioned a number of tensions concerning, for example, the treatment of context. Parker and Burman (1993) discuss a variety of problems with discourse analysis, ranging from the time-consuming nature of the work to relativism. One problem is that faced by any new approach: Instances of discourse research that are found wanting taint the whole enterprise, whereas a poor conventional study is simply a poor study. But as solid work is done and researchers become more familiar with discourse analysis and what can be done with it, it will become easier to take it up and to judge specific studies on their own merits.

The problems of taking up a new approach and of discourse analysis in particular are offset in our view by the potential of discourse analysis to contribute to positive change. Discourse analysis entails a shift in emphasis to a more social, interactional, and less individualistic orientation. It promotes a more positive view of persons in that it shows them to be more complex and accomplished than they often appear to be in conventional analyses. In preserving people's own understandings rather than seeking their view of our understandings (e.g., via questionnaires, etc.), discourse analysis can promote self-determination (Sampson, 1993). Discourse analysis encourages us to begin with particular experiences rather than social science abstractions and to ground our analyses in those experiences. At the same time, we do not want to stop there (which can be a problem in student work). The point is not so much generalization or theorizing in the traditional sense; rather, we want to work up the implications of our analyses for issues relevant to social science and culture (e.g., power, gender, social structure, etc.).

The emphasis in discourse analysis on variability can also be emancipatory. The recognition of different voices and different versions can help us to identify different approaches to problems and more possibilities for personhood. For example, the acknowledgment of variability and of the fluid, constructed, multifaceted nature of categories (including identities) means that people who undergo traumatic experiences (e.g., widowhood, the loss of employment) will not also have to see the changes in identity that these entail as a loss of (the one true) self. We have suggested some other possibilities for discourse analysis in Chapter 1. Again, a cautionary note. We need to adopt a reflexive viewpoint, that is, to analyze our own texts as well as those of others (e.g., policy makers, media members, politicians) for the ways in which they contribute for ill or for good, as we discussed in Chapter 10. But the note is also positive. In turning the lens of discourse analysis on our own work, we can also take advantage of its relevance to the construction of texts and draw on ideas from discourse analysis (e.g., techniques of fact construction, the deployment of categories, etc.) that can help us in our writing, particularly on discourse analysis.

CONCLUDING REMARKS

Let us go back to our opening statement, in which we said that this book is primarily about method. We hope that it will help practitioners to pursue the new methodological strategies with acumen and perspective. But we also wish to reiterate that the book is not just about method, but also about a new theoretical stance in the social sciences. Part of that new orientation is discourse analysis.

For some time, there has been a growing dissatisfaction with the methodology of the social sciences, grounded as it has been in the maxims of logical positivism and in efforts to emulate the successes of the natural sciences. The crisis of confidence that social psychology experienced in the 1960s and 1970s serves as an example of the larger disillusionment. It was focused first on ethical questions concerning the routine use of deception (or lying), but it progressed rapidly to questions about the very trustworthiness of positivistically constrained data. The crisis was never resolved, perhaps because of the apparent inability of many practitioners to appreciate the foundational nature of the criticisms emanating from philosophical and historical studies; because of the absence at the time of clear conceptual and methodological alternatives; and because, understandably, seasoned investigators always have a stake in maintaining the status quo.

But the pressures for change continue, inexorably. For example, it is difficult, if not impossible, to dismiss Austin's (1962) arguments against the relevance of logical positivism to the social sciences, rooted as his arguments are in the radically new conception of the nature of language bequeathed to us by Wittgenstein. It is no less difficult, as we said earlier, to dismiss the arguments of Boulding (1980) and Hampshire (1978) against the reductionist unity of science thesis. Boulding insisted that one barrier to the development of the sciences is the uncritical transfer of methodologies from one field to another. Each discipline has its own epistemological requirements, its own criteria of what counts as evidence. Hampshire articulated a distinction between studies in res naturam and in res artem, arguing that the questions they raise must be pursued by different means, conceptually and methodologically. Both plead for a patient, piecemeal approach and for abstention from outmoded dogmas.

We see discourse analysis as part of the changes that are long overdue. Our hope is to help move *Homo loquens,* the talking being, to center stage as we enter the next century.

NOTE

1. Parker (1992) provides references to descriptions of discourse groups and addresses for several discourse groups, mostly in Britain (pp. 137-138). Furthermore, van Dijk (1994) supplies information about a network for scholars and graduate students interested in CDA. Other relevant associations are the International Association of Language and Social Psychology (IALSP; c/o Dr. Jeff Pittam, Department of English, The University of Queensland, Brisbane, QLD 4072, Australia; e-mail: j.pittam@mailbox.uq.edu.au); the International Pragmatics Association (IPrA; IPrA Secretariat, P. O. Box 33 [Antwerp 11], B-2018 Antwerp, Belgium; e-mail: ipra@uia.ua.ac.be); and the International Communication Association (ICA; 8140 Burnet Road, P. O. Box 9589, Austin, TX 78766, USA).

Appendix A

Transcript Notation

The notational conventions employed in this book and in much discourse-analytic research more generally are derived from the system developed by Gail Jefferson (see Atkinson & Heritage, 1984, pp. ix-xvi). For the excerpts presented in the book, we have not followed the usual practice of using headings that refer to the original data (see the following) but have simply given the page reference for the published source in which the data are reported. (We have numbered the excerpts according to their appearance here.) We have also made occasional modifications to data segments to conform to the conventions given here. Otherwise, we have tried to present the excerpts as they appeared in the published source in order to preserve as closely as possible the original transcriptions as they were involved in analysis and to demonstrate both the variety and consistency in transcription practices.

[W98;SI;25]	Extract headings refer to the parts of the data as identified in the collection of the researcher who gathered the material
some ⌈talk⌉	Square brackets between lines or bracketing two lines of talk indicate the onset ([) and end (]) of
⌊overlap⌋	overlapping talk
end of line= =start of line	Equal signs indicate latching (no interval) between utterances
(.)	Untimed pause (just hearable; <.2 sec.)
(1.2)	Pause timed to the nearest tenth of a second
bu-	A dash shows a sharp cutoff of speech
under; pie	Underlining indicates emphasis
CAPITALS	Capital letters indicate talk that is noticeably louder than surrounding talk
°soft°	Degree signs indicate talk that is noticeably more quiet than surrounding talk

>fast< <slow>	"Less than" and "greater than" signs indicate talk that is noticeably faster or slower than the surrounding talk
ho:me	A colon indicates an extension of the sound or syllable that it follows
↑word ↓word	Upward and downward pointing arrows indicate marked rising and falling shifts in intonation in the talk immediately following
.,? !	Punctuation marks are used to mark speech delivery rather than grammar. A period indicates a stopping fall in tone; a comma indicates a continuing intonation; a question mark indicates a rising inflection; an exclamation point indicates an animated or emphatic tone.
wghord	"gh" within a word indicates guttural pronunciation
heh or hah	Indicate laughter
.hh	Audible inbreath
hh	Audible outbreath (sometimes associated with laughter)
wo(h)rd	An "h" in parentheses denotes laughter within words
rilly	Modified spelling is used to suggest pronunciation
(word)	Transcriber's guess at unclear material
( )	Unclear speech or noise
((coughs))	Double parentheses enclose transcriber's descriptions of nonspeech sounds or other features of the talk ((whispered)) or scene ((telephone rings))
[a local pub]	Brackets enclose contextual or explanatory information
. . .	Horizontal ellipses indicate talk omitted from the data segment
. .	Vertical ellipses indicate intervening turns omitted from the data segment
→	A horizontal arrow in the left margin points to an utterance discussed in the text

Note: repeated symbols, for example, :::, °°, and hhhh, indicate, respectively, greater elongation, quiet, outbreaths, and so on. Speakers may be identified by letter, pseudonym, or role (e.g., counselor). Lines are usually numbered, particularly in long excerpts.

Appendix B

Selected Varieties of Discourse Analysis

We consider here those varieties of discourse analysis that we find most relevant. For reasons of space, we emphasize the themes and devices that are likely to be useful for empirical work rather than presenting research examples or explicating the perspectives overall. (The examples given in the book, particularly Chapters 3 and 9, illustrate a good many of the resources identified here.) Our treatment is necessarily brief and selective; readers are encouraged to consult the fuller presentations of the varieties that we mention here and also to consult works in which various approaches are compared (e.g., Schiffrin, 1994; Taylor & Cameron, 1987; Tracy, 1991, 1995; van Dijk, 1985, 1997b; Wieder, 1999). Other approaches that might be useful are identified in the Glossary.

DISCOURSE ANALYSIS IN SOCIAL PSYCHOLOGY

The perspective of DASP was initially described by Potter and Wetherell (1987). Edwards and Potter (1992) subsequently used the term *discursive psychology* to indicate that the perspective involves radical rethinking of concepts, not just a methodological shift. They also used the term to signal a reconstruction of central topics in psychology, such as memory and attribution. More recently, Edwards (1997) has contributed a wholesale discursive respecification (see Potter, 1999) of a host of psychological topics conventionally treated in cognitive terms, including perception, categorization, scripts, emotion, and so on. In the same way that discursive psychology can be seen to describe the application of a discourse-analytic perspective to psychological concepts, Potter (1998b) has used the term *discursive social psychology* for "the application of ideas from discourse analysis to issues in social psychology" (p. 234). The terms do emphasize that discourse analysis involves more than method, but they can be confusing to novices if, for example, they are taken to suggest different domains or activities rather than driving home the way in which various notions are all considered in discursive, that is, social terms, and as both theory and practice. Some confusion may also arise because the term *discursive psychology* has been used by Harré (e.g., 1995) to describe a perspective that shares some of the basic assumptions of DASP (e.g., regarding language as action, the discursive mind; cf. Harré & Gillett, 1994), but that departs in other important ways (e.g., in the emphasis on rules; see Edwards, 1997). Harré's contributions are largely conceptual rather than empirical, although his explications of self (Sabat & Harré, 1992) and, particularly, of positioning (Harré & van Langenhove, 1991) have been taken up in a number of empirical studies.

The other potential problem with the terms *discursive psychology* and *discursive social psychology* is that they may suggest to some readers that the perspective is restricted to the discipline, whereas it not only draws upon multiple disciplines but also works to transcend a number of traditional disciplinary boundaries. For our purposes, we shall refer to the perspective as *discourse analysis,* with the qualifier that it is the version developed within social psychology (hence, DASP) and with the emphasis on analysis as perspective rather than method.

DASP focuses on both participants' discursive practices and the resources upon which they draw (Potter & Wetherell, 1995a). Some of the important features of participants' discursive practices and the relationships between them are captured by the Discursive Action Model, which consists of three major sections (Edwards & Potter, 1992, p. 154). *Action* stresses that the focus is on action, not cognition; treats references to internal (perceptual, cognitive) processes (e.g., attributions, rememberings) not as statements about such processes but as rhetorical devices; and situates these in sequences of explaining, blaming, and so forth. *Fact and interest* stresses the way in which dilemmas of interest are managed through reports that do attributions, are constructed as factual through various discursive techniques, and are organized to undermine alternatives. *Accountability* stresses the way in which reports attend to accountability both in the events reported and of the speaker who is reporting and emphasizes the relations between these aspects of reports.

These themes are played out through the examination of various sorts of practices and resources. A major focus has been on the variety of ways in which versions are constructed to appear factual. For example, Edwards and Potter (1992, pp. 160-163) have identified nine main techniques of fact construction:

1. category entitlements (reports by members of particular categories have a prima facie truth value; see CA below);
2. vivid description (in which details support the factual quality of the report);
3. narrative (the factual status of events is enhanced by embedding them in a particular narrative sequence);
4. systematic vagueness (which can serve to deflect the undermining of an account);

5. empiricist accounting (a style that enhances factual status by removing the influence of the observer or reporter, thus creating "objectivity"; e.g., the passive voice of scientific discourse);

6. rhetoric of argument (using the form of standard argument types, e.g., syllogisms);

7. extreme case formulations (which help to render actions commonplace; see CA below);

8. consensus and corroboration (agreement across observers, judges, etc., e.g., as in reports of interrater reliability);

9. lists and contrasts (which enhance completeness and bolster the claim at issue through comparing it with an unlikely alternative).

The focus here is on some of the devices that can be deployed to construct discourse as factual (see also Potter, 1996, for discussion and identification of additional devices).

An important issue in the construction of versions is the management of stake or interest. Referencing stake is one important way in which the significance of an action or the truth of a claim can be discounted, for example, as motivated by personal interest. One example of this sort of referencing is the reply attributed to Mandy Rice-Davies, a witness in a British court case involving prostitution and a number of public figures, to a question from Counsel, "Are you aware that Lord Astor denies any impropriety in his relationship with you?": "Well he would wouldn't he" (see Edwards & Potter, 1992, pp. 117-118 for analysis of the way in which this expression works). The effectiveness of this device (and its more general form, "they would say that, wouldn't they") for discounting has been widely recognized in that it has been taken up and deployed in a variety of contexts (see also Potter, 1997). But like all such devices, it can be turned around and used to acknowledge stake (But I would say that, wouldn't I?), thereby limiting the possibility for other speakers to undermine one's claim. Potter (1996) has discussed a variety of ways in which one can do *stake inoculation,* that is, construct one's talk or writing to prevent its undermining, for example, by presenting one's position as involving a change of mind (see also Potters', 1997, discussion of the phrases *I dunno* and *I don't know* as stake inoculation).

Accountability is another major theme in DASP. As in attribution theory, issues of agency and of blame and responsibility are viewed as central features in many reports. For example, to say that a student has failed because she did not study is to identify her as an agent and to hold her responsible for her failure. But as Edwards and Potter have pointed out (1992), there is another level of accountability here, namely that of the person who makes the statement. That is, we need to consider the accountability of both "the parties *in* the talk (in the events as recounted) and the parties *to* the talk" (p. 125). The professor who tells her chair that a student failed because she did not study is constructing her own accountability for giving the student a failing grade; the professor cannot be blamed—as would be the case if the exams were unfair, for example. That is, the two levels of accountability are related. Moreover, the professor is also accountable for the report itself. This point relates to the concept of footing, that is, the basis on which accounts are offered and received (see Chapter 7). In this example, we are likely to overlook the footing because the professor aligns herself with the report, that is, presents it as her own evaluation. We can see the important distinctions more clearly if we consider those cases in which speakers claim to be passing on the views of others, that is, in which they claim that they are not responsible for the content of the report (e.g., if the chair were to say to the student, "I'm only telling you what the professor said"). But the speaker may nonetheless be held responsible for passing on the report—and this involves an issue of accountability that may require further work by the speaker (e.g., invoking the responsibilities of office).

Emotion concepts and metaphors constitute an important set of discursive resources for deployment within narrative and rhetoric. Edwards (1997, p. 194) has identified a range of such resources in the form of rhetorical positions and contrasts:

1. emotion versus cognition (description of actions as expressions of feelings vs. thought);
2. emotion as irrational versus rational (whether emotions are treated as accountable);
3. emotion as cognitively grounded or cognitively consequential (the treatment of emotion as a reaction to or basis for cognitive assessment);
4. event-driven versus dispositional (emotion as reactive or provoked vs. stemming from character);
5. dispositions versus temporary states;
6. emotion as controllable action or passive reaction (dichotomizing emotional reactions into what is unaccountably felt and what is accountably done);
7. spontaneous versus externally caused (emotion as caused internally vs. by its object);
8. natural versus moral (emotions as automatic bodily reactions vs. social judgments);
9. internal states versus external behavior: private ("feelings") versus public ("expressions," "displays"); "true" emotions as privileged reports from the inner life of the mind vs. ascriptions based on overt behavior;
10. honest (spontaneous, reactive) versus faked (artful, not "true").

Interpretive repertoires are general resources upon which people can draw to construct discourse and to perform particular actions (see Potter & Wetherell, 1995a). We have discussed these in the context of a number of studies (e.g., Coates et al., 1994; see also discussions of Buchanan & Middleton, 1993, in Chapter 3; of Gilbert & Mulkay, 1984, in Chapter 7; and of Wood & Rennie, 1994, in Chapter 8; see also discussion of top-down and bottom-up analysis in Chapter 2).

A central theme in DASP is the rhetorical organization of discourse (Potter & Wetherell, 1995a), that is, the way in which it is constructed to counter or undermine actual or possible alternatives (Billig, 1991, 1996). (See, e.g., discussion of Tracy & Carjuzáa, 1993, and of Edwards, 1998, in Chapter 9.) The emphasis here is on the generally argumentative nature of discourse (vs. rhetoric in the sense of ornamentation, Billig, 1996), that is, the way in which it is oriented (not necessarily explicitly) to other versions or claims. For example, a description "will work as *offensive rhetoric* in so far as it undermines alternative descriptions . . . [it] may provide *defensive rhetoric* depending on its capacity to resist discounting or undermining" (Potter, 1996, p. 106). Billig's approach (e.g., 1985) also emphasizes that we should examine discourse for the way in which it particularizes as well as categorizes (see, e.g., discussion of Buchanan & Middleton, 1993, in Chapter 3).

Argument has also been addressed within DASP in relation to specific discursive devices involved in making an argument (e.g., see discussion of the Antaki & Wetherell, 1999, work on concessions in Chapter 3). For discussion of different ways of approaching rhetoric and argument, see Antaki (1994) and Edwards (1997) and also the following discussion of CA.

DASP emphasizes the flexibility and interrelatedness of both discourse and analysis. What participants are doing and the resources that they use are not only intertwined; instances of discourse can be seen as either action, resource, or both. The devices or resources that we have mentioned, for example, under fact construction can be deployed for a whole variety of discursive practices; they also illustrate the way in which DASP incorporates a variety of influences (e.g., from CA, sociology of science, linguistics). Using DASP requires an appreciation for the way in which analytic categories overlap with participants' concerns and a recognition that the approach involves a basic reframing of research questions, not simply the application of a method to traditional questions (Potter, 1997). (For guidelines on carrying out DASP, see Potter, 1997; Potter & Wetherell, 1987, 1994, 1995a.)

CONVERSATION ANALYSIS

The term "conversation analysis" is now used almost exclusively to refer to the approach developed originally by Sacks and his colleagues, an approach that is easy to identify. There are nonetheless two definitional issues that deserve brief mention. The first concerns the relationship of CA to ethnomethodology (see Glossary), which has been framed in a number of ways (see, e.g., Edwards, 1997; Heritage, 1984; Holstein & Gubrium, 1994; Taylor & Cameron, 1987; Tracy, 1995; Wieder, 1999). We have no space here to discuss ethnomethodology, but we strongly recommend that discourse analysts read about it both as background to CA and also for its general relevance (Edwards, 1997). Second, CA has sometimes been distinguished from discourse analysis (e.g., Hutchby &

Wooffitt, 1998; Levinson, 1983; Psathas, 1995). However, the sorts of discourse analysis with which it has been contrasted are linguistic approaches rather than those we have emphasized, particularly DASP. Nowadays, CA is more likely to be viewed as a variety of discourse analysis (e.g., Pomerantz & Fehr, 1997, discuss the relation of conversation analysis to "other forms of discourse analysis," p. 64; Edwards, 1998, refers to "CA and its discourse analytic (DA) relatives," p. 17).

The CA focus on interaction in talk gives particular attention to the details of talk and to the indexicality and occasionedness of talk, that is, the way in which the sense and reference of talk depends on the context or occasions of use (see Antaki & Widdicombe, 1998). CA also stresses *recipient design* (Sacks & Schegloff, 1979), the way in which turns at talk are shaped for particular aspects of the context, especially the other participants. CA is an extremely rich source of ideas about actions, structures, and devices that can serve as analytic resources. We can consider only a few of the key notions here; fortunately, there are a number of more thorough presentations and discussions of CA available (e.g., Antaki, 1994; Antaki & Widdicombe, 1998; Edwards, 1997; Nofsinger, 1991; Potter, 1996; Psathas, 1995; Sacks, 1992) as well as works that provide guidelines at various levels on how to carry it out (e.g., Drew, 1995; Heritage, 1997; Hopper et al., 1986; Hutchby & Wooffitt, 1998; Pomerantz & Fehr, 1997; Schiffrin, 1994).

There are several different strands of work in CA. The early work of Sacks was concerned with everyday practical reasoning. He developed a number of concepts to specify how members or social interactants produce descriptions of social life, for example, by constructing and connecting various social categories (Sacks, 1974, 1992; see also Antaki & Widdicombe, 1998). For example, *membership categories* are classifications of various sorts that can be used to describe persons (e.g., sister, drunk driver, discourse analyst). *Membership categorization devices* are used to group together membership categories; for example, "family" groups together mother, father, brother, sister, and so on. Membership categories are conventionally associated with a number of features or predicates, for example, activities, entitlements, knowledge, and attributes. Thus, the identification of someone as a member of a particular category can imply certain features; conversely, a description of someone's features can be used to invoke category membership. For example, to describe someone as a "doctor" is to imply that the person engages in certain activities, knows certain sorts of things, and so on. Membership categorization is a pervasive and important characteristic of discourse because it is such a useful resource (e.g., in explanation and warranting).

Another type of work in CA (often taken as prototypical) has focused on the structure and sequence of everyday conversation, with the aim of producing analyses of patterns based on "'collections' of instances of a particular conversational phenomenon" (Hutchby & Wooffitt, 1998, p. 93). Conversation analysts have identified a wide variety of action sequences (see, e.g., Nofsinger,

1991). For example, one basic structure of conversation is the *adjacency pair*: a sequence of two utterances, which are usually although not necessarily adjacent to each other and which are produced by two different speakers, such that the first utterance requires a particular (or a limited range of) second utterance(s) (Schegloff & Sacks, 1973). A summons requires a response, an invitation requires an acceptance or refusal, a question requires an answer, and so on. Failure of the second speaker to supply the second part is met with renewed attempts and also has normative consequences (e.g., the speaker may be reprimanded or criticized). Adjacency pairs themselves often occur in sequences. For example, a request-agreement pair (e.g., Will you go to the movies with me?—Love to) may be preceded by a question-answer pair (called a *presequence*) that prepares for the request (e.g., Are you busy tonight?—No, I don't think so). In some cases, the utterance of the first part of the presequence allows the recipient to project what is coming up and skip ahead to the second part of the next pair (e.g., Do you know where the paper is? [Yes; Where?] On the table). Note that this suggests a way of handling the problem of indirect speech acts. That is, it is not that the second speaker has to interpret a question asking for information as a request (the indirect act), but rather that the question projects a subsequent request (Where?), and it is this request to which the second speaker responds (see Levinson, 1983).

Adjacency pairs are involved in one of the most complicated (and interesting) concepts in CA, that is, *preference*. Conversation analysts have argued that there are two types of possible responses to the first parts of adjacency pairs: preferred and dispreferred. Put simply, preferred responses are those that are expected or conventional; dispreferred responses are those that are not. Note that preference refers to the design features of utterances, not to individual dispositions (e.g., personal wishes or expectations). For example, the preferred response to a question is an answer, to an invitation an acceptance, to a self-disparagement a denial, and so on. We all know that invitations may be issued and accepted even though both parties would be pleased if they were refused. It is obvious that both preferred and dispreferred responses do occur. What is striking is that the two sorts of response are likely to be very different in structure as well as in content. Preferred responses tend to be delivered promptly, to be brief (nothing extraneous is added), and to be clear-cut and positive rather than hedged or qualified: "Can you come for dinner on Saturday?" "We'd love to." In contrast, dispreferred responses usually contain a delay component (e.g., an initial pause), and they often begin with the term *well,* which discursively identifies the status of the response as a dispreferred one and further delays the answer.

Most important, dispreferred responses are likely to include accounts (excuses or justifications). Thus, a refusal of an invitation to dinner is likely to look something like the following: "(pause) Well, it'd be great but we already promised to have dinner with the children." The person who refuses by simply saying "No," or even, "Sorry, no," or who offers an insulting account, "Love to, but your cooking is terrible," is not likely to receive future invitations. The finding that dispreferred responses differ in structure from preferred responses is consistent, robust, and general. The finding is important, because it shows the way in which priority is given to certain second parts over others (because they are simpler and easier to manage), such that requests are more likely to be fulfilled, agreement is more likely than disagreement, and so on.

The story of preference is more complex than the one we have presented here. For example, the terms *preferred* and *dispreferred* are also used to refer specifically to the shape or structure of responses. Thus, it is possible to give a response that is dispreferred in content (i.e., performs a dispreferred action, e.g., a refusal) but that is preferred in structure, that is, it has a "preferred" format (e.g., "No"). For further discussion, see Heritage (1984), Hutchby and Wooffitt (1998), and Nofsinger (1991).

Another very important set of principles concerns the organization of turn taking. Sacks et al. (1978) proposed a model of the management of turn taking in everyday conversation that has become the foundation for the analysis of a wide variety of conversational practices. Turn construction units can be of various sizes (words, phrases, clauses, or sentences). Their important feature is that participants can project where they will end and where speaker change becomes relevant (a transition-relevant place). Sacks et al. also described three practices by which turns may be distributed or allocated: The current speaker selects the next speaker; the next speaker self-selects; the current speaker continues (see Hutchby & Wooffitt, 1998, and Nofsinger, 1991, for detailed discussion). The features described by the model are the basis for some obvious features of conversation, for example, that speaker change occurs, that usually only one person speaks at a time, that turn length varies, and so on. But the model also helps to account for other features. For example, Sacks et al. consider the way in which the treatment of silence depends upon where it occurs in relation to turn construction and allocation. A *lapse* occurs during and after a transition-relevant place (TRP) when no one speaks. A *gap* is the silence at the TRP between the talk of the current speaker and that of a self-selecting next speaker. A *pause* is a silence that occurs within a person's turn (e.g., when a speaker is silent at a non-TRP or where the speaker selected by the current speaker delays the start of her or his turn; see Nofsinger, 1991, for details). The distinctions are important because they entail different attributions for the silence; for example, the pause belongs to the person within whose turn it occurs, the gap belongs to no one, and the lapse belongs to everyone.

The turn-taking model also provides for a much finer analysis of the notion of *interruption*. Briefly, the model allows us to distinguish between overlapping or simultaneous talk that occurs at or approaching the TRP (and which arises from the normal operation of the turn-taking system) and simultaneous talk that does not (and which apparently violates turn-taking norms; cf. Schegloff, 1987). The model is also implicated in the organization of conversational repair. There has been a good deal of work on repair; we can only mention some basics here. Schegloff et al. (1977) described four different types of repair:

1. *Self-initiated self-repair:* The initiation—the marking of a *trouble source*—and the carrying out of repair are both done by the speaker of the trouble source. For example, "Is it l-is it in a liquid form?" (from Nofsinger, 1991, p. 125).

2. *Other-initiated self-repair:* The repair is initiated by recipient but carried out by speaker of trouble source. For example,

1		Ken:	Is Al here today?
2		Dan:	Yeah
3			(2.0)
4	→	Roger:	he is? hh eh heh
5		Dan:	Well he was.

In this example (from Hutchby & Wooffitt, 1998, p. 62), we see Roger in Line 4 initiating the repair (an example of what is called a next-turn repair initiator, i.e., it comes in the next turn after the trouble source) and Dan in Line 5 carrying it out.

3. *Self-initiated other-repair;* for example,

1	B:	He had dis uh Mistuh W-m whatever k—I can't
2		think of his first name, Watts on, the one that
3		wrote ⌈that piece.
4	A:	⌊Dan Watts.

In this example (from Hutchby & Wooffitt, p. 63), the speaker initiates repair by referring to his trouble remembering the name, and the second speaker carries out the repair.

4. *Other-initiated other-repair;* for example,

1		Milly:	and then they said something about Kruschev has
2			leukemia so I thought oh it's all a big put on.
3	→	Jean:	Breshnev.
4		Milly:	Breshnev has leukemia.

In Line 3, Jean (the second or other speaker) simultaneously initiates and carries out the repair of the trouble source in the first speaker's utterance (from Hutchby & Wooffitt, p. 63).

The four types of repair are different in several ways. For example, the last type is more explicit in attending to an error by the speaker (see Hutchby & Wooffitt, 1998), and the turn-taking system provides for more self-repair than other-repair (see discussions in Drew, 1995; Hutchby & Wooffitt; and Nofsinger, 1991, for explication and discussion of implications; see also Chapter 7).

There is also CA work on argument. For example, Jackson and Jacobs (1980) consider argument in the sense of speech events relevant to disagreement. Argument can involve making an argument (offering reasons for a claim) or having an argument (as a matter of interactional disagreement) and often the combination of both (Nofsinger, 1991; see also Hutchby, 1996). And there are a host of other useful notions, for example, extreme case formulations (ways of referring to an object or event that take it to the extreme of some dimension or property; cf. Pomerantz, 1986; see also previous discussion on fact construction in section on DASP and discussion of Buchanan & Middleton, 1993, in Chapter 3). We cannot begin to describe all of them here; Atkinson and Heritage (1984), Nofsinger (1991), and Hutchby and Wooffitt (1998) cover a variety of devices and types of resources (e.g., alignment, conversational closings, topic organization, story structure), and there are numerous individual articles, for example, by Lerner (e.g., on responsive list construction, 1994; on compound turn construction, 1996) and Maynard (on news delivery sequences, 1997).

Not all work in CA involves collection-based analyses of particular features of everyday conversation. CA can also take the form of single-case analysis, the examination of a single conversation (or a portion of one) in order to analyze extended sequences of talk and to "track in detail the various conversational strategies and devices which inform and drive its production" (Hutchby & Wooffitt, 1998, p. 121). Yet another form of work involves what Heritage and Greatbach (1991) refer to as the branching out of CA studies from the "'home base' of ordinary conversation to 'institutional' settings in which more or less official or formal task-based or role-based activities are undertaken" (pp. 93-94). Organizations and institutions are studied both in their own right and also for purposes of comparison with everyday interaction and with each other (Heritage & Greatbach, 1991; Hutchby & Wooffitt, 1998). As we have discussed elsewhere, the idea here involves the ways in which institutionality is oriented to and produced by the participants themselves. Heritage (1997) has identified six places in which to probe the institutionality of interaction:

1. turn-taking organization;
2. overall structural organization (phases or sections);
3. sequence organization;
4. turn design (kinds of actions performed and means by which performed);
5. lexical choice (e.g., "police officer" vs. "cop");

6. interactional asymmetries (of participation, of interactional and institutional "knowhow," of knowledge, of rights of access to knowledge).

There is now a good body of such research. For example, Heritage and Greatbach (1991) have considered the distinctive turn-taking procedures in news interviews; Atkinson and Drew (1979) considered features of turn organization and design in court, including the production of accusations and of defenses; ten Have (1991) has addressed issues of asymmetry in doctor-patient interaction. Other work has involved classrooms, counseling sessions, and calls to emergency services (see Heritage, 1997; Hutchby & Wooffitt, 1998).

CA can sometimes seem to entail either trivial observations (e.g., with respect to turn taking) or esoteric notions, and it may thus seem to be rather removed from the concerns of both everyday interactants and other discourse analysts, particularly those doing CDA. In contrast, we want to stress the utility of both the individual concepts and of the approach as a whole. CA has contributed major insights to our understanding of talk in both everyday and institutional contexts. It has also provided new ways to consider specific social problems. One example is an analysis of investigations of child sexual abuse. Lloyd (1992) examined the ways in which preference and turn structure served to confirm child sexual abuse through adults' offering of particular sorts of responses in the first part of question-answer sequences. Another is the use of CA to develop a feminist perspective on sexual refusal (Kitzinger & Frith, 1999) that draws on the body of work in CA on the dispreferred status of refusals and their structure in everyday conversation.

CRITICAL DISCOURSE ANALYSIS

CDA is a term that is most often used to identify a set of perspectives that emphasizes the relations between language and power and the role of discourse analysis in social and cultural critique. CDA can be defined in part by its focus on social issues and social problems (e.g., racism, sexism, nuclear disarmament), although these topics are also addressed by discourse analysts who work within other traditions. Fairclough and Wodak (1997) discuss eight theoretical approaches to CDA: French discourse analysis; critical linguistics; social semiotics; sociocultural change and change in discourse; socio-cognitive studies; discourse-historical method; reading analysis; and the Duisburg School. (The list is not exhaustive; as Fairclough & Wodak note, critical feminist studies also belong to CDA; see Glossary). These approaches differ in a number of ways, for example, the extent to which they incorporate a historical perspective, their relative emphasis on reproduction versus innovation, their view of the mediation between the text and the social, and the extent to which they stress the multifunctionality of texts. We comment briefly on those that are most accessible or closest to the sort of analysis we have discussed in the book.

Critical linguistics (Fowler, Hodge, Kress, & Trew, 1979) can be seen as both a precursor to and a form of CDA. The emphasis is on the relation between linguistic form and ideology, and the concern is to demonstrate the ways in which various aspects of grammar (syntax and semantics) are connected to power and control. For example, to be described consistently (e.g., in the media, in policy documents) as the object rather than the subject of a verb is to be positioned as a victim rather than as an agent. Fowler (1996) has continued to develop the original approach, which was based on Halliday's (1985) work.

Social semiotics is the term used by Hodge and Kress (1988) to describe the extension of critical linguistics in the social dimension; that is, the goal is to analyze systems of meaning from the viewpoint of social structures and processes rather than taking the structure of language as the starting point for analysis, and to extend the analysis beyond verbal language, that is, to other sign systems. Hodge and Kress identify a very broad set of components for their "alternative semiotics" and apply these to the analysis of a wide range of topics and texts, including poems by Sylvia Plath and family photographs.

Sociocultural change and change in discourse refers to the work of Fairclough, whose overall aim has been to link linguistic analysis to social analysis (e.g., 1992a, 1992b, 1993, 1995). His system for doing so is extensive and elaborate. Briefly, Fairclough views discourse (language use) as social practice, as a "socially and historically situated mode of action" that is "socially shaped, but . . . also socially shaping, or *constitutive*" (1993, p. 134). He uses a three-dimensional framework to analyze linkages between discourse, ideology, and power; the framework draws on a variety of sources, including Foucault (e.g., 1979) and Halliday and Hasan (1985). "The aim is to map three separate forms of analysis onto one another: analysis of (spoken or written) language texts, analysis of discourse practice (processes of text production, distribution and consumption) and analysis of discursive events as instances of sociocultural practice" (Fairclough, 1995, p. 2). The first (extended linguistic analysis) focuses on the analysis of form—the structure and organization of the text both up to and above the level of the sentence—and includes some of the concerns of pragmatics (e.g., utterance force) and conversation analysis (e.g., turn taking). The second includes "explication of how participants produce and interpret texts" (Fairclough, 1993, p. 136), as done in pragmatics and conversation analysis, and it also includes intertextual analysis, that is, the way in which texts draw upon orders of discourse—"the particular configurations of conventionalized practices (genres, discourses, narratives . . .) which are available to text producers and interpreters in particular social circumstances" (Fairclough, 1992a, p. 194). The third considers issues of hegemony, ideology, power, and systems of power relations at different levels of social organization (situational, institutional, and societal contexts; Fairclough, 1993).

Socio-cognitive studies refers to the CDA work of van Dijk, who has carried out an extensive program of work on ethnic prejudice, racism, and related topics. As illustrated in his (1993b) analysis of the reproduction of racism in parliamentary discourse, his work involves multiple levels and types of analysis, for example, participants' positions, speech acts, topics, text schemata (argumentation), propositional structures of clauses and sentences, variations of syntax and lexicon, and rhetorical features. In contrast to the perspective we have adopted in this book, van Dijk's work is marked by an emphasis on cognition as the mediator of discourse and social structures. Furthermore, van Dijk rejects the notion of poststructuralism (1993a) that runs through a number of discourse-analytic perspectives, including DASP and some versions of CDA. Briefly, poststructuralist approaches can be characterized as "suspicious both of claims to reveal a world outside language and of claims that we can experience any aspect of ourselves as outside language. . . . Post-structuralism provokes a deconstruction of the 'truths' we take as given" (Burman & Parker, 1993, p. 6; see also Potter, 1996).

CDA is "not a homogeneous method, nor a school or a paradigm, but at most a shared perspective on doing linguistic, semiotic or discourse analysis" (van Dijk, 1993a, p. 131). There is, rather, an emphasis on principles (only some of which also characterize other perspectives). For example, van Dijk (1993b) proposes a number of principles such as multidisciplinarity, an explicit sociopolitical stance, a focus on social (between groups) rather than personal power and on both the abuse and challenge of power, and an examination of privileged access to discourse and communication. Fairclough and Wodak (1997) identify "a version of CDA based on eight principles of theory or method" (p. 268), including the ideas that power relations are discursive, that discourse constitutes society and culture, that discourse does ideological work, and that the link between text and society is mediated (e.g., by orders of discourse). It draws on various sorts of work in linguistics, philosophy, and sociology—including CA. Thus, we do not see CDA as useful in the sense that it provides us with unique sets of specific analytical concepts for the sort of work we discuss in this book. CDA has also been subjected to a number of critiques, for example, that it imposes a priori linguistic categories and relies on analysts' own understanding of texts and assumptions about the reality of social circumstances (see, e.g., Potter, 1996) and that it involves a "mostly taken-for-granted approach to power and social reality" (Edwards, 1997, p. 229). But CDA is important both for its general stance and for the work done within this perspective on a variety of specific issues. It represents a range of possibilities, as can be seen in a recent collection of readings edited by Caldas-Coulthard and Coulthard (1996), which includes a range of theoretical accounts of CDA and its application (e.g., by Wodak, who has carried out a number of studies of racism under the rubric of CDA). We give just one brief example here to convey a bit of the flavor of CDA.

Fairclough (1993) examined the marketing efforts of British universities via promotional discursive practices in advertisements for academic posts, materials for an academic conference, a curriculum vitae, and undergraduate calendar entries. We mention only a few aspects of his analysis of the first of these texts. At the level of discourse practice, he identifies various genres and discourses, such as commodity advertising (realized, e.g., in "catchy" headlines), that contribute to a hybrid construction of the advertisements that is partly promotional. At the level of text, he considers such features as personal pronouns, modality, agentless passives, transitivity, and narrative style for the ways in which they construct institutional and personalized identities. At the level of social practice, he discusses the appearance of the advertisements in relation to the breakdown of the division between polytechnics and universities and the links between the former and the business community. Fairclough's approach is appealing in part because of its sweep and inclusiveness, but these features also make it somewhat unrealistic in practice and also subject to the danger of less-than-thorough analysis. In the meantime, it is likely that discourse analysts will continue to draw selectively on the elements of Fairclough's approach.

PRAGMATICS

Pragmatics has been defined as "the study of the principles and practice underlying *all* interactive linguistic performance—this including all aspects of language usage, understanding, and appropriateness" (Crystal, 1987, p. 120). Pragmatics can even be seen to include CA. For example, Levinson (1983) has referred to CA as "the outstanding empirical tradition in pragmatics" (p. 285).

According to Levinson (1983), pragmatics is essentially concerned with the problem that the meaning of an utterance (language as used) cannot be fully accounted for by looking at the "literal" meaning of the sentence or words by which that utterance is performed. Utterance meaning is not the same as sentence meaning (or ironic communication would be very difficult): "Meaning is not something which is inherent in the words alone, nor is it produced by the speaker alone, nor by the hearer alone" (Thomas, 1995, p. 22). Although all work in pragmatics is concerned with the issue of meaning in use, there are a number of different approaches to the issue, approaches that differ in numerous ways, including their relative emphasis on the central concepts. And in addition to what we might see as core (or linguistic) pragmatics (e.g., Leech, 1983), there are numerous other strands of pragmatics, for example, applied (Levinson, 1983); cross-cultural (e.g., Blum-Kulka, House, & Kasper, 1989); developmental (e.g., Ochs & Schieffelin, 1979); psychological-cognitive (Clark, 1979); social-psychological (Turnbull & Saxton, 1997). Some of this work may be useful to readers, depending on their particular interests. But our focus here is on central themes and devices.

Austin's (1962) theory of speech acts is arguably the centerpiece of work in pragmatics. We have described some of the basic notions of the theory in Chapter 1, namely the ideas that language is used to do as well as to say things and that there are conditions that must be met in order for illocutionary acts to be successful. Speech-act theory is problematic for use in discourse analysis (see, e.g., Potter, 1996), but it is worth reviewing for the basic ideas (see Nofsinger, 1991, for accessible description).

Conversational implicature (a particular type of pragmatic inference) is a central concept in pragmatics, both because it is a "paradigmatic example" of the way in which principles that concern social interaction can affect the structure of language and because it provides an account of how it is possible for an utterance to mean more than it says (Levinson, 1983, p. 97). Grice (1975) argues that there is a general principle (the Cooperative Principle [CP]) that conversational participants are expected to observe: "Make your conversational contribution such as is required, at the stage at which it occurs, by the accepted purpose or direction of the talk exchange in which you are engaged" (p. 307). The CP consists of a number of more specific maxims related to the quantity, quality, relevance, and manner of contributions. It is clear that participants often fail to follow these maxims. However, Grice's argument is *not* that people follow them in a strict way, but that they orient to these principles in a way that gives rise to implicature. (Note that the term *implicature* refers to inferences that go beyond semantic content; it contrasts with terms such as *logical implication, entailment,* and *logical consequence,* which refer to inferences derived solely from logical content; see Levinson, 1983.) Specifically, even though it may appear that the maxims are not being followed, people generally nonetheless assume that the maxims (or the overall CP) are being followed in some way and make the appropriate inferences to support this assumption. We have space for only one example (see Grice, 1975; Nofsinger, 1991). An adviser who writes a letter of recommendation for a student stating only that the student has an excellent command of English is flouting the Quantity maxim. The violation cannot be explained on the basis of a clash with other maxims (e.g., the adviser is unable to say more or does not know that more is required). It is difficult to reconcile with the assumption that the speaker is observing the CP, *unless* one assumes that the writer has information that he or she is reluctant to put in writing, which in turn suggests that the adviser thinks poorly of the student. This is what is implicated.

There is much more that could be said about the theory (and its problems; see, e.g., Levinson, 1983). We point here to the importance of implicature for the understanding of conversation (and other forms of discourse) by both participants and analysts. Implicature is an instance of the more general principle that expressions or utterances only make sense against certain background assumptions. (The precise nature and status of these assumptions, e.g., as cognitive entities, cultural discourses, etc., varies considerably, but the principle appears implicitly or explicitly in all discourse work, e.g., in the notion of the taken-for-granted in CA.)

The term *deixis* concerns the ways in which certain features of language (referred to variously as deictics, deictic forms, indexicals, or indexical expressions) refer directly (point) to the characteristics of the situation. There are three traditional categories of deixis: person (e.g., use of words such as *I* or *you*); place (e.g., *this* vs. *that, here* vs. *there*); and time (e.g., *now, then,* verb tense). Two additional categories have recently received attention. *Social deixis* refers to the encoding of the social relationship between the speaker and addressee (grammatically or via pronouns [e.g., *tu* vs. *vous*] or address forms [e.g., Ms. Jones vs. Sally]). Discourse deixis concerns the encoding of reference to other portions of the discourse (e.g., "I said no and *that* is what I meant"; the use of *anyway* at the beginning of an utterance to signal that the utterance is not related to the discourse that immediately precedes it, but to discourse that is one or more steps back; time and place deictics [e.g., terms like *earlier, in the last paragraph*]; see Levinson, 1983).

The term *markers* refers to words or phrases that do not contribute to propositional meaning, but that function in other ways, for example, as commentary on the propositional meaning (e.g., "*Unfortunately,* I am cold"), as a signal of the force of the basic message (e.g., "*I promise* that I will be there on time"), or (as noted previously in the discussion of discourse deixis) to indicate or impose a "relationship between some aspect of the discourse segment they are a part of . . . and some aspect of a prior discourse segment" (Fraser, 1999, p. 938; e.g., "We left late. *However,* we arrived on time"). Fraser (e.g., 1996, 1999) provides discussions of a wide variety of such expressions that can be examined for the way in which they serve social functions. These discussions are rather technical, but discourse analysts can gloss over the fine distinctions (e.g., between discourse and pragmatic markers) and simply look for the expressions and suggestions about their functions.

We mention briefly two examples of work on specific expressions. The discourse marker *well,* when used in the initial position of an utterance, has neither a specific semantic meaning nor a grammatical status (Schiffrin, 1987), but it serves a number of functions, many of which concern the flow and organization of conversation (e.g., as a preclosing device, Schegloff & Sacks, 1973; to shift talk to another topic, Labov & Fanshel, 1977; to mark the insufficiency of a speaker's response, Cathers, 1995, and Jucker, 1993; as a delay device, Jucker, 1993; and as a frame for summing up a previous topic, Cathers, 1995, or introducing a new topic or level of conversation, Jucker, 1993). As we noted previously, *well* can serve to preface an utterance that is a dispreferred response and, in so doing, to signal its appearance and mitigate its force (e.g., Jucker, 1993). Finally, *well* can be used alone as a speech act to invite or challenge another to speak (Cathers, 1995).

The term *like* (unless used as simile or as a colloquial substitute for *for example*) is often viewed as a sort of random utterance, as a pause filler or meaningless interjection, as poor style. However, a number of analysts have argued that *like* has specific functions in the organization of discourse. For example, Miller and Weinert (1995) have shown that the use of *like* is not random. Their analysis identifies two major functions of *like*. First, *like* is used in clause-final position to counter objections and assumptions, for example, "just something to leave a memory of us LIKE"; *like* is used here to counter an inference that the news sheet that is being described will be remarkable (p. 389; the word *just* fulfills a similar function). Second, *like* is used in other positions as a focusing device, to highlight information that elucidates a previous comment (e.g., "like I knew that I coulnae apply for Edinburgh because . . .") or to ask for details elucidating a previous comment (e.g., "like are there strict rules"; Miller and Weinert, p. 388).

Modality refers to the linguistic encoding of "speakers' claims about the necessity, probability or possibility of beliefs and actions" (Turnbull & Saxton, 1997, p. 145). The primary modal elements are auxiliary verbs (e.g., *must, will, shall, ought to, can, may*); Turnbull and Saxton also consider certain adjectives (e.g., *necessary*), adverbs (e.g., *probably*), and parenthetical expressions (e.g., *I think*) as modal or modal-like linguistic elements (see pp. 147-151 for discussion and other examples). Modality is an important resource for fact construction (e.g., see Edwards & Potter, 1992, pp. 105-106, for discussion of hierarchies of modalization), for identity construction (e.g., what one *can* do) and for a variety of other discursive actions (e.g., denying responsibility).

In sum, we encourage attention to the grammatical and pragmatic features of discourse. As we have stressed throughout, any detail can be important, even those that appear at first glance to be mere aberrations in the smooth flow of discourse or to involve some sort of linguistic nit-picking. But as we have also argued, we are interested in linguistic features not in their own right, but as they are in relation to their social functions. And as for all features of discourse, we cannot rely on the literature in pragmatics to supply us with ready-made interpretations but must work up and ground these in the discourse at hand. Nonetheless, these features can be used to develop and support our arguments concerning, for example, social comparisons (e.g., the use of tense and durative verbs in the comparison of old vs. new members in the Widdicombe & Wooffitt study, 1990), the construction of character descriptions (e.g., the syntax of "You're not lonely, are you?" in the Coupland et al., 1991, study), and the working up of particular versions of events and responsibility (e.g., via basic grammatical devices such as agentless passives) and of utterances themselves (e.g., the simple conjunction *but* in the classic disclaimer, "I'm not a racist, but . . ."). There is also a role for analyses in which the focus is on particular expressions (such as *well* and *like*) rather than on the overall discourse in which they appear. Such analyses are not in principle different from the focus on a particular structural feature or sort of expression (e.g., idioms) that has been the concern of some CA work; such analyses can make a contribution to discourse-analytic work as long as they follow the more general requirements for analysis, including attention to discourse sequence and context.

Glossary

Terms for Discourse Analysis

Account Analysis: The term *account* most broadly refers to a person's version of events in the world, of the self, of others, and so on. May also refer to a version directed toward making events both interpretable and warrantable, that is, understandable and justifiable (cf. Antaki, 1994) and toward promoting the presentation of self as a rational and worthy being (cf. Harré, 1978). Still more narrowly, it may refer to an anticipation of or response to a reproach for failure, with an emphasis on excuses and justifications (e.g., Schönbach, 1990; Scott & Lyman, 1968). Usually verbal but may also be material (e.g., a urine sample offered to support a claim that one is a woman; cf. Garfinkel, 1967).

Action-Implicative Discourse Analysis: A method developed by Tracy (1995, 1997a, 1997b) within grounded practical theory, a metatheoretical frame on communicative practices. Focuses on what is problematic for communicators. Tracy's approach also incorporates notions of identity and rhetoric (e.g., Tracy & Anderson, 1999; Tracy & Carjuzáa, 1993).

Applied Linguistics: The application of linguistic work to language issues in other fields (e.g., problems of communication; cf. Tannen, 1984b).

Cognitive Sociology: Developed by Cicourel (1992) and applied to a variety of contexts (e.g., medical, legal, educational). Blends microsociology and cognitive science. Stresses a broad interactive model involving relationships among linguistic, cognitive, and sociocultural elements and draws on interactional data, ethnographic information, interviews, and textual materials, with attention to the information-processing and reasoning capacities of participants.

213

Comprehensive Discourse Analysis: Approach of Labov and Fanshel (1977) in which utterances in text are expanded from what is said to what is meant by linking information from different levels of abstraction (e.g., syntactical, propositional, sequential, biographical, and social-cultural). Employed (with some modifications) by Grimshaw (1989), who has also referred to it as *sociological discourse analysis* (1992).

Deconstruction: A technique for the analysis of texts developed within literary theory as attack on structuralism (see Semiotics) and associated largely with Derrida (e.g., 1978). Takes texts apart with emphasis on oppositions and absences (see Parker, 1989; Potter, 1996).

Discourse Dynamics: Parker's (1992) version of discourse analysis. A critical approach that both challenges prevailing practices within the academy (including some discourse-analytic work) and emphasizes social critique and change. Includes a number of criteria for discourse-analytic work, but relatively few systematic research examples.

Discourse Process(ing): Analysis in the experimental tradition of the comprehension, recall, and production of text. Emphasis is on theories and models of knowledge and reasoning (e.g., Schank & Burstein, 1985); most frequently involves brief, constructed samples of noninterpersonal discourse, such as stories and scripts. Sometimes used much more broadly, as in the journal *Discourse Processes* and the series *Advances in Discourse Processes*.

Dramaturgical Analysis: Primarily associated with Goffman (1959, 1967, 1981), who emphasized the presentation of self in interpersonal interaction and the structure of conversational interchange, partially in analogy to theater performance. Goffman's approach is often considered to be self-contained, but a number of traditions of discourse analysis incorporate notions (e.g., face, frames, remedial and supportive exchanges) and particular concepts (e.g., footing) from Goffman's work.

Ecolinguistics: An emerging field examining, for example, the way in which the natural environment and ecological problems are represented in texts (see Coupland & Coupland, 1997).

Ethnography: Goal is to describe a particular community, with emphasis on its social and cultural practices (including language use) and systems of norms, beliefs and values. *Ethnography of communication* (Hymes, 1974) is concerned with the ways in which the features of language use, such as the medium of communication, its structural patterns (phonology, lexicon, grammar), and its subject matter, are related to the interaction of situational factors, such as the setting, participants, goals, norms, and activities involved. It shares with ethnolinguistics (Crystal, 1987) a focus on social interaction, but it is not restricted to the study of ethnic groups.

Ethnomethodology: Originated in sociology with work of Garfinkel (1967); stresses the way in which the social world and social order are joint, systematic accomplishments of the members of particular communities; focuses on the methods used by social actors to produce and impute orderliness (see Antaki & Widdicombe, 1998; Edwards, 1997; Heritage, 1984; Holstein & Gubrium, 1994; Hutchby & Wooffitt, 1998; Potter, 1996; Watson & Seiler, 1992).

Exchange Structure: Approach originating in the Birmingham school, a group of linguists that includes Coulthard, McTear, Montgomery, Sinclair, and Stubbs (Taylor & Cameron, 1987). Employs a notion of speech acts in which acts are defined by their sequential or distributional function in the discourse (Sinclair & Coulthard, 1975). Strongly grammatical (e.g., the idea of using a small number of categories to generate a large number of structures; discourse as segmentable and hierarchically structured). Has been applied, for example, to classroom and medical interactions.

Feminist Discourse Analysis: Focuses critically on issues of gender, gender relations, and power and on social issues with gender implications (e.g., poverty, anorexia). Draws on a variety of traditions, including poststructuralism (Foucauldian and psychoanalytic; e.g., Gavey, 1989), DASP (Wetherell, 1998), CA (Kitzinger & Frith, 1999; Widdicombe, 1995), and CDA (e.g., Bergvall & Remlinger, 1996). Two recent volumes (Radtke & Stam, 1994; Wilkinson & Kitzinger, 1995) present a variety of examples of feminist theoretical and empirical work.

Forensic Linguistics: The application of basic linguistic principles to the law, with a concern for the social context and consequences of language use (e.g., Shuy, 1993).

Interactional Sociolinguistics: Approach of Gumperz (1982; see also Tannen, 1984a) focusing on the way in which uses of language in social interaction are related to issues of identity construction and miscommunication, with an emphasis on variations in social and cultural context. Schiffrin (1994) includes contributions by Goffman (e.g., 1959, 1967, 1981) under this heading because of his general emphasis on interaction, self, face, and social context.

Semiotics or Semiology: Rooted in classical work of Saussure as the founder of the science of signs. Basic idea is that meaning derives from the structure of language, seen as a formal system of differences made up by relationships between signs. Signs are not limited to linguistic signs (Silverman, 1993); semiotics deals with "patterned human communication in all its modes (sound, sight, touch, smell, and taste) and in all contexts (e.g., dance, film, politics, eating, clothing)" (Crystal, 1987, p. 399). Barthes (e.g., 1977) was a major influence in the development of semiology and also in the poststructuralist movement away from static structuralist notions (cf. Potter, 1996).

Sociolinguistics: Broadly defined as the study of language in society. In contrast to sociology of language, emphasizes linguistic versus social structures (Hudson, 1985). The basic strategy is to treat linguistic (e.g., pronunciation) and social (e.g., age, status) categories as independent systems and to identify relationships between them using statistical techniques.

Stylistics: The analysis of style (broadly, any situationally distinctive use of language that is characteristic of groups and individuals or language use that is characteristic of social contexts; Coupland, 1988; Crystal, 1987), including study of genres (see Fairclough, 1992a) and registers (see Brown, 1986).

Systemic-Functional Grammar or Systemic Linguistics: Developed by Halliday (e.g., 1985). Emphasizes the function of grammatical elements, their social implication, and their choice from the possibilities of grammatical systems. Draws attention to what is and is not selected; also attends to the role of intonation.

Text Grammar or Textlinguistics: A primarily linguistic approach that emphasizes the way in which sentences are connected to form coherent text (e.g., Halliday & Hasan, 1976). Analyses tend to focus on the structure of written texts, including literary work; primary aim is to produce a grammar at the level of text rather than the level of sentence.

References

Antaki, C. (1994). *Explaining and arguing: The social organization of accounts*. London: Sage.

Antaki, C., & Rapley, M. (1996). "Quality of life" talk: The liberal paradox of psychological testing. *Discourse & Society, 7,* 293-316.

Antaki, C., & Wetherell, M. (1999). Show concessions. *Discourse Studies, 1,* 7-27.

Antaki, C., & Widdicombe, S. (1998). Identity as an achievement and as a tool. In C. Antaki & S. Widdicombe (Eds.), *Identities in talk* (pp. 1-14). London: Sage.

Aronson, E. (1992). *The social animal* (6th ed.). New York: Freeman.

Atkinson, J. M. (1984). *Our masters' voices*. London: Methuen.

Atkinson, J. M., & Drew, P. (1979). *Order in court: The organization of verbal interaction in judicial settings*. London: Macmillan.

Atkinson, J. M., & Heritage, J. (Eds.). (1984). *Structures of social action: Studies in conversation analysis*. Cambridge, UK: Cambridge University Press.

Austin, J. (1962). *How to do things with words*. Oxford, UK: Clarendon Press.

Bakhtin, M. (1981). *The dialogic imagination: Four essays* (M. Holquist, Ed., C. Emerson & M. Holquist, Trans.). Austin: University of Texas Press.

Barthes, R. (1977). *Image, music, text*. London: Fontana.

Bavelas, J. B. (1990). Nonverbal and social aspects of discourse in face-to-face interaction. *Text, 10,* 5-8.

Bavelas, J. B. (1994). Gestures as part of speech: Methodological implications. *Research on Language and Social Interaction, 27,* 201-221.

Bavelas, J. B., Chovil, N., Lawrie, D. A., & Wade, A. (1992). Interactive gestures. *Discourse Processes, 15,* 469-489.

Beattie, G. (1983). *Talk*. Stony Stratford, UK: Open University Press.

Bergvall, V. L., & Remlinger, K. A. (1996). Reproduction, resistance and gender in educational discourse: The role of Critical Discourse Analysis. *Discourse & Society, 7,* 453-479.

Bickhard, M. H. (1992). Myths of science: Misconceptions of science in contemporary psychology. *Theory & Psychology, 2,* 321-337.

Billig, M. (1985). Prejudice, categorization and particularization: From a perceptual to a rhetorical approach. *European Journal of Social Psychology, 15,* 79-103.

Billig, M. (1988). Methodology and scholarship in understanding ideological explanation. In C. Antaki (Ed.), *Analysing everyday explanation: A casebook of methods* (pp. 199-215). London: Sage.

Billig, M. (1991). *Ideologies and opinions.* London: Sage.

Billig, M. (1996). *Arguing and thinking: A rhetorical approach to social psychology* (2nd ed.). Cambridge, UK: Cambridge University Press.

Blakar, R. M. (1973). An experimental method for inquiring into communication. *European Journal of Social Psychology, 3,* 415-425.

Blum-Kulka, S., House, J., & Kasper, G. (Eds.). (1989). *Advances in discourse processes: Vol. 31. Cross-cultural pragmatics: Requests and apologies.* Norwood, NJ: Ablex.

Boulding, K. (1980). Science: Our common heritage. *Science, 207,* 831-836.

Brockmeier, J., & Harré, R. (1997). Narrative: Problems and promises of an alternative paradigm. *Research on Language and Social Interaction, 30,* 263-283.

Brown, G., & Yule, G. (1983). *Discourse analysis.* Cambridge, UK: Cambridge University Press.

Brown, P., & Levinson, S. (1987). *Politeness: Some universals in language usage.* Cambridge, UK: Cambridge University Press.

Brown, R. (1986). *Social psychology* (2nd ed.). New York: Free Press.

Brown, R., & Gilman, A. (1960). The pronouns of power and solidarity. In T. A. Sebeok (Ed.), *Style in language* (pp. 253-276). Cambridge: MIT Press.

Buchanan, K., & Middleton, D. J. (1993). Discursively formulating the significance of reminiscence in later life. In N. Coupland & J. F. Nussbaum (Eds.), *Discourse and lifespan identity* (pp. 55-80). Newbury Park, CA: Sage.

Burman, E., & Parker, I. (1993). Introduction—Discourse analysis: The turn to the text. In E. Burman & I. Parker (Eds.), *Discourse analytic research* (pp. 1-13). London: Routledge.

Buttny, R. (1998). Putting prior talk into context: Reported speech and the reporting context. *Research on Language and Social Interaction, 31,* 45-58.

Caldas-Coulthard, C. R., & Coulthard, M. (Eds.). (1996). *Texts and practices: Readings in critical discourse analysis.* London: Routledge.

Cathers, T. (1995). *Gender and talk in close relationships: Orientations to status and solidarity in discourse about talk and in the use of "well."* Unpublished master's thesis, University of Guelph, Guelph, Ontario, Canada.

Cernetig, M. (1998, December 10). China's words on human rights louder than its actions. *The Globe and Mail,* p. A24.

Cicourel, A. V. (1992). The interpenetration of communicative contexts: Examples from medical encounters. In A. Duranti & C. Goodwin (Eds.), *Rethinking context* (pp. 291-310). Cambridge, UK: Cambridge University Press.

Clark, H. H. (1979). Responding to indirect speech acts. *Cognitive Psychology, 11,* 430-477.

Coates, L., Bavelas, J. B., & Gibson, J. (1994). Anomalous language in sexual assault trial judgements. *Discourse & Society, 5,* 189-206.

Cohen, J. (1994). The earth is round ($p < .05$). *American Psychologist, 49,* 997-1003.

Coupland, J., Coupland, N., & Grainger, K. (1991). Intergenerational discourse: Contextual versions of ageing and elderliness. *Ageing and Society, 11,* 189-208.

Coupland, J., Coupland, N., & Robinson, J. D. (1992). "How are you?": Negotiating phatic communion. *Language in Society, 21,* 207-230.

Coupland, J., Holmes, J., & Coupland, N. (1999). Readings of extrapolated contexts: A response to Michael Lloyd. *Journal of Pragmatics, 31,* 1237-1240.

Coupland, N. (Ed.). (1988). *Styles of discourse.* London: Croom Helm.

Coupland, N., & Coupland, J. (1997). Bodies, beaches and burn-times: 'Environmentalism' and its discursive competitors. *Discourse & Society, 8,* 7-25.

Cranach, M. von, & Kalbermatten, U. (1982). Ordinary interactive action: Theory, methods and some empirical findings. In M. von Cranach & R. Harré (Eds.), *The analysis of action* (pp. 115-160). Cambridge, UK: Cambridge University Press.

Crystal, D. (1987). *The Cambridge encyclopaedia of language.* Cambridge, UK: Cambridge University Press.

Davies, B., & Harré, R. (1990). Positioning: The discursive production of selves. *Journal for the Theory of Social Behaviour, 20,* 43-63.

Denzin, N. K., & Lincoln, Y. S. (1994). Introduction: Entering the field of qualitative research. In N. K. Denzin & Y. S. Lincoln (Eds.), *Handbook of qualitative research* (pp. 1-17). Thousand Oaks, CA: Sage.

Derrida, J. (1978). *Writing and difference.* London: Routledge & Kegan Paul.

DeVault, M. L. (1990). Talking and listening from women's standpoint: Feminist strategies for interviewing and analysis. *Social Problems, 37,* 96-116.

Douglas, J. D. (1970). Understanding everyday life. In J. D. Douglas (Ed.), *Understanding everyday life* (pp. 3-44). Chicago: Aldine.

Drew, P. (1987). Po-faced receipts of teases. *Linguistics, 25,* 219-253.

Drew, P. (1995). Conversation analysis. In J. A. Smith, R. Harré, & L. van Langenhove (Eds.), *Rethinking methods in psychology* (pp. 64-79). London: Sage.

Drew, P., & Holt, E. (1988). Complainable matters: The use of idiomatic expressions in making complaints. *Social Problems, 35,* 398-417.

Dupuis, S. (1997). *The roles of adult daughters in long-term care facilities: Alternative caregiver career paths.* Unpublished doctoral dissertation, University of Guelph, Guelph, Ontario, Canada.

Duranti, A., & Goodwin, C. (Eds.). (1992). *Rethinking context.* Cambridge, UK: Cambridge University Press.

Edley, N., & Wetherell, M. (1997). Jockeying for position: The construction of masculine identities. *Discourse & Society, 8,* 203-217.

Edwards, D. (1991). Categories are for talking: On the cognitive and discursive bases of categorization. *Theory & Psychology, 1,* 515-542.

Edwards, D. (1997). *Discourse and cognition.* London: Sage.

Edwards, D. (1998). The relevant thing about her: Social identity categories in use. In C. Antaki & S. Widdicombe (Eds.), *Identities in talk* (pp. 15-33). London: Sage.

Edwards, D., & Potter, J. (1992). *Discursive psychology.* London: Sage.

Fairclough, N. (1992a). Discourse and text: Linguistic and intertextual analysis within discourse analysis. *Discourse & Society, 3,* 193-217.

Fairclough, N. (1992b). *Discourse and social change.* Cambridge, UK: Polity Press.

Fairclough, N. (1993). Critical discourse analysis and the marketization of public discourse: The universities. *Discourse & Society, 4,* 133-168.

Fairclough, N. (1995). *Critical discourse analysis: The critical study of language.* London: Longman.

Fairclough, N., & Wodak, R. (1997). Critical discourse analysis. In T. A. van Dijk (Ed.), *Discourse studies: A multidisciplinary introduction: Vol. 2. Discourse as social interaction* (pp. 258-284). London: Sage.

Festinger, L. (1954). A theory of social comparison processes. *Human Relations, 7,* 117-140.

Firth, A. (1995). 'Accounts' in negotiation discourse: A single-case analysis. *Journal of Pragmatics, 23,* 199-226.

Foucault, M. (1979). *Discipline and punish* (A. Sheridan, Trans.). New York: Vintage Books.

Fowler, R. (1996). On critical linguistics. In C. R. Caldas-Coulthard & M. Coulthard (Eds.), *Texts and practices: Readings in critical discourse analysis* (pp. 3-14). London: Routledge.

Fowler, R., Hodge, R., Kress, G., & Trew, T. (1979). *Language and control.* London: Routledge.

Fraser, B. (1996). Pragmatic markers. *Pragmatics, 6,* 167-190.

Fraser, B. (1999). What are discourse markers? *Journal of Pragmatics, 13,* 931-952.

Freed, A. F., & Greenwood, A. (1996). Women, men, and type of talk: What makes the difference? *Language in Society, 25,* 1-26.

Funk & Wagnall standard college dictionary (Can. ed.). (1974). Toronto, Canada: Fitzhenry & Whiteside.

Garfinkel, H. (1967). *Studies in ethnomethodology.* Englewood Cliffs, NJ: Prentice Hall.

Gavey, N. (1989). Feminist poststructuralism and discourse analysis. *Psychology of Women Quarterly, 13,* 459-475.

Gilbert, D. T. (1995). Attribution and interpersonal perception. In A. Tesser (Ed.), *Advanced social psychology* (pp. 99-147). New York: McGraw-Hill.

Gilbert, G. N., & Mulkay, M. (1984). *Opening Pandora's box: A sociological analysis of scientists' discourse.* Cambridge, UK: Cambridge University Press.

Gill, R. (1995). Relativism, reflexivity and politics: Interrogating discourse analysis from a feminist perspective. In S. Wilkinson & C. Kitzinger (Eds.), *Feminism and discourse* (pp. 165-186). London: Sage.

Glaser, B. G., & Strauss, A. L. (1967). *The discovery of grounded theory: Strategies for qualitative research.* Chicago: Aldine.

Goffman, E. (1959). *The presentation of self in everyday life.* Garden City, NY: Doubleday.

Goffman, E. (1967). *Interaction ritual.* New York: Doubleday.

Goffman, E. (1981). *Forms of talk.* Oxford, UK: Basil Blackwell.

Goodwin, C. (1993). Recording human interaction in natural settings. *Pragmatics, 3,* 181-209.

Goodwin, C., & Goodwin, M. H. (1997). Contested vision: The discursive construction of Rodney King. In B. -L. Gunnarsson, P. Linell, & B. Nordberg (Eds.), *The construction of professional discourse* (pp. 292-316). New York: Addison-Wesley Longman.

Greatbach, D., & Dingwall, R. (1998). Talk and identity in divorce mediation. In C. Antaki & S. Widdicombe (Eds.), *Identities in talk* (pp. 121-132). London: Sage.

Grice, H. P. (1975). Logic and conversation. In P. Cole & J. L. Morgan (Eds.), *Syntax and semantics: Vol. 3. Speech acts* (pp. 41-58). New York: Academic Press.

Grimshaw, A. (1989). *Advances in discourse processes: Vol. 32. Collegial discourse.* Norwood, NJ: Ablex.

Grimshaw, A. (1992). Research on the discourse of international negotiations: A path to understanding international conflict processes? *Sociological Forum, 7,* 87-119.

Guba, E. G. (1981). Criteria for assessing the trustworthiness of naturalistic inquiries. *Educational Communication and Technology Journal, 29,* 75-91.

Gubrium, J. F., & Holstein, J. A. (1990). *What is family?* Mountain View, CA: Mayfield.

Gumperz, J. (1982). *Discourse strategies.* Cambridge, UK: Cambridge University Press.

Haberland, H. (1999). Text, discourse, *discourse*: The latest report from the Terminology Vice Squad. *Journal of Pragmatics, 31,* 911-918.

Hacking, I. (1992). World-making by kind-making: Child abuse for example. In M. Douglas & D. Hull (Eds.), *How classification works* (pp. 180-238). Edinburgh, Scotland: Edinburgh University Press.

Hacking, I. (1999). *The social construction of what?* Cambridge, MA: Harvard University Press.

Halliday, M. A. K. (1985). *An introduction to functional grammar.* London: Edward Arnold.

Halliday, M. A. K., & Hasan, R. (1976). *Cohesion in English.* London: Longman.

Halliday, M. A. K., & Hasan, R. (1985). *Language, context and text.* Deakin, Victoria, Australia: Deakin University Press.

Hampshire, S. (1978, October 12). The illusion of sociobiology. *New York Review of Books, 25,* 64-69.

Handel, W. (1982). *Ethnomethodology: How people make sense.* Englewood Cliffs, NJ: Prentice Hall.

Harré, R. (1978). Accounts, actions, and meanings: The practice of participatory psychology. In M. Brenner, P. Marsh, & M. Brenner (Eds.), *The social contexts of method* (pp. 44-65). London: Croom Helm.

Harré, R. (1979). *Social being: A theory for social psychology.* Oxford, UK: Blackwell.

Harré, R. (1995). Discursive psychology. In J. A. Smith, R. Harré, & L. van Langenhove (Eds.), *Rethinking psychology* (pp. 143-159). Thousand Oaks, CA: Sage.

Harré, R., Clarke, D., & De Carlo, N. (1985). *Motives and mechanisms.* London: Methuen.

Harré, R., & Gillett, G. (1994). *The discursive mind.* Thousand Oaks, CA: Sage.

Harré, R., & Secord, P. F. (1972). *The explanation of social behaviour.* Oxford, UK: Blackwell.

Harré, R., & van Langenhove, L. (1991). Varieties of positioning. *Journal for the Theory of Social Behaviour, 21,* 393-407.

Harwood, J., & Giles, H. (1992). 'Don't make me laugh': Age representations in a humorous context. *Discourse & Society, 3,* 403-436.

Heath, C. (1997). The analysis of activities in face to face interaction using video. In D. Silverman (Ed.), *Qualitative research* (pp. 183-200). London: Sage.

Hepburn, A. (1997). Teachers and secondary school bullying: A postmodern discourse analysis. *Discourse & Society, 8,* 27-48.

Heritage, J. (1984). *Garfinkel and ethnomethodology.* Cambridge, UK: Polity Press.

Heritage, J. (1997). Conversation analysis and institutional talk: Analysing data. In D. Silverman (Ed.), *Qualitative research* (pp. 161-182). London: Sage.

Heritage, J., & Atkinson, J. M. (1984). Introduction. In J. M. Atkinson & J. Heritage (Eds.), *Structures of social action: Studies in conversation analysis* (pp. 1-15). Cambridge, UK: Cambridge University Press.

Heritage, J., & Greatbach, D. (1991). On the institutional character of institutional talk: The case of news interviews. In D. Boden & D. Zimmerman (Eds.), *Talk and social structure* (pp. 93-137). Cambridge, UK: Polity Press.

Heritage, J. C., & Roth, A. L. (1995). Grammar and institution: Questions and questioning in the broadcast news interview. *Research on Language and Social Interaction, 28,* 1-60.

Hodge, R., & Kress, G. (1988). *Social semiotics.* Cambridge, UK: Polity Press.

Holstein, J. A., & Gubrium, J. F. (1994). Phenomenology, ethnomethodology and interpretive practice. In N. K. Denzin & Y. S. Lincoln (Eds.), *Handbook of qualitative research* (pp. 262-272). Thousand Oaks, CA: Sage.

Holstein, J. A., & Gubrium, J. F. (1995). *The active interview.* Thousand Oaks, CA: Sage.

Holt, E. (1996). Reporting on talk: The use of direct reported speech in conversation. *Research on Language and Social Interaction, 29,* 219-245.

Hoonaard, W. C. van den. (1997). *Working with sensitizing concepts.* Thousand Oaks, CA: Sage.

Hopper, R. (1989). Conversation analysis and social psychology as descriptions of interpersonal communication. In D. Roger & P. Bull (Eds.), *Conversation: An interdisciplinary perspective* (pp. 48-54). Clevedon, UK: Multilingual Matters.

Hopper, R. (1992). *Telephone conversation.* Bloomington: Indiana University Press.

Hopper, R. (1999). Going public about social interaction. *Research on Language and Social Interaction, 31,* 77-84.

Hopper, R., Koch, S., & Mandelbaum, J. (1986). Conversation analysis methods. In D. G. Ellis & W. A. Donohue (Eds.), *Contemporary issues in language and discourse processes* (pp. 169-186). Hillsdale, NJ: Lawrence Erlbaum.

Hopper, R., & LeBaron, C. (1998). How gender creeps into talk. *Research on Language and Social Interaction, 31,* 59-74.

Houtkoop-Steenstra, H., & Antaki, C. (1997). Creating happy people by asking yes-no questions. *Research on Language and Social Interaction, 30,* 285-313.

Huberman, A. M., & Miles, M. B. (1994). Data management and analysis methods. In N. K. Denzin & Y. S. Lincoln (Eds.), *Handbook of qualitative research* (pp. 428-444). Thousand Oaks, CA: Sage.

Hudson, R. A. (1985). *Sociolinguistics.* New York: Cambridge University Press.

Hutchby, I. (1996). Power in discourse: The case of arguments on a British talk radio show. *Discourse & Society, 7,* 481-497.

Hutchby, I. (1999). Beyond agnosticism?: Conversation analysis and the sociological agenda. *Research on Language and Social Interaction, 31,* 85-93.

Hutchby, I., & Wooffitt, R. (1998). *Conversation analysis.* Cambridge, UK: Polity Press.

Hymes, D. (1974). *Foundations of sociolinguistics: An ethnographic approach.* Philadelphia: University of Pennsylvania Press.

Jackson, S. (1986). Building a case for claims about discourse structures. In D. G. Ellis & W. A. Donohue (Eds.), *Contemporary issues in language and discourse processes* (pp. 129-147). Hillsdale, NJ: Lawrence Erlbaum.

Jackson, S., & Jacobs, S. (1980). Structure of conversational argument: Pragmatic bases for the enthymeme. *Quarterly Journal of Speech, 66,* 251-265.

Jacobs, S. (1986). How to make an argument from example in discourse analysis. In D. G. Ellis & W. A. Donohue (Eds.), *Contemporary issues in language and discourse processes* (pp. 149-167). Hillsdale, NJ: Lawrence Erlbaum.

Jacoby, J., & Ochs, E. (1995). Co-construction: An introduction. *Research on Language and Social Interaction, 28,* 171-183.

Janoff-Bulman, R. (1979). Characterological versus behavioral self-blame: Inquiries into depression and rape. *Journal of Personality and Social Psychology, 37,* 1798-1809.

Jefferson, G. (1978). Sequential aspects of story telling in conversation. In J. Schenkein (Ed.), *Studies in the organisation of conversational interaction* (pp. 219-248). New York: Academic Press.

Jefferson, G. (1984). On the organization of laughter in talk about troubles. In J. M. Atkinson & J. Heritage (Eds.), *Structures of social action: Studies in conversation analysis* (pp. 346-369). Cambridge, UK: Cambridge University Press.

Jefferson, G. (1996). A case of transcriptional stereotyping. *Journal of Pragmatics, 26,* 159-170.

Jucker, A. H. (1993). The discourse marker *well:* A relevance-theoretical account. *Journal of Pragmatics, 19,* 435-452.

Kelly, J., & Local, J. K. (1989). On the use of general phonetic techniques in handling conversational material. In D. Roger & P. Bull (Eds.), *Conversation: An interdisciplinary perspective* (pp. 197-212). Clevedon, UK: Multilingual Matters.

Kendon, A. (1979). Some theoretical and methodological aspects of the use of film in the study of social interaction. In G. P. Ginsburg (Ed.), *Emerging strategies in social psychological research* (pp. 67-91). New York: John Wiley.

Kitzinger, C. (1998). Inaccuracies in quoting from data transcripts: *OR* Inaccuracy in quotations from data transcripts. *Discourse & Society, 9,* 136-143.

Kitzinger, C., & Frith, H. (1999). Just say no? The use of conversation analysis in developing a feminist perspective on sexual refusal. *Discourse & Society, 10,* 293-316.

Knorr-Cetina, K. D. (1996). *Epistemic cultures: How scientists make sense.* Cambridge, MA: Harvard University Press.

Kress, G. (1989). *Linguistic processes in sociocultural practice.* Oxford, UK: Oxford University Press.

Kroger, R. O. (1982). Explorations in ethogeny: With special reference to the rules of address. *American Psychologist, 37,* 810-820.

Kroger, R. O., & Wood, L. A. (1992). Are the rules of address universal? IV: Comparison of Chinese, Korean, Greek and German usage. *Journal of Cross-Cultural Psychology, 23,* 148-162.

Kroger, R. O., & Wood, L. A. (1998). The turn to discourse in social psychology. *Canadian Psychology, 39,* 266-279.

Labov, W., & Fanshel, D. (1977). *Therapeutic discourse: Psychotherapy as conversation.* New York: Academic Press.

Lakoff, G., & Johnson, M. (1980). *Metaphors we live by.* Chicago: University of Chicago Press.

Lamb, S. (1991). Acts without agents: An analysis of linguistic avoidance in journal articles on men who batter women. *American Journal of Orthopsychiatry, 61,* 250-257.

Latour, B. (1987). *Science in action.* Milton Keynes, UK: Open University Press.

Lazar, M. (1993). Equalizing gender relations: A case of double-talk. *Discourse & Society, 4,* 443-465.

Lee, D. A., & Peck, J. J. (1995). Troubled waters: Argument as sociability revisited. *Language in Society, 24,* 29-52.

Leech, G. (1983). *Principles of pragmatics.* London: Longman.

Lerner, G. H. (1994). Responsive list construction: A conversational resource for accomplishing multifaceted social action. *Journal of Language and Social Psychology, 13,* 20-33.

Lerner, G. H. (1996). Finding "face" in the preference structures of talk-in-interaction. *Social Psychology Quarterly, 59,* 303-321.

Levinas, M. (1995). *Sexual harassment in academia: A discursive approach.* Unpublished master's thesis, University of Guelph, Guelph, Ontario, Canada.

Levinson, S. C. (1983). *Pragmatics.* Cambridge, UK: Cambridge University Press.

Lloyd, R. M. (1992). Negotiating child sexual abuse: The interactional character of investigative practices. *Social Problems, 39,* 109-124.

Lowry, R. P. (1974). *Social problems.* Lexington, MA: Heath.

MacMartin, C. (1999). *Discursive constructions of child sexual abuse: Conduct, credibility and culpability in trial judgments.* Unpublished doctoral dissertation, University of Guelph, Guelph, Ontario, Canada.

MacMartin, C., Wood, L. A., & Kroger, R. O. (in press). Facework. In H. Giles & W. P. Robinson (Eds.), *Handbook of language and social psychology* (2nd ed.). Chichester, UK: Wiley.

MacMartin, C., & Yarmey, A. D. (1999). Rhetoric and the recovered memory debate. *Canadian Psychology, 40,* 343-358.

MacMillan, K., & Edwards, D. (1999). Who killed the Princess? Description and blame in the British press. *Discourse Studies, 1,* 151-174.

MacWhinney, B. (1991). *The Childes project: Tools for analysing talk.* Hillsdale, NJ: Lawrence Erlbaum.

Madigan, R., Johnson, S., & Linton, P. (1995). The language of psychology: APA style as epistemology. *American Psychologist, 50,* 428-436.

Maynard, D. W. (1997). The news delivery sequence: Bad news and good news in conversational interaction. *Research on Language and Social Interaction, 30,* 93-130.

McClelland, D. C. (1961). *The achieving society.* New York: Free Press.

Milgram, S. (1974). *Obedience to authority.* New York: Harper & Row.

Miller, G. (1997). Building bridges: The possibility of analytic dialogue between ethnography, conversation analysis and Foucault. In D. Silverman (Ed.), *Qualitative research* (pp. 24-44). London: Sage.

Miller, J., & Weinert, R. (1995). The function of LIKE in dialogue. *Journal of Pragmatics, 23,* 365-393.

Mühlhäusler, P., & Harré, R. (1990). *Pronouns & people.* Oxford, UK: Blackwell.

Myers, G. (1989). The pragmatics of politeness in scientific articles. *Applied Linguistics, 10,* 1-35.

Nofsinger, R. E. (1991). *Everyday conversation.* Newbury Park, CA: Sage.

Ochs, E., Schegloff, E. A., & Thompson, S. A. (Eds.). (1996). *Interaction and grammar.* Cambridge, UK: Cambridge University Press.

Ochs, E., & Schieffelin, B. B. (Eds.). (1979). *Developmental pragmatics.* New York: Academic Press.

O'Connell, D. C., & Kowal, S. (1994). Some current transcription systems for spoken discourse: A critical analysis. *Pragmatics, 4,* 81-107.

Oskamp, S. (1997). Applied social psychology today and tomorrow. In S. W. Sadava & D. R. McCreary (Eds.), *Applied social psychology* (pp. 310-329). Upper Saddle River, NJ: Prentice Hall.

Parker, I. (1989). *The crisis in modern social psychology, and how to end it*. London: Routledge.

Parker, I. (1992). *Discourse dynamics*. London: Routledge.

Parker, I. (Ed.). (1998). *Social constructionism, discourse and realism*. London: Sage.

Parker, I., & Burman, E. (1993). Against discursive imperialism, empiricism and constructionism: Thirty-two problems with discourse analysis. In E. Burman & I. Parker (Eds.), *Discourse analytic research* (pp. 155-172). London: Routledge.

Penelope, J. (1990). *Speaking freely*. New York: Pergamon.

Peters, R. S. (1960). *The concept of motivation*. London: Routledge & Kegan Paul.

Pfaffenberger, B. (1988). *Microcomputer applications in qualitative research*. Newbury Park, CA: Sage.

Philp, M. (1998, August 20). Banks urged to offer cheap, no-frills accounts. *The Globe and Mail*, p. A9.

Pomerantz, A. (1986). Extreme case formulations: A new way of legitimating claims. *Human Studies, 9*, 219-230.

Pomerantz, A., & Fehr, A. (1997). Conversation analysis: An approach to the study of social action as sense making practices. In T. A. van Dijk (Ed.), *Discourse studies: A multidisciplinary introduction: Vol. 2. Discourse as social interaction* (pp. 64-91). London: Sage.

Potter, J. (1984). Testability, flexibility: Kuhnian values in psychologists' discourse concerning theory choice. *Philosophy of the Social Sciences, 14*, 303-330.

Potter, J. (1994). Conversation and society [Review of the book *Harvey Sacks, Lectures on conversation*]. *Discourse & Society, 5*, 407-411.

Potter, J. (1996). *Representing reality: Discourse, rhetoric and social construction*. London: Sage.

Potter, J. (1997). Discourse analysis as a way of analysing naturally occurring talk. In D. Silverman (Ed.), *Qualitative research* (pp. 144-160). London: Sage.

Potter, J. (1998a). Cognition as context (Whose cognition?) *Research on Language and Social Interaction, 31*, 29-44.

Potter, J. (1998b). Discursive social psychology: From attitudes to evaluative practices. *European Review of Social Psychology, 9*, 233-266.

Potter, J. (1999). Beyond cognitivism. *Research on Language and Social Interaction, 32*, 119-127.

Potter, J., & Reicher, S. (1987). Discourses of community and conflict: The organization of social categories in accounts of a 'riot.' *British Journal of Social Psychology, 26*, 25-40.

Potter, J., & Wetherell, M. (1987). *Discourse and social psychology*. Newbury Park, CA: Sage.

Potter, J., & Wetherell, M. (1994). Analysing discourse. In A. Bryman & R. G. Burgess (Eds.), *Analysing qualitative data* (pp. 47-66). London: Routledge.

Potter, J., & Wetherell, M. (1995a). Discourse analysis. In J. A. Smith, R. Harré, & L. van Langenhove (Eds.), *Rethinking methods in psychology* (pp. 80-92). London: Sage.

Potter, J., & Wetherell, M. (1995b). Natural order: Why social psychologists should study (a constructed version of) natural language, and why they have not done so. *Journal of Language and Social Psychology, 14,* 216-222.

Psathas, G. (1995). *Conversation analysis: The study of talk-in-interaction.* Thousand Oaks, CA: Sage.

Radtke, H. L., & Stam, H. J. (Eds.). (1994). *Power/gender: Social relations in theory and practice.* Thousand Oaks, CA: Sage.

Richards, T., & Richards, L. (1990). *NUD•IST 2.1: Manual* [Software manual]. Melbourne, Australia: Replee.

Roger, D., & Bull, P. (Eds.). (1989). *Conversation: An interdisciplinary perspective.* Clevedon, UK: Multilingual Matters.

Rosenthal, R., & Rosnow, R. L. (1991). *Essentials of behavioural research: Methods and data analysis* (2nd ed.). New York: McGraw-Hill.

Sabat, S., & Harré, R. (1992). The construction and deconstruction of self in Alzheimer's disease. *Ageing and Society, 12,* 443-461.

Sacks, H. (1974). On the analysability of stories by children. In R. Turner (Ed.), *Ethnomethodology* (pp. 216-232). Harmondsworth, UK: Penguin.

Sacks, H. (1984). Notes on methodology. In J. M. Atkinson & J. Heritage (Eds.), *Structures of social action: Studies in conversation analysis* (pp. 21-27). Cambridge, UK: Cambridge University Press.

Sacks, H. (1992). *Lectures on conversation* (G. Jefferson, Ed., Vols. 1-2). Oxford, UK: Blackwell.

Sacks, H., & Schegloff, E. A. (1979). Two preferences in the organisation of reference to persons in conversation and their interaction. In G. Psathas (Ed.), *Everyday language: Studies in ethnomethodology* (pp. 15-21). New York: Irvington.

Sacks, H., Schegloff, E. A., & Jefferson, G. (1978). A simplest systematics for the organization of turn-taking for conversation. In J. Schenkein (Ed.), *Studies in the organization of conversational interaction* (pp. 7-55). New York: Academic Press.

Sampson, E. E. (1993). Identity politics: Challenges to psychology's understanding. *American Psychologist, 12,* 1219-1230.

Sarbin, T. R. (Ed.). (1986). *Narrative psychology.* New York: Praeger.

Saussure, F. de. (1974). *Course in general linguistics.* London: Fontana.

Schank, R., & Burstein, M. (1985). Artificial intelligence: Modeling memory for language understanding. In T. A. van Dijk (Ed.), *Handbook of discourse analysis: Vol. 1. Disciplines of discourse* (pp. 145-166). London: Academic Press.

Schegloff, E. A. (1968). Sequencing in conversational openings. *American Anthropologist, 70,* 1075-1095.

Schegloff, E. A. (1980). Preliminaries to preliminaries: Can I ask you a question? *Sociological Inquiry, 50,* 104-152.

Schegloff, E. A. (1987). Recycled turn beginnings: A precise repair mechanism in conversation's turn-taking organisation. In G. Button & J. R. E. Lee (Eds.), *Talk and social organisation* (pp. 70-85). Clevedon, UK: Multilingual Matters.

Schegloff, E. A. (1989). Harvey Sacks—Lectures 1964-1965: An introduction/memoir. *Human Studies, 12,* 185-209.

Schegloff, E. A. (1992). In another context. In A. Duranti & C. Goodwin (Eds.), *Rethinking context* (pp. 191-227). Cambridge, UK: Cambridge University Press.

Schegloff, E. A. (1993). Reflections on quantification in the study of conversation. *Research on Language and Social Interaction, 26,* 99-128.

Schegloff, E. A. (1995). Discourse as an interactional achievement. III: The omnirelevance of action. *Research on Language and Social Interaction, 28,* 185-211.

Schegloff, E. A. (1997). Whose text? Whose context? *Discourse & Society, 8,* 165-187.

Schegloff, E. A. (1998). Reply to Wetherell. *Discourse & Society, 9,* 413-416.

Schegloff, E. A. (1999). What next?: Language and social interaction study at the century's turn. *Research on Language and Social Interaction, 32,* 141-148.

Schegloff, E. A., Jefferson, G., & Sacks, H. (1977). The preference for self-correction in the organization of repair in conversation. *Language, 53,* 361-382.

Schegloff, E. A., & Sacks, H. (1973). Opening up closings. *Semiotica, 7,* 289-327.

Schenkein, J. (Ed.). (1978). *Studies in the organisation of conversational interaction.* New York: Academic Press.

Schiffrin, D. (1987). *Discourse markers.* Cambridge, UK: Cambridge University Press.

Schiffrin, D. (1994). *Approaches to discourse.* Oxford, UK: Blackwell.

Schönbach, P. (1990). *Account episodes.* Cambridge, UK: Cambridge University Press.

Scott, M. B., & Lyman, S. M. (1968). Accounts. *American Sociological Review, 33,* 46-62.

Seidel, J. V., & Clark, J. A. (1984). The ETHNOGRAPH: A computer program for the analysis of qualitative data. *Qualitative Sociology, 7,* 110-125.

Sherrard, C. (1991). Developing discourse analysis. *Journal of General Psychology, 118*(2), 171-179.

Shuy, R. W. (1993). *Language crimes: The use and abuse of language evidence in the courtroom.* Oxford, UK: Blackwell.

Silverman, D. (1993). *Interpreting qualitative data.* London: Sage.

Sinclair, J. McH., & Coulthard, M. (1975). *Towards an analysis of discourse.* London: Oxford University Press.

Spector, M., & Kitsuse, J. (1973). Social problems: A reformulation. *Social Problems, 21,* 145-159.

Spradley, J. P. (1979). *The ethnographic interview.* New York: Holt, Rinehart & Winston.

Stubbs, M. (1983). *Discourse analysis: The sociolinguistic analysis of natural language.* Chicago: University of Chicago Press.

Svartvik, J., & Quirk, R. (1980). *A corpus of conversational English.* Lund, Sweden: Gleerup.

Tannen, D. (1984a). *Conversational style: Analysing talk among friends.* Norwood, NJ: Ablex.

Tannen, D. (1984b). The pragmatics of cross-cultural communication. *Applied Linguistics, 5,* 189-195.

Tannen, D. (1989). *Talking voices.* Cambridge, UK: Cambridge University Press.

Tannen, D. (1990). *You just don't understand: Women and men in conversation.* New York: Ballantine.

Tannock, S. (1997). Positioning the worker: Discursive practice in a workplace literacy program. *Discourse & Society, 8,* 85-116.

Taylor, T. J., & Cameron, D. (1987). *Analysing conversation: Rules and units in the structure of talk.* Oxford, UK: Pergamon.

228

ten Have, P. (1991). Talk and institution: A reconsideration of the 'asymmetry' of doctor-
  patient interaction. In D. Boden & D. Zimmerman (Eds.), *Talk and social structure*
  (pp. 138-163). Cambridge, UK: Polity Press.
Thomas, J. (1995). *Meaning in interaction: An introduction to pragmatics.* London:
  Longman.
Tracy, K. (1988). A discourse analysis of four discourse studies. *Discourse Processes,
  11,* 243-259.
Tracy, K. (1990). The many faces of facework. In H. Giles & W. P. Robinson (Eds.),
  Handbook of language and social psychology (pp. 209-226). Chichester, UK: Wiley.
Tracy, K. (1991). Discourse. In B. M. Montgomery and S. Duck (Eds.), *Studying inter-
  personal interaction* (pp. 179-195). New York: Guilford.
Tracy, K. (1995). Action-implicative discourse analysis. *Journal of Language and Social
  Psychology, 14,* 195-215.
Tracy, K. (1997a). *Colloquium: Dilemmas of academic discourse.* Norwood, NJ: Ablex.
Tracy, K. (1997b). Interactional trouble in emergency service requests: A problem of
  frames. *Research on Language and Social Interaction, 30,* 315-343.
Tracy, K. (Ed.). (1998). Analysing context [Special issue]. *Research on Language and
  Social Interaction, 31*(1).
Tracy, K., & Anderson, D. L. (1999). Relational positioning strategies in police calls: A
  dilemma. *Discourse Studies, 1,* 201-225.
Tracy, K., & Carjuzáa, J. (1993). Identity enactment in intellectual discussion. *Journal of
  Language and Social Psychology, 12,* 171-194.
Tracy, K., & Tracy, S. J. (1998). Rudeness at 911: Reconceptualizing face and face attack.
  Human Communication Research, 25, 225-251.
Turnbull, W., & Saxton, K. L. (1997). Modal expressions as facework in refusals to com-
  ply with requests: I think I should say 'no' right now. *Journal of Pragmatics, 27,* 145-
  181.
van Dijk, T. A. (1977). *Text and context: Explorations in the semantics and pragmatics of
  discourse.* London: Longman.
van Dijk, T. A. (Ed.). (1985). *Handbook of discourse analysis* (Vols. 1-4). London: Academic Press.
van Dijk, T. A. (1993a). Editor's foreword. *Discourse & Society, 4,* 131-132.
van Dijk, T. A. (1993b). Principles of critical discourse analysis. *Discourse & Society, 4,*
  249-283.
van Dijk, T. A. (1994). Critical discourse analysis. *Discourse & Society, 5,* 435-436.
van Dijk, T. A. (1997a). Analysing discourse analysis. *Discourse & Society, 8,* 5-6.
van Dijk, T. A. (Ed.). (1997b). *Discourse studies: A multidisciplinary introduction* (Vols.
  1-2). London: Sage.
Wagner, W. (1995). Everyday folk-politics, sensibleness and the explanation of action—
  An answer to Cranach. *Journal for the Theory of Social Behaviour, 25,* 295-301.
Walker, A. G. (1986). The verbatim record: The myth and the reality. In S. Fisher & A. D.
  Todd (Eds.), *Discourse and institutional authority: Medicine, education and law*
  (pp. 205-222). Norwood, NJ: Ablex.
Watson, G. (1992). Introduction. In G. Watson & R. M. Seiler (Eds.), *Text in context*
  (pp. xiv-xxvi). Newbury Park, CA: Sage.
Watson, G., & Seiler, R. M. (Eds.). (1992). *Text in context.* Newbury Park, CA: Sage.
Webster's new twentieth century dictionary (2nd ed.). (1976). New York: Collins World.

Wetherell, M. (1998). Positioning and interpretative repertoires: Conversation analysis and post-structuralism in dialogue. *Discourse & Society, 9,* 387-412.

Wetherell, M., & Potter, J. (1988). Discourse analysis and the identification of interpretative repertoires. In C. Antaki (Ed.), *Analysing everyday explanation: A casebook of methods* (pp. 168-183). London: Sage.

Wetherell, M., & Potter, J. (1992). *Mapping the language of racism: Discourse and the legitimation of exploitation.* Hemel Hempstead, UK: Harvester.

Widdicombe, S. (1995). Identity, politics and talk: A case for the mundane and the everyday. In S. Wilkinson & C. Kitzinger (Eds.), *Feminism and discourse* (pp. 106-127). London: Sage.

Widdicombe, S., & Wooffitt, R. (1990). 'Being' vs. 'doing' punk: On achieving authenticity as a member. *Journal of Language and Social Psychology, 9,* 257-277.

Widdicombe, S., & Wooffitt, R. (1995). *The language of youth subcultures.* Hemel Hempstead, UK: Harvester.

Wieder, D. L. (1999). Ethnomethodology, conversation analysis, microanalysis, and the ethnography of speaking (EM-CA-MA-ES): Resonances and basic issues. *Research on Language and Social Interaction, 31,* 163-171.

Wilkinson, S., & Kitzinger, C. (Eds.). (1995). *Feminism and discourse.* London: Sage.

Wilson, A. J., & Zeitlyn, D. (1995). The distribution of person-referring expressions in natural conversation. *Research on Language and Social Interaction, 28,* 61-92.

Wittgenstein, L. (1953). *Philosophical investigations* (G. E. M. Anscombe & R. Rhees, Eds., G. E. M. Anscombe, Trans.). Oxford, UK: Blackwell.

Wood, L. A., & Kroger, R. O. (1994). The analysis of facework in discourse: Review and proposal. *Journal of Language and Social Psychology, 13,* 248-277.

Wood, L. A., & Kroger, R. O. (1995). Discourse analysis in research on aging. *Canadian Journal on Aging, 14*(Suppl. 1), 82-99.

Wood, L. A., & Rennie, H. (1994). Formulating rape: The discursive construction of victims and villains. *Discourse & Society, 5,* 125-148.

Index

Absences, paying attention to, 91
Accountability, 21, 102, 169, 196, 197-198
    footing and, 102
Account analysis, 213
Accounts, 99
Action identifications, 12
Action-implicative discourse analysis, 213
Adjacency pairs, 99, 106, 201
Agent-patient distinction, 101-102
    power issues and, 102
Analogy, 46
Analysis:
    determining focus of, 88
    levels of, 18
Analytical concepts, 99-107. *See also*
    specific analytical concepts
Analytical procedures:
    bottom-up
    top-down, 24
Analytical process, 95-99
    as painstaking, 99
    as time-consuming, 99
    multiple listenings/viewings/readings, 98
    starting, 98-99
    See also Scaffolding
Analytic induction, 120, 173
Anderson, D. L., 213
Antaki, C., 38, 39, 40, 41, 93, 104, 105, 106,
    110, 120, 122, 128, 129, 154, 172, 183,
    199, 200, 213, 215
Applied linguistics, 213
Archives, 71-72
Argument, 204
Argumentation, 207
Aronson, E., x
Atkinson, J. M., 83, 84, 86, 96, 110, 193, 205
Attitudes, 17, 21
Attributions, 17, 21, 102, 146, 159, 195

Attribution theory, 197
Austin, J., ix, 4, 5, 191, 208

Bakhtin, M., 66
Barthes, R., 216
Bavelas, J. B., 11, 42, 43, 44, 45, 60, 63, 70,
    74, 82, 83, 87, 92, 93, 94, 135, 198
Beattie, G., 60, 61, 63
Bergvall, V. L., 215
Bickhard, M. H., xi, xiii
Billig, M., 20, 177, 199
Blakar, R. M., 74
Blum-Kulka, S., 208
Boulding, K., xii, xiii, xvi, 192
Bricolage, 25-26
Brockmeier, J., 104
Brown, G., 56
Brown, P., 48, 51, 104
Brown, R., 59, 60, 61, 63, 149, 216
Buchanan, K., 45, 46, 47, 151, 198, 199, 204
Bull, P., 70
Burman, E., 19, 190, 207
Burstein, M., 214
Buttny, R., 103

Caldas-Coulthard, C. R., 207
Cameron, D., 195, 199, 215
Carjuzáa, J., 51, 65, 137, 138, 139, 141, 143,
    144, 145, 146, 154, 199, 213
Categories, 105-106, 199
    analysts' versus participants', 129
    participants', 105
Categorization, 18, 29-30, 32, 195
    as problematic, 106, 139-140
    participants', 94
    provisional, 30
Cathers, T., 75, 210
Cernetig, M., 5

231

Child Language Data Exchange System
  (CHILDES), 71
Chovil, N., 74
Cicourel, A. V., 213
Clark, H. H., 208
Clark, J. A., 142
Clarke, D., xii, xiv
Coates, L., 42, 43, 44, 45, 87, 92, 93, 94,
  135, 198
Cognition, 16-17
Cognitive sociology, 213
Cohen, J., 136
Collected dossiers, 106-107
Comprehensive discourse analysis, 214
Computer-assisted analysis, 141-142
  software, 142
Concession, 38-42
Consensus, 17
Constructed dialogue. See Reported speech
Constructing motive, 99
Content, 6-7, 32, 92, 109, 171
  discourse level, 6
  function and, 8
  illocutionary level, 109
  lexical level, 6
  locutionary level, 109
  perlocutionary level, 109
  pragmatic level, 6
  social level, 6
  structure and, 93
Content analysis:
  versus discourse analysis, 32-33
Context, 18, 96, 127-136, 190
  as ever-changing, 135
  as problematic notion, 135-136
  as process, 135
  extrinsic, 127, 128
  gender as relevant, 131
  intrinsic, 127
Conversational repair, 202-203, 204
  other-initiated other repair, 203
  other initiated self-repair, 203
  self-initiated other repair, 203
  self-initiated self-repair, 203
Conversation analysis (CA), 21, 22, 23, 24,
  26, 27, 62, 77, 83, 84, 86, 96, 103, 116,
  121, 122, 123, 126, 128, 130, 180, 182,
  196, 197, 199-205, 207, 208, 211, 215
  Antaki and Wetherell study as example,
    38-42
  Buchanan and Middleton study as
    example, 46-47
  Drew study as example, 35-38, 41-42
  narrative concepts in, 104

participants' meaning in, 109
primary focus, 21, 23
recipient design, 200
Conversation analysts, 77, 93, 120, 145, 200
  use of positioning, 101
Conversation analytic mentality, 96
Cooperative Principle (CP), 209
Coulthard, M., 207
Coulthard, R. M., 215
Counterfactual thinking, 105
Coupland, J., 47, 48, 74, 78, 102, 132, 146,
  147, 148, 149, 151, 154, 183, 211, 214
Coupland, N., 26, 47, 48, 74, 78, 102, 132,
  146, 147, 148, 149, 151, 154, 183, 211,
  214, 216
Course-grained analysis, 80
Court transcripts, 56
Cranach, M., von, 75
Critical discourse analysis (CDA), 21, 22, 23,
  96, 134, 182, 205-208, 215
  critiques, 207
  emphasis in, 21, 22, 23
  feminist researchers and, 102
  overlap with PS, 22
  theoretical approaches to, 205
Critical discourse researchers, 24
Critical linguistics, 205, 206
Crystal, D., 61, 71, 208, 215, 216

Data collection, 18. See also Data collection
  procedures
Data collection procedures, 69-75
  nature of sample, 78-79
  researcher-instigated, 72-75
  sample size, 80-81
  sampling issues, 76-78
  See also Archives; Discourse recording
Davies, B., 100
De Carlo, N., xii, xiv
Deconstruction, 93, 214
Deixis, 209-210
Denzin, N. K., 25, 28, 176
Derrida, J., 214
Description, 15, 21
DeVault, M. L., 73
Dingwall, R., 130
Direct reported speech, 47
Discourse:
  as action, 159, 166
  as focus/topic, 8-10
  as practice, 22-23
  basic assumptions, 4-13
  factual, 16
  meaning of, 19-20

multiple definitions, 3
multiple functions, 145
See also Spoken discourse; Written
    discourse
Discourse analysis, x, xiv, xv
    as constructionist perspective, 159
    as open-ended activity, 179
    as recursive activity, 179
    as time-consuming, 190
    collaboration, 188
    definition, 3-4
    emphasis in, 5
    first attempts at, 187-189
    flexibility of, 159
    glossary, 213-216
    inductive spirit of, 34
    major assumption of, 4
    methods, 25-33
    origins of, 18
    other qualitative perspectives and, 27-32
    overall goal, 95
    practical issues, 13-16
    teachability of, 189-190
    varieties, 18-25
    versus content analysis, 32-33
    See also specific methods and varieties of
        discourse analysis; Analytical
        process; Discourse analysis, examples
        of; Discourse analytic orientation
Discourse analysis, examples of, 30-31, 123-
    127
    Antaki and Wetherell on making
        concessions, 38-42
    Brown and Levinson on face and
        politeness, 48
    Buchanan and Middleton on metaphor and
        reminiscence, 45-47
    Coates et al. on legal constructions of
        sexual assault, 42-45
    Coupland et al. on metaphor and
        reminiscence, 37-48
    Drew on responding to teasing, 35-38
    Myers on face and politeness, 48-51
    See also Discourse analysis research,
        identity as topic of
Discourse analysis in social psychology
    (DASP), 20, 22, 72, 96, 102, 103, 105,
    115, 123, 149, 180, 195-199, 200, 204,
    207, 215
    accountability in, 102
    Antaki and Wetherell study as example, 42
    Buchanan and Middleton study as
        example, 45-46, 47
    central concepts, 20-21

Coates et al. study as example, 42-45
    defensive rhetoric, 199
    flexibility in, 199
    narrative concepts in, 104
    offensive rhetoric, 199
    positioning and, 101
Discourse analysis in social psychology
    researchers, 24
Discourse analysts, 9, 10, 95, 145, 163, 164,
    175, 187
    aim of, 6
    basic premise for, 167
    using film analyst devices, 58
    using literary analyst devices, 58
Discourse analysis research, identity as topic
    of, 143, 158-159
    age identities, 146-149
    authenticity, 151-154
    identity as achievement, 143-154
    identity as tool, 154-158
    intellectual and institutional identity, 143-
    146
    pronouns and selves, 149-151
Discourse analytic orientation
    adopting, 91-95
    See also Sensitizing devices
Discourse & Society, 14
Discourse data, 55, 64-65
    fictional, 65
    naturalness, 57-59
    nonverbal, 59-63
    recording/records, 55-56, 64
    sources, 65-68
Discourse dynamics, 214
Discourse-historical method, 205
Discourse marker, 124
Discourse process(ing), 214
Discourse recording, 58-59, 64, 69-70
    ethical issues, 70
    problems, 69-70
    technical constraints, 69
    technical issues, 70
    video, 70
Discursive Action Model, 196
Discursive metatheory, 9, 176
Discursive mind, 196
Discursive psychology, 195, 196
Discursive social psychology, 195, 196
Dispreferred response, 62
Douglas, J. D., 76
Dramaturgical analysis, 214
Drew, P., 6, 35, 36, 37, 38, 41, 77, 92, 200,
    204, 205
Duisburg School, 205

Dummy it, 124
Dupuis, S., 30, 31
Duranti, A., 128

Ecolinguistics, 214
Edley, N., 24, 18
Edwards, D., xiv, 9, 13, 15, 16, 17, 20, 24,
    57, 66, 67, 104, 105, 106, 107, 108, 129,
    130, 154, 155, 156, 157, 158, 165, 183,
    184, 195, 196, 197, 198, 199, 200, 207,
    211, 215
Emotion categories, 21, 195, 198
Epistemological relativism, 166
Ethnographic research, 130
Ethnography, 214
Ethnomethodological indifference, 67
Ethnomethodologists, 8
Ethnomethodology, 199, 215
Exchange structure, 215
Experiments, xiii-xiv, 74-75
    ethical concerns, 75

Face-threatening acts (FTAs), 48, 49, 50
    claims, 48, 49
    denials of claims, 48, 49
    strategies for carrying out, 48
Facework, 104
Fact construction, 21, 204
    main techniques, 196-197
Fairclough, N., 7, 19, 21, 24, 96, 134, 135,
    176, 178, 182, 205, 206, 207, 208, 216
Fallacy of abstractionism, 76
Fallacy of misplaced precision, 141
Fanshel, D., 210, 214
Fehr, A., xii, 21, 96, 200
Felicity conditions, 5
Feminist discourse analysis, 215
Feminist researchers, 178
Festinger, L., 151
Fictional discourse, 58
    special uses for, 58
Figures of speech, 19, 46
Fine-grained analysis, 80
Firth, A., 71
Footing, 102
Forensic linguistics, 215
Foucault, M., 206
Fowler, R., 206
Framing, 45, 124
Fraser, B., 210
Freed, A. F., 139
French discourse analysis, 205
Freud, S., 101
Frith, H., 205, 215

Function, 7-8
    as action, 7-8
    content and, 8
    domains of, 8
    global, 8
    linguistic, 8
    pragmatic, 8
    social, 8
    specific, 8
Funk & Wagnall, 167

Gap, 202
Garfinkel, H., 8, 213, 215
Gavey, N., 25, 215
Generalizability, 76, 77
Gibson, J., 42, 43, 44, 45, 87, 92, 93, 94,
    135, 198
Gilbert, D. T., 11, 12
Gilbert, G. N., 50, 111, 112, 198
Giles, H., 138, 139
Gill, R., 16, 178
Gillett, G., xii, 9, 196
Gilman, A., 149
Glaser, B. G., 27, 30, 95
Glosses, 42
Goffman, E., 102, 214, 215
Goodwin, C., 70, 108, 127, 128
Goodwin, M. H., 108
Grainger, K., 74, 102, 146, 147, 148, 149,
    151, 154, 183, 211
Grammar, 94, 171, 187
    social implications of, 23-24, 94-95
Greatbach, D., 130, 204, 205
Greenwood, A., 139
Grice, H. P., 22, 209
Gricean pragmatics, 50, 93, 145, 209
Grimshaw, A., 59, 214
Grounded theory, 27, 29, 81, 95, 142
Grounding interpretations, 112-116, 175
    double role, 113
    versus coherence, 173, 174
Guba, E. G., 169, 170, 178
Gubrium, J. F., 29, 72, 199, 215
Gumperz, J., 215

Haberland, H., 20
Hacking, I., 16, 166
Halliday, M. A. K., 206, 216
Hampshire, S., xi, 192
Handel, W., xv
Harré, R., x, xii, xiv, 9, 19, 100, 101, 104,
    107, 137, 149, 151, 196, 213
Harwood, J., 138, 139
Hasan, R., 206, 216

Heath, C., 70
Hedged responses, 48, 201
Hedging, 48, 49, 115, 149
Hepburn, A., 190
Heritage, J., 82, 83, 84, 96, 109, 110, 128,
    130, 133, 193, 199, 200, 202, 204, 205,
    215
Heritage, J. C., 139, 140
Hesitations, 61
Hodge, R., 206
Holmes, J., 132
Holstein, J. A., 29, 72, 199, 215
Holt, E., 6, 103
Hoonaard, W. C. van den, 99
Hopper, R., 23, 26, 58, 71, 85, 120, 131, 200
House, J., 208
Houtkoop-Steenstra, H., 183
Huberman, A. M., 95, 141, 142, 170, 176
Hudson, R. A., 216
Hutchby, I., 23, 38, 82, 84, 85, 86, 96, 104,
    113, 114, 119, 122, 127, 130, 199, 200,
    202, 203, 204, 205, 215
Hymes, D., 214

Idiomatic formulations, 6
Indexicals, 209
    higher-order, 150
    iterated, 150
    simple, 150
Initial reading, 87-88, 93, 98
Initiation, 7
Intensifiers, 99, 106
Intention, 115
Interactional sociolinguistics, 215
Interest, management of, 21, 196
Interpretation, doing, 99-107. *See also*
    Analytical concepts; Grounding
    interpretations
Interpretation strategies, 107-112
    appearance of new problems, 112
    content, 109
    multiple functions, 108-109
    participants' meaning 109-110
    reframing, 107-108
    similarity and difference, 111-112
    substitution, 107
Interpretive repertoires, 19, 20-21, 43-45, 47,
    80, 87, 96, 111, 175, 189, 198
    contingent, 111
    empiricist, 111
    See also Metaphor
Interruption, 202
Intertextual analysis, 58, 132, 134-135, 172,
    174, 176, 178

examples, 134-135
    See also Intertextuality
Intertextuality, 124
    multiple meanings, 134
    See also Intertextual analysis
Interviews, 72-74
    active, 72
    as conversational encounters, 72
    feminist strategies, 73
    interventionist approach, 72
Intonation, 20, 61, 84, 149
Invented discourse, 58

Jackson, S., 58, 116, 120, 168, 173, 204
Jacobs, S., 120, 172, 185, 204
Jacoby, J., 74
Janoff-Bulman, R., 76
Jefferson, G., 21, 62, 83, 85, 93, 110, 114,
    120, 122, 123, 202, 203
Johnson, M., 48, 105
Johnson, S., 181
Jucker, A. H., 210

Kalbermatten, U., 75
Kasper, G., 208
Kelly, J., 83
Kendon, A., 70, 85
Kitsuse, J., 177
Kitzinger, C., 84, 86, 205, 215
Knorr-Cetina, K. D., xiii
Koch, S., 120, 200
Kowal, S., 82, 85
Kress, G., 19, 206
Kroger, R. O., x, 9, 12, 13, 14, 25, 50, 51, 71,
    104, 123, 127, 133, 134, 135, 149

Labov, W., 210, 214
Lakoff, G., 48, 105
Lamb, S., 102
Language:
    and behavior, 11-13
    as action, 4-8, 11, 18, 196
    as social practice, 4
    pragmatic function, ix
    psychology and, x
Language games, 116
Lapse, 202
Laughter, 48
Lawrie, D. A., 74
Lazar, M., 20
LeBaron, C., 131
Lee, D. A., 59, 64
Leech, G., 208
Lerner, G. H., 204

Levinas, M., 79
Levinson, S., 48, 51, 104
Levinson, S. C., 109, 175, 200, 201, 208, 209, 210
Lincoln, Y. S., 25, 28, 176
Linton, P., 181
Lloyd, R. M., 205
Local, J. K., 83
Lowry, R. P., 141
Lyman, S. M., 213

MacMartin, C., 14, 15, 25, 45, 50, 51, 104, 133
MacMillan, K., 24
MacWhinney, B., 71
Madigan, R., 181
Mandelbaum, J., 120, 200
Markers, 210
  temporal, 153
Maynard, D. W., 204
McLelland, D. C., 32
Meaning, 171
Membership categories, 200
Membership categorization devices, 200
Memory, 15, 195
Metaphors, 19, 45-48, 104-105, 134
  distance, 125
  temporal, 125
Middleton, D. J., 45, 46, 47, 151, 198, 199, 204
Miles, M. B., 95, 141, 142, 170, 176
Milgram, S., xiii, 11, 164
Miller, G., 24
Miller, J., 210, 211
Modality, 211
Modals, 101
Mühlhäusler, P., 149
Mulkay, M., 50, 111, 112, 198
Myers, G., 48, 49, 50, 51, 94

Narrative, 94, 104, 206
Narrative analysis, 27, 104
  information-processing/cognitive approaches, 104
  literary approaches, 104
  social-constructionist approaches, 104
Natural discourse, 57-59
Naturalistic research, 169
Negative appraisals:
  qualified initial, 48
Negative case analysis, 118-120
  example, 118-119
  See also Analytic induction
Negative cases, 118

Nofsinger, R. E., 110, 113, 114, 130, 200, 202, 203, 204, 209
Nonverbal data, 59-63
  body language, 60, 61-62
  DA meaning of, 61-62
  implications of, 62-63
  problems, 60
  See also Silence

Ochs, E., 24, 74, 208
O'Connell, D. C., 82, 85
Orders of analysis, 133-134
  first-order, 133
  second-order, 133
Orders of discourse, 134
Orientation, participants', 113-114, 136, 171.
  See also Orienting
Orienting, 145. See also Orientation, participants'
Overlapping speech, 29, 84, 202

Paralanguage, 61
  vocal, 61
Parker, I., 16, 19, 27, 28, 190, 192, 207, 214
Passive voice, 102
Patterns:
  analysis, 96, 200
  claim checking and, 172
  diachronic, 117
  interpretation of, 95, 96
  nonnumerical expression description, 138
  numerical expression description, 138
  of laughter, 121-122
  synchronic, 117
  See also Patterns, identification of
Patterns, identification of, 95, 117-118
  alertness and, 117
  See also Negative case analysis; Patterns
Pauses, 20, 61, 83, 202
  filled, 48
Peck, J. J., 59, 64
Penelope, J., 30, 102, 124
People points, xii
Perception, 195
Persuading, 8
Peters, R. S., 101
Pfaffenberger, B., 141
Philp, M., 6
Pomerantz, A., xii, 21, 31, 39, 47, 96, 126, 200, 204
Positioning, 100-101
Poststructuralism (PS), 19, 21-22, 23, 24, 133, 207, 215, 216
  focus, 23

overlap with CDA, 22
positioning and, 101
Potter, J., x, xiv, xv, 3, 4, 6, 8, 10, 12, 13, 15,
  16, 17, 18, 19, 20, 21, 23, 44, 51, 57, 58,
  66, 72, 73, 75, 78, 80, 85, 87, 88, 95, 96,
  98, 99, 100, 102, 105, 106, 109, 111, 112,
  113, 117, 118, 127, 128, 129, 132, 134,
  136, 137, 165, 166, 168, 169, 171, 173,
  174, 175, 176, 181, 184, 185, 188, 189,
  195, 196, 197, 198, 199, 200, 207, 209,
  211, 214, 215, 216
Pragmatics, 22, 208-211, 206
  focus, 23
  forms, 22
Preference structure, 77, 106, 201-202
Presequence, 201
Pronouns, personal, 149-151. *See also*
  Indexicals
Proposals, writing, 188-189
Proposition, 42
Prosody, 61
Psathas, G., 57, 67, 200
Psycholinguistics, xi

Qualitative perspectives, discourse analysis
  and other, 27-32. *See also* Grounded
  theory; Narrative analysis
Qualitative researcher:
  as bricoleur, 25-26
Quantification, 18, 136-141
  data selection and, 139
  detection of patterns, 139
  ethnoquantification, 138
  problems, 137-138
Quirk, R., 38

Radtke, H. L., 215
Rapley, M., 183
Reading analysis, 205
Realism, 16
Recorded data, 55-56, 62, 64
  high-fidelity, 56
Recycling:
  levels of analysis, 96
  See also Scaffolding
Reflectivity, xv
Reflexivity, xv, 30, 51, 191
Reframing, 17, 107-108, 199
Reicher, S., 98
Relativism, 16, 190
Relativized appraisals, 48
Reliability, 97, 163, 164-166, 167
  judgments about, 165
  See also Repetition

Remlinger, K. A., 215
Rennie, H., 44, 76, 78, 87, 123, 127, 131,
  132, 133, 134, 135, 175, 180, 198
Repetition, 164-166
Report, writing the, 18, 179-186
  analysis, 181-186
  demonstration, 183-186
  discourse excerpts, 183-184, 185
  discussion section, 180
  final analysis section, 185
  introduction, 179-180
  methodology section, 180
  notes section, 181
  reference list, 181
  results section, 180
  reworking analysis, 184
  writing out the analysis, 186
Reported speech, 103-104
  direct, 103
  indirect, 103
Reprimand, 7
Res artem, xi-xii, 11
Res naturam, xi, xii, 11, 12, 163, 164
Reversals, 17, 107
Rhetorical positions/contrasts, 198
Richards, L., 142
Richards, T., 142
Robinson, J. D., 47, 48
Roger, D., 70
Rosenthal, R., 77, 163
Rosnow, R. L., 77, 163
Roth, A. L., 139, 140

Sabat, S., 101, 150, 151, 196
Sacks, H., 21, 23, 62, 65, 67, 93, 99, 107,
  110, 200, 201, 202, 203, 210
Sampling, 18, 76-78
  identification, 76
  nature of sample, 78-79
  selection, 79
  size, 76, 77, 80-81
  See also Generalizability; Saturation
Sampson, E. E., 4, 14, 190
Sarbin, T. R., 27, 104
Saturation, 81
Saussure, F. de, 19, 215
Saxton, K. L., 75, 208, 211
Scaffolding, 96-98, 113, 133
Scenarios, 75
Schank, R., 214
Schegloff, E. A., 21, 24, 25, 26, 32, 62, 66,
  77, 79, 83, 93, 106, 110, 114, 116, 118,
  119, 127, 128, 129, 130, 131, 132, 133,

136, 137, 138, 139, 140, 200, 201, 202,
   203, 210
Schenkein, J., 96
Schieffelin, B. B., 208
Schiffrin, D., 195, 200, 210, 215
Schönbach, P., 213
Scientific method, xii-xiv
Scott, M. B., 213
Scripts, 195
Secord, P. F., xiv
Seidel, J. V., 142
Seiler, R. M., 127, 215
Semantics, 206
Semiotic harmony, 63
Semiotics, 92, 214, 215-216
Sensitizing devices, 91-95
   adopt comparative stance, 94
   adopt questioning stance, 94
   adopt reversal strategy, 94
   alertness to multiple functions of
      discourse, 93
   attention to the obvious, 92
   attention to what is included, 93
   attention to what is missing, 92-93
   develop new terms/concepts, 94
   draw on own knowledge, 95
   examine participant's categorization, 94
   examine text's structure, 93
   focus on literal meaning, 92
   focus on variation, 94
   knowledge of grammar, 94-95
   play with the text, 93
   reactions to texts, 91-92
   seeing text as writing essay, 93-94
   self-permission to be analyst, 95
Sherrad, C., 115, 174
Shifts in discourse, trivial, 151
Shuy, R. W., 215
Silence, 62, 93
Silverman, D., 56, 215
Sinclair, J., 215
Social comparison, 105, 106, 126, 151-154,
   159
Social constructionism, 16
Social cultural change/change in discourse,
   205, 206
Social science work, 105
Social semiotics, 205, 206
Socio-cognitive studies, 205, 206-207
Sociolinguistics, 216
Sociological discourse analysis, 214
Soundness, criteria of, 167-168, 169, 170-177
   coherence, 173-174
   demonstration, 170-173

fruitfulness, 171, 175-176
orderliness, 170, 176
plausibility, 174-175
Spector, M., 177
Speech act, 7, 207
Speech act theory, 4, 5, 208-209
Speech onset, 84
Spoken discourse, 55
Spradley, J. P., 73
Stake, management of, 21, 197
Stake innoculation, 197
Stam, H. J., 215
Strategy of reversal, 88
Strauss, A. L., 27, 30, 95
Stress, 61
Structure:
   as active process, 8
   content and, 93
   hierarchical, 8, 99
   sequential, 8, 99
Stubbs, M., 19, 57
Style, 7
Stylistics, 216
Svartvik, J., 38
Syntax, 93, 206
Systemic-functional grammar, 216
Systemic linguistics, 216

Talk:
   as action, xv, 5, 16, 17, 18
   as event of interest, 16
   multiple functions of, 5
   See also Language is action
Tannen, D., 22, 47, 57, 67, 75, 82, 94, 103,
   165, 213, 215
Tannock, S., 58, 100
Taylor, T. J., 195, 199, 215
ten Have, P., 205
Testing, xiii
Text grammar, 216
Textlinguistics, 216
Text schemata, 207
Thomas, J., 208
Thompson, S. A., 24
Threat, 7
Timbre, 61
Topics, 207
Tracy, K., 14, 28, 51, 65, 85, 92, 104, 127,
   128, 131, 133, 137, 138, 139, 141, 143,
   144, 145, 146, 154, 155, 163, 168, 171,
   173, 174, 175, 177, 178, 195, 199, 213
Tracy, S. J., 51, 85
Transcribing:
   Jefferson system, 84-85

requirements for making, 85
   suggestions for, 84-87
   transcriber and, 86
Transcription, 18, 82-87
   accuracy in, 86
   as analytical activity, 84
   as complicated, 82
   as theoretical activity, 84
   as time-consuming, 82
   notation, 193-194
   orthographic approach, 83
   phonetic approach, 83
   phonological approach, 83
   requirements for using, 85
   thoroughness, 86
Transcripts, 60, 63, 82, 84
   published, 71
   See also Court transcripts
Transition-relevant place (TRP), 202
Trew, T., 206
Triangulation, 176
Trustworthiness, criteria of, 167-168, 169-
   170
   audits, 169-170
   documentation, 169
   orderliness, 169
Turnbull, W., 75, 208, 211
Turns, 84
Turn taking, 8, 80, 99, 106, 202-204
Turn to language, x. *See also* Discourse

University of Texas Conversation Library, 71
Utterances, 4-5, 8, 11, 13, 66, 91, 92, 96,
   107, 108, 109, 110, 114, 115, 145, 208,
   211
   as actions, 29
   condemnation of, 14
   contextualization of, 128
   illocutionary force, 5
   locutionary/referential meaning, 5
   multiple functions, 9-10
   perlocutionary force, 5

Validity, 97, 163, 166, 167
   in psychological research, 166
van Dijk, T. A., 19, 115, 184, 192, 195, 206,
   207
van Langenhove, L., 100, 196
Variability, 10-11, 16, 17, 28, 60, 111-112,
   159, 191
Video recordings, 146
   of face-to-face interaction, 38
Voice quality, 61

Wade, A., 74
Wagner, W., 108
Walker, A. G., 86
Warrantability, 166, 178, 183
   conceptual criteria, 168
   empirical criteria, 168
   logical criteria, 168
   method and, 168
   moral criteria, 177-178
   reflexive elements, 168
   scientific criteria, 167-168
   theory and, 168
   See also Soundness, criteria of;
      Trustworthiness, criteria of
Warranting, 18, 76-77, 113, 117, 149, 177,
   200
   grounding in, 170-171
   in psychology, 163
   methods, 169
   See also Warrantability
Watson, G., 127, 129, 215
Webster's, 167
Weinert, R., 210, 211
Wetherell, M., 3, 4, 6, 8, 10, 12, 17, 18, 19,
   20, 24, 25, 38, 39, 40, 41, 57, 66, 72, 73,
   75, 78, 80, 85, 87, 88, 93, 95, 96, 100,
   101, 102, 105, 109, 111, 112, 113, 120,
   122, 132, 137, 168, 169, 171, 172, 173,
   174, 175, 176, 181, 182, 185, 188, 189,
   195, 196, 198, 199, 215
Widdicombe, S., 25, 73, 151, 152, 153, 154,
   159, 200, 211, 215
Wieder, D. L., 25, 195, 199
Wilkinson, S., 215
Wilson, A. J., 139, 140
Wittgenstein, L., 116, 191
Wodak, R., 21, 205, 207
Wood, L. A., x, 9, 12, 13, 14, 25, 44, 50, 51,
   71, 76, 78, 87, 104, 123, 127, 131, 132,
   133, 134, 135, 149, 175, 180, 198
Wooffitt, R., 23, 38, 73, 82, 84, 85, 86, 96,
   104, 113, 114, 119, 122, 127, 130, 151,
   152, 153, 154, 159, 200, 202, 203, 204,
   205, 211, 215
Writing. *See* Proposals, writing; Report,
   writing the
Written discourse, 55
   equivalents to nonverbal aspects of spoken
      language, 62

Yarmey, A. D., 15
Yule, G., 56

Zeitlyn, D., 139, 140

About the Authors

Linda A. Wood (Ph.D., York University, Canada) is Professor of Psychology at the University of Guelph. Her research concerns issues of language and social interaction, and discourse and social structure. She has published articles and chapters on loneliness, identity, forms of address, politeness, facework, aging, abuse, and sexual assault. Her current work is focused on discourses of child sexual abuse in legal, scholarly and media accounts, and on the reproduction of gender in discursive practices of address and naming as represented, for example, in expressions such as *guys* and in surnames. She is a member of the International Association of Language and Social Psychology (IALSP), the International Communication Association, and the International Pragmatics Association.

Rolf O. Kroger (Ph.D., University of California, Berkeley) is Professor Emeritus of Psychology at the University of Toronto. The general focus of his research has been on the social conditions of self-report as found, for example, in personality testing, hypnosis experiments, and everyday self-disclosure, as well as on discursive issues (politeness, facework). His current work is concerned with the discursive respecification of personality and the social psychology of address forms. He is a member of IALSP and of CHEIRON. The two authors have collaborated since the early 1980s on studies of discourse and on the critical examination of the metatheory and methodology of social psychology.